FIREBIRD

A SOURCE BOOK

EDITED AND ANNOTATED BY

Thomas E. Bonsall

Bookman Publishing/Baltimore, Maryland

Printed in the U.S.A.
Copyright 1981 in U.S.A. by Bookman Dan!, Inc.

ISBN O-934780-07-2

First Edition
Third Printing

Inquiries may be directed to:
Bookman Dan!, Inc.
P.O. Box 13492
Baltimore, Maryland 21203

Preface

Probably no car in America is more closely associated with the concept of high performance than the Pontiac Firebird, and, in particular, the Firebird Trans Am. I am making a distinction here between four-seater, grand touring transportation and the out and out sports cars of the Corvette genre, although I am not at all sure that the Trans Am hasn't achieved a reputation among enthusiasts rivalling that of the fabled 'Vette. None of this is accidental. It has been a result of years of devotion and hard work by enthusiasts within Pontiac Motor Division who fought to keep their dream car going even when the market seemed to have deserted it in the early 1970's. They persevered even after the disastrous 1972 model run when a pathetic 1,286 Trans Ams were built. In time, they came to be recognized as the only band of GT car loyalists left in the industry. When the high performance car was rediscovered in the mid-seventies, Pontiac was there with the goods and reaped tremendous, and well deserved, rewards for its loyalty to the high performance concept. Indeed, the Firebird is perhaps the only specialty car Pontiac has ever built on a body shared with Chevrolet that has assumed its own distinct identity in the mind of the public. The beautifully styled and finished Pontiac Safaris of 1955-57, for example, are generally referred to as little more than footnotes to the Chevrolet Nomad story. But, the Firebird...it has, by virtue of its own inherent qualities, transcended its status as a Camaro sibling and emerged as a revered marque in its own right. As this is being written, Pontiac is preparing the introduction of an entirely new Firebird for the 1982 model year that promises to carry the legend to new heights.

The original Firebird was not created in a void but, rather, was very much a product of the general situation in which Pontiac Motor Division found itself as it prepared to enter its fifth decade, in the mid-sixties. The original Pontiac, announced in 1926, was created as a marketing ploy by GM's legendary Alfred P. Sloan to prove that the public would buy a six cylinder car if it were offered at a price just a little above that of the four cylinder Fords and Chevys. It worked so well that the Pontiac's parent car, the Oakland, was soon gone and forgotten. When the low price market shifted to sixes and eights, Pontiac brought out its straight eight engine and, for over twenty years, Pontiac specialized in dull, middle class transportation. And especially dull. Pontiacs were always well built and nicely finished. Occasionally, they were even pretty—in a homey sort of way. The wholesome girl next door as opposed to the flashy, Hollywood starlet. All that changed in the summer of 1956.

When Semon E. ("Bunkie") Knudsen took charge of Pontiac Motor Division, he was determined to radically alter the car's image. "You can sell a young man's car to old people," his famous dictum went, "but you can't sell an old car to young people." He therefore set about making the Pontiac the youngest car in the industry. The first thing he did, almost literally, was to remove the traditional Pontiac hood stripes ("suspenders," Knudsen disdainfully called them). Next, he set to work, aided by his proteges Pete Estes and John DeLorean, to begin exploration of the potential inherent in the V-8 engine Pontiac had announced in 1955. They found a lot of it. So much, in fact, that Pontiacs were soon the hottest machines on the stock car racing circuit. A radical, youthful restyling in 1959 really turned Pontiac's fortunes around. By the time the Tempest and its *tour de force* engineering appeared in 1961, Pontiac was in third place in national sales rankings.

Pontiac's youthful and, at times, ingenious engineering was followed in 1963 by a styling revolution initiated with the new Grand Prix. It is hard to remember now, but until that time the price and status of cars were functions of ornamentation. As a car moved up the price ladder, it gathered trim doodads until, eventually, it looked like a rummage sale at the First M. E. Church. The 1963 Grand Prix changed all that. Here was the most expensive Pontiac series...and it was distinguishable by the absence of unnecessary trim. Instead, the Grand Prix's sculptured lines were allowed to cary the message. And, a beautiful message it was, too. In addition to the famous Pontiac split grille and wide-track stance, the new Grand Prix sported vertically stacked head lamps, hidden tail lights, venturi (or, "Coke bottle") side contours and a concave rear window. Most of these became styling hallmarks of other Pontiac lines, as well.

In 1964, Pontiac management defied a GM ban on high performance intermediates and launched the legendary GTO option on its stylish LeMans series. The result of all this innovation was that Pontiac came to completely dominate the medium price field in a way that no other marque has ever done, before or since. Indeed, it appeared that there were no worlds left for Pontiac to conquer. In fact, there were.

Pontiac management had, for several years, been trying to obtain clearance from GM management for a Pontiac two- or four-seater sports type car. Several different designs were advanced, but none received a go-ahead. Whether this would have led to a Corvette type sports car or a Mustang type ponycar is unanswerable at this juncture, but Pontiac designers were clearly working along those lines to no avail.

The fantastic success of the first, 1964½ Ford Mustang changed all that. Although Chevrolet's response, the 1967 Camaro, was surprisingly slow in coming, no one doubted its arrival. Pontiac management pushed for, and won, approval for a wide-track version of this Camaro body shell.

At first, the Pontiac ponycar was to be called the "Banshee," after a show car of the same name. This was changed when someone looked "banshee" up in the dictionary and learned that it was a wailing spirit of death, usually female, in Welsh mythology! This was

Preface

not the sort of connotation Pontiac wanted for its new car, so the Firebird name was appropriated from three GM experimental cars of the late fifties. (Many people, in fact, remain under the misapprehension that these early Firebirds were Pontiac experimentals. Pontiac PR helped propogate this misapprehension when a Firebird prototype was posed with one of the Firebird experimentals in an early publicity photo. That photo appears on the cover of this book, too, because it really is a lovely shot. Incidentally, the Firebird depicted was fitted with Camaro seats! Factory photos aren't always perfect but, at least, when they make mistakes the mistakes are AUTHENTIC mistakes!)

Despite the obvious visual similarity of the early Camaro and Firebird ponycars, the Firebird was much different beneath the skin. Pontiac engines were used, including the remarkable Pontiac overhead cam six, and Pontiac engineers completely went over the chassis doing whatever they deemed necessary to bring Firebird roadability up to wide-track standards. Firebirds were even fitted with fatter tires, an alteration that gave them a lean, muscular look that was so appropriate to the times.

The Firebird was an immediate hit and, while it has since had its ups and downs commercially, it has continued to gain wide respect as one of the few true high performance cars available in an age that seems to be shifting decisively to boring econoboxes. Pontiac Motor Division doesn't mind being the keeper of the flame, as it were, and we are all the richer for its devotion. It is fitting that the second book in this high performance cars series should cover the Firebird.

This book's predecessor, the GTO source book published last fall, was designed to fill a void in the publishing field. While interest in certain marques remains at high levels long after the cars themselves are "new," and even increases, it is harder and harder to find the original factory sales literature on them. When such material is found, it is often priced out of the enthusiast's reach. The GTO book was intended to reprint all of the important factory sales literature along with editing and commentary recounting, in brief form, the history of the marque and clarifying the importance of the various items reproduced. What the reader was left with was a carefully assembled and annotated collection of the essential GTO literature that would have cost hundreds of dollars if assembled individually (assuming that could have been done) combined with an informative, easy to read history of the car. Not surprisingly, the GTO volume met with instantaneous public favor. As this is written, it is the fourth best selling enthusiast car book in the country.

As a consequence of the success of the GTO book, a whole series of similar source books is being launched. This Firebird volume will be joined by Chrysler 300 and AMX editions, with others to follow at a later date. These books are not pretentious, but they are affordable and jam-packed with useful information. It is a potent combination.

Firebirds often had their own sales brochure, apart from the full-line Pontiac item for the year in question. In other years, they were included in the full-line literature. What this book sets out to do is reproduce the relevant sections from the most important or informative brochures for each year. At the beginning of each chapter, the front covers of all of the important Firebird-related brochures are reproduced and they are further described in the text. This should be of help to those enthusiasts who wish to seek out the original items for any particular year or model. In addition to the customer sales literature, the fleet or dealer ordering guides have frequently contained informative and useful information not included in the customer literature and these Firebird spreads have been included for several of the model years.

The items contained herein are not reproduced at the original size (necessarily) but are reduced to fit the available space while still remaining fully readable. Every attempt has been made to ensure the absolute accuracy of the information contained in this book. I will be anxious to hear of any discrepencies so that future editions may be brought up to date. For those wishing more historical information about the Pontiac Firebird or about Pontiacs in general, I would modestly recommend my book, "PONTIAC: The Complete History, 1926-1979," which is available from the same people who published this book and also through better book stores everywhere. It remains the only complete history of the Pontiac and its derivatives ever published.

Washington, D.C.

July, 1981

Contents

In 1967, Pontiac market penetration reached the highest point in its history: 9.98%, or virtually one out of every ten cars sold in the United States was a Pontiac. The sixties had been a fabulous decade for the old indian. Indeed, there were few areas of the market in which Pontiac influence was not felt. One such area, however, was the burgeoning ponycar market which, until that year, had been the sole preserve of the Ford Mustang. The fall of 1966 saw the competition stiffen a bit, what with Chevrolet (Camaro) and Mercury (Cougar) preparing to do battle. The Cougar was not really intended for the Mustang buyer—interdivisional rivalry was not the tradition at Ford that it was at GM—but was designed to be more of an upscale companion car. The Firebird, announced in February of 1967 as a midyear entry, was closer to the Mustang/Camaro concept than it was to that of the Cougar. But whereas the Cougar was basically a Ford beneath the skin, the Firebird was substantially different from its stablemate, the Camaro.

The Firebird shared most of the Camaro's exterior sheet metal and interior trim. The grille and tail lights were unique to the Firebird and, on the inside, details such as the pleating of the seats served to make a little bit of a distinction. The real difference, and what made a Firebird a Firebird, was found in the drivetrain. There were five different Pontiac engines, and, appropriately, five official Firebird models, each known by its engine. The base Firebird came with the 165 hp, 230 cid overhead cam six. The Firebird Sprint featured the four-barrel, 215 hp version of this engine. The Firebird 326 used the standard, two-barrel version of the 326 cid V-8 rated at 250 hp. The Firebird HO was quite a bit quicker with the high output, four-barrel version rated at 285 hp. And, finally, for the real speed freaks, there was the Firebird 400 with its 400 cid V-8 rated at 325 hp. This latter model could also be had with the Ram Air engine rated jokingly at the same horsepower (the insurance companies were supposed to be fooled by this). Actual Ram Air output was considerably more. All models came with standard 3-speed manual transmissions, although a 4-speed was available on all but the base Firebird. A 2-speed automatic was also available on all models save the Firebird 400, which had an optional Turbo Hydra-Matic. The base Firebird listed at $2,666 (for the coupe) and $2,903 for the convertible. The Firebird 326 listed at $2,761 and $2,998, respectively. All Firebirds were available with standard and custom trim options and all models featured GM's new space saver collapsible spare tire.

Firebird production hit 82,560 for the abbreviated 1967 model run. Of this number, 67,032 were coupes and 15,528 were convertibles.

Firebird customer sales literature consisted of a nice color catalogue (see pages 8-15), a color Sunday newspaper supplement at announcement time (see pages 16-22), five color post cards and a contest mailer (see pages 23-26) and a folder listing Firebird accessories (see pages 27-29).

Leave it to Pontiac to do it right. To build a sports car that's completely different. And build it in five exciting versions so that one of the five Firebirds is just right for any kind of driving. Five new sports cars with different driving personalities—one of them yours.

They all share features like wide oval tires, a wood grain dash and deep carpets as standard equipment. And all five are available as a convertible or hardtop coupe in regular or custom trim versions. The convertible has an expanded Morrokide interior and bucket seats as standard, the coupe gives you a choice of these bucket seats or the extra-cost bench.

Which Firebird is for you? Well, as a starter, we even made one of these sleek, exotic machines an economical fun car! But don't let the word economy bother you. This Firebird has the same exciting features and options as the rest of the magnificent Firebird line.

In fact, the main reason for the economy title is because it has a thrifty, one-barrel carburetor, regular fuel version of our astonishing Overhead Cam Six engine. It's astonishing because it serves up traditional six-cylinder economy while the Overhead Cam gives it the muscle to keep up with V-8s. And that's not traditional. At 165 horsepower, the Firebird is pretty spirited economy.

230 cu. in. OHC 6/1-bbl carburetor/regular fuel/ 165-hp/3-speed, column shift.

Firebird

How about a car that's a sports car for you, a family car for your wife? That's the Firebird 326.

We took the features that make driving fun and added them to the elements that make a car practical for a family. Like putting in expanded Morrokide front bucket seats as standard, and then giving you the option of ordering our fold-down rear seat for extra cargo space. And, in the coupes, the extra-cost option of the thin profile front bench seat and fold-down center armrest.

And using a 326 cubic inch V-8 that delivers 250 horsepower, and does it on regular gas. The all-synchro three-speed transmission is standard but if you want something a little special, order the automatic.

Or go all the way with a custom interior-exterior trim package or even air conditioning. Whatever you add to it, the Firebird 326 makes room for a family in a sports car.

326 cu. in. V-8/2-bbl carburetor/regular fuel/250-hp/3-speed, column shift.

Firebird 326

Imagine what you'd have if you took a specially high-tuned version of our exotic, Overhead Cam Six engine and then built a lightweight touring car around it. We'll stop imagining—here it is.

With special high rate springs, sticky wide oval tires and a floor-mounted, all-synchro three-speed.

There's nothing like it this side of the Atlantic. And on the other side, a rally-inspired machine like this would carry a custom price tag.

It's called the Firebird Sprint. And when you try out the 215 horsepower in the high-revving engine, you'll see why it's called Sprint.

Options available for the Sprint include a four-speed manual transmission, Rally II, mag-type steel wheels, front disc brakes, a special gauge cluster and a hood-mounted tach. And more. See the back of the catalog.

Front bucket seats are standard, and you can take your choice of the convertible or the hardtop coupe.

230 cu. in. OHC 6/4-bbl carburetor/premium fuel/215-hp/3-speed, floor shift/h.d. suspension.

Firebird Sprint

The HO in Firebird HO stands for high output. That's what makes it our light heavyweight.

The output comes from a 326 cubic inch V-8 with a 4-barrel and dual exhausts and totals 285 horsepower We coupled this to a manual three-speed with wide oval tires and heavy rate springs and added the sports striping. Now you can see what the HO is all about.

If you'd rather, you can add options like a four-speed manual or an automatic transmission, stereo tape, redline tires and any of the dozens of other options available for the Firebirds.

And naturally, this list includes items like hood-mounted tachometer, your choice of axle ratios and our limited slip differential. So start with the HO, and go.

326 cu. in. V-8/4-bbl carburetor/premium fuel/ 285-hp/3-speed, column shift/dual exhaust.

Firebird HO

Firebird 400

When it talks, you listen.

400 cubic inches, 10.75:1 compression, rated at 325 horsepower @ 4800 rpm, 410 lb. ft. of torque @ 3400 rpm, dual exhausts. (And those dual hood scoops become functional if you order the Ram Air option.)

Special, extra-firm suspension, redline wide oval tires, a floor-mounted, heavy-duty, all-synchro three-speed and front bucket seats. All standard!

And if that isn't enough, consider options like front disc brakes, a heavy-duty four-speed or the three-speed Turbo Hydra-Matic, mag-type steel wheels, hood-mounted tach, exhaust splitters, shoulder belts and a special gauge cluster.

And of course, the Firebird 400 gives you your choice of convertible or hardtop, regular or custom trim, and any one of 15 paint colors—if it really matters.

400 cu. in. V-8/4-bbl carburetor/ premium fuel/325-hp/h.d. 3-speed, floor shift/dual exhaust/h.d. suspension.

These bucket seats are standard in all Firebirds. As is this expanded Morrokide interior, seat back safety latches and seat belts, front and rear.

The custom trim option includes these slim buckets, molded door interior panels, integral front armrests, deluxe steering wheel and decorative exterior trim moldings. Worth the extra cost.

The thin profile bench seat is available in any of the Firebird coupes. The bench seat is extra-cost but the rest of the interior you're looking at comes standard.

The sports wheel, and the special gauge cluster are extra-cost. But if you're the rally type you won't think they're much extra. And that wood grain style dash is standard.

The extra-cost, 2-speed automatic. With the Firebird 400, you can order the 3-speed Turbo Hydra-Matic. For floor shift, you need the extra-cost console. (So we made it specially attractive.)

A 3-speed manual is standard. On the floor of the Sprint and the 400, on the steering column of the rest. A 3- or 4-speed manual is extra-cost and on the floor. (Naturally, the console is available, extra-cost, as is that walnut shift knob.)

If AM-FM radio isn't enough, order the extra-cost stereo tape deck. It includes a rear speaker and its eight tracks can give you up to 60 minutes of anything that can go on tape.

The formal look in a fun car. A rich, Cordova vinyl roof covering available, at extra-cost, in black, white or cream.

Rally II wheels. Mag styled, but all steel for strength. Extra-cost. Redline wide ovals (or white-walls) are standard on the 400, otherwise optional at extra cost.

The deluxe steering wheel and standard instrument cluster. A place for everything and everything in its place.

Have the coolest sports car on the block —add our extra-cost custom air conditioner.

The hood-mounted tach lets you shift properly without looking down from the road. (You do use a tach for shifting, don't you?)

The assist grip (it's too good looking to call it a grab bar) is part of the extra-cost custom trim package.

The extra-cost, fold-down rear seat. It makes a carpeted cargo space that's perfect for big dogs, small children and all sorts of packages.

Those scoops are real with the 400's Ram Air option. This induction system, combined with a different cam and valve springs, lifts the hp peak above 5000 rpm. Extra-cost, but you get what you pay for.

A very sporting extra-cost combination. Redline wide oval tires and polished steel Rally I wheels. The wheels are available only with disc brakes. (The wide ovals are standard on all Firebirds.)

Want more of the sports car look? Add the chromed exhaust splitters and gleaming wire wheel discs.

The Space Saver Spare. Adds 3 cubic feet of usable space to the luggage compartment. Deflated, but if you ever need it, a pressure can, packed with the tire, inflates it in seconds.

Five Firebirds for every kind of driving.

	Firebird	Firebird Sprint	Firebird 326	Firebird HO	Firebird 400
Engine Size (cu. in.)	230	230	326	326	400
Engine type	OHC 6, 1-BBL Regular fuel	OHC 6, 4-BBL Premium fuel	V-8, 2-BBL Regular fuel	V-8, 4-BBL Premium fuel	V-8, 4-BBL Premium fuel
Std. transmission	3-speed Man. (column)	3-speed Man. (floor)	3-speed Man. (column)	3-speed Man. (column)	Heavy-duty 3-speed (floor)
Opt. transmissions (extra cost)	2-speed Auto.	4-speed Man., or 2-speed Auto.	4-speed Man., or 2-speed Auto.	4-speed Man., or 2-speed Auto.	4-speed Man. or 3-speed Turbo Hydra-Matic
Bore & stroke (inches)	3.88 x 3.25	3.88 x 3.25	3.72 x 3.75	3.72 x 3.75	4.12 x 3.75
Horsepower	165 @ 4700 rpm	215 @ 5200 rpm	250 @ 4600 rpm	285 @ 5000 rpm	325 @ 4800 rpm (325 @ 5200 rpm, Ram Air)
Torque (lb. ft.)	216 @ 2600 rpm	240 @ 3800 rpm	333 @ 2800 rpm	359 @ 3200 rpm	410 @ 3400 rpm (410 @ 3600 rpm, Ram Air)
Compression ratio	9.0:1	10.5:1	9.2:1	10.5:1	10.75:1
Oil capacity (less filter)	5 Quarts	5 Quarts	6 Quarts	6 Quarts	6 Quarts
Camshaft duration, degrees—intake	228	244	269	269	273
exhaust	228	244	277	277	289
overlap	14	26	47	47	54
Camshaft lift @ zero lash—intake	.400	.438	.375	.375	.410
exhaust	.400	.438	.410	.410	.413
Valve head diameter—intake	1.92	1.92	1.92	1.92	2.11
exhaust	1.60	1.60	1.64	1.64	1.77
Carburetor, bore dia.—primary	1.75	1.38	1.69	1.44	1.38
secondary		2.25		1.69	2.25
jetting—primary	stick: .069, auto: .065	.071	.057	.092	.070
secondary		.1365		stick: .080, auto: .083	.1365
Spring rates, lbs./in. deflection, front wheel	73	85	85	85	92
rear wheel	100	115	115	115	135
Shipping weight (lbs./hp.) Coupe	2929 (17.7)	3006 (13.9)	3119 (12.4)	3143 (11.0)	3186 (9.8)
Convertible	3203 (19.4)	3280 (15.2)	3393 (13.5)	3417 (11.9)	3460 (10.6)
with 4-spd trans.		+9.0	+6.0	+6.0	−26.0
with auto. trans.	−12.0	−12.0	−30.0	−30.0	+25.0
Radiator cap., qts.	12.1	12.1	18.6	18.6	17.9
Axle ratio† Manual trans. (MPH/1000 rpm, high gear)	3.08:1 (24.1)	3.55:1 (20.9)	3.23:1 (23.0)	3.36:1 (22.1)	3.36:1 (22.1)
Auto. trans.	2.56:1 (29.0)	3.23:1 (23.0)	2.56:1 (29.0)	3.23:1 (23.0)	3.08:1 (24.1)
Optional ratios	3.36:1 (22.1) 2.93:1* (25.4) 3.23:1† (23.0)	2.78:1 (26.7) 3.23:1† (23.0)	3.08:1 (24.1) 2.93:1 (25.4)	3.55:1 (20.9) 3.90:1 (19.0)	3.55:1 (20.9) 3.23:1‡ (23.0) 3.90:1‡ (19.0) 4.33:1‡ (17.0)

†Some ratios require extra-cost items like a h.d. cooling package, limited slip differential, etc. Special 4.11:1 ratio available, dealer installed.
*w/automatic   †w/air conditioning   ‡w/Ram Air

All five Firebirds, like every '67 Pontiac, have a host of standard safety features to help make your driving safer and more comfortable. Some of these are:

Shoulder belt anchors; Padded sun visors; Dual-speed windshield wipers; Windshield washer; Pushbutton seat belt buckles—front and rear (retractors on front); Safety door locks and hinges. Passenger-guard door locks—all doors. Corrosion-resistant brake lines; Folding seat back latches; Padded instrument panel; Four-way hazard warning system; Dual master cylinder brake system with warning light; Backup lights; Outside rearview mirror. Energy absorbing steering column; Energy absorbing steering wheel. Lane-change signal in direction signal control; Inside, day-night, shatter-resistant vinyl-edged mirror with breakaway support.

In addition to the options and accessories on the previous pages, you can personalize your Firebird with these:

Cruise control, Disc brakes (front wheel); Electric clock; Head restraints; Heavy-duty battery; Heavy-duty radiator; Limited slip differential; Luggage carriers; Power brakes; Power steering; Power windows; Safeguard speedometer; Ski carriers; Soft Ray glass (all around or windshield only); Tonneau Cover.

For more information, ask your dealer to show you the rest of the Firebird accessory list.

Get a Firebird model customizing kit. A selection of engines lets you build a beautifully detailed model of any one of the Magnificent Five Firebirds. Or, if you'd rather, order the assembled Firebird model. The customizing kit or the finished model are each only $1.25.

Just print your name and address, enclose $1.25 in cash, check or money order (no stamps, please) and mail to Firebird Model, Model Products Corp., 126 Groesbeck Hwy., Mt. Clemens, Mich. 48043. With the finished model, indicate your choice of Firebird Red Convertible or Tyrol Blue Hardtop.

Firebird General Specifications

Wheelbase		108.1
Tread: Front		59
Rear		60
Tire size*		E 70 x 14, wide-oval
Luggage compartment		9.9 cubic feet, usable
Length, overall		188.8
Width, overall		72.6
Overall height:	Coupe	51.5
	Convertible	51.4
Headroom:	front Coupe	37.0
	Convertible	37.5
	rear Coupe	36.7
	Convertible	36.8
Leg room:	front Coupe	42.5
	Convertible	42.5
	rear Coupe	29.5
	Convertible	29.8
Fuel tank capacity		18.5 gallons
Steering gear ratio:	manual	24:1 w/6 cyl., 28:1 w/V-8
	power	17.5:1
Brake,	diameter: drums 9.5 inches, 269.2 sq. in. swept area (total, std. system) front, disc 11.12 inches; 323.6 sq. in. swept area (total, opt. system)	

*Space Saver Spare is standard, conventional spare tire is a no extra-cost option.

You're a Firebird driver if :

Check the appropriate boxes : ☐ You're in love with sports cars. ☐ You think all cars should have bucket seats, carpeting and a wood grain  styled dash. ☐ You're tired of docking the Queen Mary every time you park. ☐ You're an attractive young secretary. ☐ You *have* an attractive young secretary. ☐ A 3-speed is your speed (but you might pay extra for a silky-smooth automatic). ☐ You love a convertible. But you can find happiness in a sleek hardtop. ☐ You find it hard to believe that a six can act like an eight—but you're willing to be convinced. ☐ You love to run your toes through yards of nylon blend carpeting.☐You  think the loudest noise you hear at 60 should be the thumping of your heart. ☐ Happiness is choosing from an option list that includes everything from rally wheels to power steering. ☐ You like to do something while you're driving—like driving. ☐ And you're a Firebird driver if you don't want to pay an arm and a leg for what you see in the picture down there—plus things like a space-saver collapsible spare and a sophisticated Overhead Cam Six that squeezes 165 hp out of regular fuel. (You don't believe 165 hp? Maybe you're not ready for a brand new Firebird!)

Are you a Firebird winner? Read on!

You're a Firebird Sprint driver if :

Check the appropriate boxes : ☐ Italian movie actresses turn you on. ☐ You look smashing in sunglasses. ☐ You think the greatest engine ever invented is the overhead cam. ☐ You take your vacations at Sebring. Watching cars. ☐ You know a "carrozzeria" isn't some place where you buy bread. ☐ There are times when you'd rather listen to a well tuned engine than a radio. ☐ You sometimes find yourself talking to your car. ☐ You flip

for heavy-duty suspension that welds your car to the road. ☐ You don't want to buy a $12,000 sports car, just drive one. ☐ You sneer at any engine that can't put out over 5,000 rpms. ☐ You crave extra-cost options like front wheel disc brakes and a hood-mounted tach. ☐ You think "vita" can't be "dolce" unless you've got something like you see in the picture, under power of a 4-barrel 215-horsepower Overhead Cam Six. ☐ Does this sound like you, Sport ?

Are you a Firebird Sprint winner? Read on!

You're a Firebird 326 driver if :

Check the appropriate boxes : ☐ You'd like to find a sports car that could please both you and your wife. ☐ You think kids are great, but station wagons are dull. ☐ You could go for V-8 zap if you didn't have to pay for it at the gas station. ☐ You wanted to run away  to sea when you were 40. ☐ You want a sports car that can carry five and an Irish setter. ☐ At the class reunion you were shocked at how old everyone else is getting. ☐ You think a "family" car ought to start with all-Morrokide upholstery, bucket seats or optional bench, carpeting and the complete GM safety package. ☐ You like the Beatles as well as you did Glenn Miller. ☐ You get the urge to shout "contact" every time you start the engine. ☐ You just realized you only live once. ☐ And you're a Firebird 326 driver if you're just waiting for us to clinch it by telling you about its Wide-Track ride and the 326 cubic inch V-8 that delivers a glorious 250 horses on regular (yes, regular!) gas. ☐ Could we be talking about you, Flash ?

Are you a Firebird 326 winner? Read on!

You're a Firebird HO driver if :

Check the appropriate boxes : ☐ You'd sleep with your car—if they'd let you. ☐ You wear chukka boots on dates. ☐ You like the way a trained athlete moves. ☐ You know what 4-bbl carburetion, dual exhausts, heavy rated springs and wide-oval tires are for. ☐ You wear driving gloves even when you're not driving. ☐ You think stripes look better on cars than on ties. ☐ You've been thinking of taking up sky diving. ☐ You just might want a 4.11 rear axle ratio some afternoon, and like to know it's available. ☐ You know a gymkhana isn't something that you eat with rice. ☐ You like knowing you can equip your car with a 4-speed, disc brakes and a hood-mounted tachometer. ☐ You insist cars should be heard as well as seen. ☐ You know in your heart "HO" stands for High Output. (It does.) ☐ And you're a Firebird HO driver if, after one look down there, you want to ask your dealer to open the hood and show you the V8 where all those 285 horses hide out.

Are you a Firebird HO winner? Read on!

You're a Firebird 400 driver if:

Check the appropriate boxes : ☐ You get a kick from champagne. ☐ You know what a chicane is. And what to do when you meet one. ☐ You think all gearshifts belong on the floor. ☐ You're a stick lover but you'd pay more for a 3-speed Turbo Hydra-Matic. ☐ Your wife knows better than to tell you how to drive. ☐ You think scoops on the hood ought to be standard. ☐ You usually come out ahead when you go to Las Vegas. ☐ You think the sound of music is the chirp of wide-oval tires. ☐ You like to gun the engine just to hear the rumble of dual exhausts. ☐ You know what "GT" stands for. And can translate it. ☐ You used to spend your allowance on recordings of engine sounds. ☐ You know the Grand Prix circuit isn't an electrical connection. ☐ A Ram Air induction system does the same thing for your spirits that it does for the engine. ☐ You think all engines should be chromed. ☐ And you're a Firebird 400 driver if you think anything that looks as great as what you see down there deserves nothing less than a 400 cubic inch V-8, complete with a 4-barrel carb, 325 hp and 410 foot pounds of torque. (Just lift the hood!) Is this the real you, Spunky?

Are you a Firebird 400 winner? Read on!

THE NEW YORK TIMES MAGAZINE

You may already have won in Pontiac's Personality Payoff!

Five First Prizes! Winner's choice of a new 1967 Pontiac Firebird, Firebird Sprint, Firebird 326, Firebird HO or Firebird 400. **50 Second Prizes!** Choice of one of five exciting American Airlines one-week tours for two: Astrojet Western Holiday in California and the southwest. Or an Autojet Holiday combining a flight to California and the use of a Firebird for a week. Or an Astrojet Set Tour of seven cities in seven days. Or an Astrojet Acapulco Holiday south of the border. Or the Great Golf Tour—a week for two at one of the country's greatest courses. **150 Third Prizes!** Choice of: Sleek Alumacraft S-12 sailboat and 11-piece Aqualung Skin diving Outfit. Or a surfboard and Magnavox Stereo Set. Or a mink stole and Kodak Home Movie Outfit, complete with camera, projector and screen. Or a complete Garcia Ski Outfit and a Magnavox 19" Color Television. Or a complete Apache Eagle Camping Trailer. **200 Fourth Prizes!** Choice of: Smart 7-piece Samsonite His-and-Her Matched Luggage. Or a Remington Model 1100 12-gauge shotgun and an Irish setter. Or a Kroydon Executive Golf Set and His-and-Her Swimsuit Ensemble by Catalina. Or General Electric 12" Portacolor TV and National Football League Season Tickets for two. Or a Bernz-O-Matic Camping Outfit (including heater, grill, refrigerator, stove and lantern) plus a Garcia Custom Spinning Reel and Rod set. **20,000 Fifth Prizes!** Choice of: Dashing Firebird Glove and Scarf Set for driving (two sets). Or a Hickock Travel Bar and Hickock Game Chest. Or a Polaroid Swinger Camera. Or a Magnavox Portable AM-FM Radio. Or a Garcia Mitchell Fishing Rod and Reel Set.

How do you win? Turn the page!

Prize Claim

"I am a

_____ **driver."**

Official Entry—Pontiac's Firebird Personality Payoff

RULES: This prize offer ends May 15, 1967, and is restricted to licensed drivers 18 years old or older, living in the U.S.A. The offer is void in Wisconsin, and wherever prohibited by federal, state or local law or regulations. Florida residents may check their entry at a Pontiac dealership, or by mailing said entry to a Pontiac dealership for judging. Those not eligible for this offer are personnel of Pontiac dealerships, Pontiac Motor Division, its advertising agency, its suppliers or Visual Services, Inc., and their families. Prizes will be awarded only after final judging and verification of entry form by Visual Services, Inc., 753 Penobscot Building, Detroit, Michigan, whose decision is final. Winners will be responsible for all applicable federal, state and/or local taxes. Only one prize per family.

Here's your Personality Payoff Claim—fill it in now!

If you've taken the test on the preceding pages, the Firebird with the greatest number of "yes" answers is the one that matches your personality best. Now—see if you've already won it for your very own. Simply fill in the name of your Firebird on the Personality Payoff Claim. Then take it to your authorized Pontiac dealer. He'll check it in his Personality Payoff viewer and be able to tell you right away if you've won. Or, if you miss First Prize, your Pontiac dealer will be able to tell you if you've won one of the 20,400 other exciting prizes described on page 7 of this section. But hurry—quiz yourself now! Read the rules carefully . . . then head for your Pontiac dealer's. The Pontiac Firebird Personality Payoff closes midnight, May 15, 1967!

Take this to your Pontiac dealer and see if you've already won a Firebird or any of 20,400 prizes!

Pontiac Motor Division

67

Thank you for entering

Firebird
Personality Payoff

Firebird 400

Come on back...
you may be the
winner of this
Firebird or any of
20,400 prizes!

Which one of these Five Magnificent Firebird first prizes matched your personality best? You may already have won it!

See inside for your

Prize Claim

Leave it to Pontiac to come up with five new sports cars for every kind of driving. From a road-rigged 325-hp **Firebird 400** for grand touring, to a 165-hp regular-gas **Firebird** for funning around. In between there's **Firebird 326,** our 250-hp regular-gas family sportster. **Firebird Sprint,** our European-style 215-hp Overhead Cam Six with floor shift and sports suspension. And our 285-hp light-heavyweight, **Firebird HO.** All come with the complete GM safety package.

Firebird 400

Firebird 326

Firebird Sprint

Firebird HO

Firebird

Prize Claim

Firebird Personality Payoff

"The Firebird that I would like to own is _____."

Official Entry—Pontiac's Firebird Personality Payoff

RULES: This prize offer ends May 15, 1967, and is restricted to licensed drivers 18 years old or older, living in the U.S.A. The offer is void in Wisconsin, and wherever prohibited by law, taxed or regulated. Florida residents may check their entry at a Pontiac dealership, or by mailing said entry to a Pontiac dealership for their entry. These not eligible for this offer are personnel of Pontiac Motor Division, Pontiac Retail Stores, Pontiac dealers, its suppliers or Visual Services, Inc., and their families. Prizes will be awarded only after final judging and verification of entry forms by Visual Services, Inc., 704 Penobscot Building, Detroit, Michigan 48226, whose decision are final. Winners will be responsible for all applicable federal, state and/or local taxes. Only one name per family.

Here's your Personality Payoff Claim—Fill it in now!

Fill in the name of the Firebird that you would like to own. Now . . . see if you have already won it for your very own. Your authorized Pontiac Dealer will check it in his Personality Payoff Viewer and be able to tell you right away if you have won. Or, if you miss First Prize, your Pontiac Dealer will be able to tell you if you have won one of the 20,400 other exciting prizes described in this folder. But hurry—head for your Pontiac Dealer. The Pontiac Firebird Personality Payoff closes Midnight, May 15, 1967!

Take this to your Pontiac dealer and see if you have already won a Firebird or any of 20,400 prizes!

PROTECTION

DOOR EDGE GUARDS (Code 382)
These bright, stainless steel strips help prevent nicks and scratches on door edges. (F,D)

**FLOOR MATS, FRONT (Code 631)
REAR (Code 632)**
Keep car looking new. Easily removed for washing. Available in seven Firebird colors to harmonize with interiors. (F,D)

POWER OPTIONS

POWER BRAKES (Code 502)
Includes bright metal trim plate on brake pedal when factory-installed. Recommended with disc brakes. (Code 521) (F,D)

POWER STEERING (Code 501)
One or two pounds of effort is all you need for the easiest steering you'll ever experience. Makes driving, turning and parking a breeze. (F,D)

POWER WINDOWS (Code 551)
Gives the driver fingertip control of all vertical side windows from a single control panel at his side. Each window has its own control button. Inoperable when ignition is off. (F)

LAMPS

LUGGAGE LAMP (Code 401)
Lights automatically when trunk lid is lifted. Permits free use of both hands for loading and unloading luggage at night. (F,D)

IGNITION SWITCH LAMP (Code 402)
Illuminates the ignition switch area for greater convenience and easier location of key slot. (F)

UNDERHOOD LAMP (Code 421)
Unit similar to Luggage Lamp, but located under engine hood. (F,D)

COMFORT

CUSTOM AIR CONDITIONER (Code 582)
It's combined with heater to give full range comfort control. It heats and cools air, reduces humidity, limits window fogging and filters the air. Lets you ride in cool or warm, cleaner, noise-free comfort. (F)

REAR WINDOW DEFOGGER (Code 374)
A blower under the rear package shelf channels air through a grille to the rear window. Helps give you a clearer view all the time. Not available on Convertibles. (F,D)

SOFT-RAY GLASS (Code 531)
Reduce glare and enjoy more comfortable driving with fully tinted windows. The upper area of the windshield is shaded for added glare reduction. Recommended with air conditioning. Also available in windshield only. (Code 532) (F)

CRUISE CONTROL (Code 441)
Maintain a selected speed automatically by depressing a button located at the end of your turn signal indicator lever. Cruise Control releases to accelerator control with slightest brake pressure. Great for turnpike driving. Available only with Turbo-Hydra-Matic or automatic transmissions, V-8 engines. (F,D)

SAFEGUARD SPEEDOMETER (Code 442)
Warns of excess speed. Control knob lets you select desired speed. Buzzer signals when car exceeds this speed. (F)

CONVENIENCE

FOLD DOWN REAR SEAT (Code 654)
Fully carpeted seat back adds convenience when you want to carry bulky objects. (D)

POWER CONVERTIBLE TOP (Code 544)
Fold top down or put it up without leaving the driver's seat. The control is on the instrument panel. (F)

Custom Seat Belts

Floor Mat

Rear Window Defogger

Pushbutton AM-FM Radio

Fold Down Rear Seat

Cruise Control

Custom Air Conditioner

ELECTRIC CLOCK (Code 474)
Floor mounted, it has a sweep second hand and a built-in automatic self-regulator. Dial is illuminated for easy night reading. (F,D)

REMOTE-CONTROL OUTSIDE MIRROR (Code 394)
Mounts on left-hand door. Convenient and easy to adjust from inside car. (F)

VISOR VANITY MIRROR (Code 391)
Mounts on back of visor. Out of sight when not in use. Ideal for checking makeup, combing hair, etc. (F,D)

RADIOS, REAR SPEAKERS STEREO TAPE PLAYERS

PUSHBUTTON RADIO AND MANUAL ANTENNA (Code 342)
Superior tone and fidelity. Completely transistorized. Wide dial provides space for precise tuning. (F,D)

PUSHBUTTON AM-FM RADIO WITH MANUAL ANTENNA (Code 344)
Offers dual listening enjoyment on either AM or FM frequencies. Completely transistorized. Pushbuttons can be set to either AM or FM or combinations of both. Unusually fine quality and fidelity. (F,D)

REAR SPEAKER (Code 351)
Brilliant tone and depth control. Fader switch lets you play front, rear or both speakers. (F,D)

DELCO STEREO TAPE PLAYER (Code 354)
Mounted under the instrument panel with or without console. The Delco Stereo Tape Player comes with two rear speakers, plus two front speakers. It's available only with any of the several radio options. It has its own built-in amplifiers and plays the new 8-track Stereo Tape Cartridges. It has a "Balance" control that lets you vary the volume between the front and rear speakers. It also has a track selector and tone and volume controls. Not available on heaterless cars, or cars with air conditioning, electric clock or manual transmission with floor shift. (F,D)

STEREO MULTIPLEX ADAPTER
Used with AM-FM Radio, has two front and two rear speakers. Passengers completely surrounded by sound. Light indicates when FM station is broadcasting a Multiplex signal. Can be used with Delco Tape Player. (D)

STEERING WHEELS

DELUXE STEERING WHEEL (Code 462)
Horn activator bars recessed into each of the two wheel spokes. Included in Custom Option. (Order by trim number.)

CUSTOM SPORTS STEERING WHEEL (Code 471)
Handsome "just-like-wood" appearance. Has three equally spaced, brushed stainless steel spokes. Horn button in center. (F)

TILT STEERING WHEEL (Code 504)
Adjusts to seven different positions for individual driving comfort. Permits easier entry and exit, better visibility for shorter people. Not available with standard steering, 3-speed column shift or Turbo Hydra-Matic without console. (F)

MISCELLANEOUS

SAFE-T-TRACK DIFFERENTIAL (Code 731)
Minimizes the hazard of getting stuck. Power is directed to the driving wheel with the best grip on the road surface. Sure handling through rutted roads, on sand or gravel, over bumps or chuck holes, through heavy snow, on wet or icy roads. (F)

RALLY STRIPES (Code 491)
Get the sports car appearance. Rally stripes go from rear wheel opening to front opening. Available in red, white or black. Standard on Firebird HO. (F)

RALLY GAUGE CLUSTER AND HOOD-MOUNTED TACHOMETER (Code 444)
Provides gauges for engine temperature, oil pressure and ammeter in place of indicator lights. Positioned with fuel gauge. Includes Code 704 tachometer. (F)

TACHOMETER (Code 704)
New hood-mounted design, installed outside the car in front of the windshield, in line with the driver. Offers easy, instant reading —minimum of distraction. (F,D)

CUSTOM GEARSHIFT KNOB (Code 524)
Extra-large, walnut shift knob for floor shift manual transmissions. Good looking, fits your hand. (F,D)

TRANSMISSION CONSOLE (Code 472)
Available with bucket seats and floor shift. Finished with wood grain appearance. On both 3- and 4-speed manual transmission, the standard shift knob features a shifting diagram. (F)

DUAL EXHAUSTS (Code 481)
Cuts down back pressure in exhaust system, adds to engine efficiency. Available on 326 V-8 regular fuel engine only. Standard on HO and 400. (F)

EXHAUST TAILPIPE EXTENSIONS (Code 482)
Two gleaming exhaust "splitters" for dual exhaust systems: one "splitter" for 6 cylinder OHC engine. (F,D)

RIDE AND HANDLING PACKAGE (Code 621)
Higher rate front and rear springs, stiffer shock absorber action gives true sports car roadability. (F)

CUSTOM FRONT AND REAR SEAT BELTS (Code 431)
Custom Seat Belts with pushbutton buckle releases and retractors in front seat, no retractors in rear seat. Seat belt colors harmonize with interiors. (F)

FRONT SEAT SHOULDER STRAPS (Code 434)
Give extra security by keeping the torso erect in case of sudden stops. Available with all seat belts for driver and front seat passenger. One end is anchored to the floor, the other end is anchored at the roof rail above the driver or passenger, on all models except convertibles, where it anchors at the rear, inner quarter panel. The shoulder strap is worn diagonally across the torso in conjunction with your seat belt. It has a pushbutton buckle release. (F)

Delco Stereo Tape Player

Custom Gearshift Knob

Electric Clock

Transmission Console

FRONT DISC BRAKES (Code 521)
Air flows around the outside surfaces of the discs and integrally cast internal cooling fins force air between disc surfaces, helps keep them cooler and fade-resistant. Limiting valve adjusts initial line pressures for smooth, even stops. Power brakes (Code 502) recommended. (F)

HOOD RETAINERS
Dual stainless steel posts keep the hood secure. Chrome finished. (D)

DUAL HORNS (Code 494)
Emit a loud, commanding sound. Available on all cars, standard with Custom Option. (F,D)

CUSTOM TRIM

VINYL ROOF (Top No's. 1, 2 and 7)
Comes in your choice of white, black or cream. A handsome addition to any sport coupe's roof.

CUSTOM OPTION
(Order by Trim Number.)
Includes all-expanded Morrokide interiors, full length molded vinyl door trim panels with integral armrests, instrument panel assist grip, recessed door handles and carpeted scuff panels. Deluxe steering wheel, front and rear wheel opening moldings, bright interior roof rail and windshield garnish molding (hardtop coupe only), deluxe wheel covers and dual horns. (F)

STRATO-BENCH FRONT SEAT
Attractive, thin profile bench seat with folding center armrest and individual backrests, available in hardtop coupe only. Order by trim number. (F)

HEAVY-DUTY OPTIONS

HEAVY-DUTY FAN (Code 684)
Gives increased cooling at lower car speeds. For Firebird or Sprint only. (F)

HEAVY-DUTY THERMOSTATICALLY CONTROLLED FAN (Code 514)
Available for 326 and HO, this fan gives increased cooling at low speeds and saves power by disengaging when engine temperature is low. (F)

HEAVY-DUTY ALTERNATOR (Code 674)
55 amp. alternator for use when greater than usual power output is needed. Includes 61 amp. hr. heavy-duty battery. Standard with air, conditioning. (F)

HEAVY-DUTY RADIATOR (Code 681)
Larger capacity gives increased cooling for extreme operating conditions. Standard with air conditioning. (F)

DUAL STAGE, HEAVY-DUTY AIR CLEANER (Code 361)
Dual filter design consists of wetted paper inner filter surrounded by a special polyglycol wetted polyurethane foam outer filter. These two filters give finer filtration, extended service. (F,D)

HEAVY-DUTY BATTERY (Code 678)
This 61 amp. hr. battery provides longer life, greater power and increased cranking ability. Keeps your power accessories operating efficiently. (F,D)

RALLY II WHEELS (Code 453)
These are specially styled. 14-inch steel wheels with a center emblem. They have a stainless steel trim ring and chrome wheel nuts. Available with Front Wheel Disc Brakes. (F)

RALLY I WHEELS (Code 454)
Large openings provide maximum cooling for brakes. Includes stainless steel full trim ring, unique center wheel cap and chrome plated wheel nuts. Available with Front Wheel Disc Brakes. (F)

DELUXE WHEEL DISCS (Code 461)
Pontiac Deluxe disc spinner is made of chrome-flashed stainless steel with radial ribs and cutouts. A red plastic insert forms the center hub ornament with "PMD" letters framed in chrome. (F,D)

CUSTOM WHEEL DISCS (Code 458)
Made of chrome-flashed stainless steel with gray matte finish; black matte panels are surrounded with gleaming chrome. A spinner adds a look of ruggedness. The center of the spinner is black plastic insert with red "PMD" letters framed in chrome. (F,D)

WIRE WHEEL DISCS (Code 452)
For that special flair and sports car look. Gleaming wire spokes handsomely styled and structurally strong. (F,D)

MARK OF EXCELLENCE

**Pontiac Motor Division
General Motors Corporation**

Pontiac Motor Division of General Motors Corporation reserves the right to make changes at any time, without notice, in prices, colors, materials, equipment, specifications and models, and also to discontinue models.

Custom Option

Strato-bench Seat

Vinyl Roof Top

Rally II Wheels

Rally I Wheels

Deluxe Wheel Disc

Custom Wheel Disc

Wire Wheel Disc

Pontiac set a record for model year production in 1968 as 910,977 Wide-Tracks were built. While this was a piece of good cheer, market penetration was down slightly—not so much as to do any damage, but enough to warn of future problems.

The Firebird, which had been all-new in mid-1967, was hardly changed at all for 1968. The two alterations of any significance were not done specifically for the Firebird, but effected all Pontiacs: the 326 cid V-8 was upgraded to 350 cid and the front vent windows were eliminated. The former change necessitated renaming the middle Firebird the "Firebird 350." The latter change, shared with the Grand Prix, was a harbinger of things to come in the industry as manufacturers, under increasingly severe inflationary pressures, sought to shave nickels and dimes wherever possible in order to keep profit margins high and retail prices low. From the vantage point of 1981, they seem to have failed miserably on both counts. The special irony of this particular move involved the amount of publicity GM had given vent windows when they were first introduced in 1933 ("Fisher No Draft Ventilation," as they were originally known). It is amusing, to say the least, to compare the initial ballyhooing with GM's later attempt to paint a return to the pre-1933 system as some sort of improvement.

Additional modifications for 1968 included a refined rear suspension and revised interiors. The standard Firebird now listed at $2,781 for the coupe and $2,996 for the convertible. The Firebird 350 listed at $105 more, while the Firebird 400 cost $273.

Firebird production climbed to 107,112 units for the model run. Of these, 90,152 were coupes, 16,960 were convertibles.

Firebird customer sales literature for 1968 consisted of a two-page spread in the Pontiac full-line saver catalogue (see pages 32-33), a special Firebird catalogue (see pages 34-36), two different post cards (see page 37) and coverage in the 1968 Pontiac high performance catalogue, the front cover of which is reproduced below along with the other Firebird related literature. The Firebird sections from the color and trim brochure are reproduced on page 38.

FIREBIRD 400 CONVERTIBLE

Firebirds/The Magnificent Five

Never satisfied, our engineers. Having created one of the most successful new sports cars of 1967, they might have paused to savor the cheers of a growing multitude of Firebird owners. But no. Perfectionists to the core, they have labored long and lovingly on a host of refinements which make The Magnificent Five even more so for 1968. New rear suspension enhances the ride of The Five this year. New engines move them. New interiors of glove-smooth expanded Morrokide add new luxury. A new upper-level ventilation system lets us eliminate the vent windows, leaving you with a big, picture-window view of the world (while a host of new safety features lets you explore it with added security). What else? Examples abound on the following pages. Explore them. And when you discover which of these Great American Sports is for you—drive it.

The standard—but hardly ordinary—Firebird interior (below) sports slimline buckets in expanded Morrokide, copious carpeting and a simulated burl wood grain dash. Also standard: wide-oval tires and an ingenious space-saver spare.

All Firebirds come with slimline bucket seats, but order our custom trim option and they'll be covered with the elegant new woven vinyl upholstery on display on the next page. You'll also get such styling slickeries as molded door interior panels, integral front armrests, deluxe steering wheel, assist grip and decorative exterior trim moldings. The console isn't included in the custom trim package, but it, too, is well worth the extra cost. Of course, you can practically design your own Firebird. Our option list is filled with magnificent suggestions.

FIREBIRD 400 CONVERTIBLE

FIREBIRD H.O. HARDTOP COUPE

FIREBIRD 350 CONVERTIBLE

FIREBIRD SPRINT HARDTOP COUPE

FIREBIRD HARDTOP COUPE

19

Feature this:

All Firebirds come with slimline bucket seats, but order our custom trim option and they'll be covered with the elegant new woven-vinyl upholstery on display at right. You'll also get such styling slickeries as molded door interior panels, integral front armrests, deluxe steering wheel, assist grip and decorative exterior trim moldings. The console isn't included in the custom trim package, but it, too, is well worth the extra cost.

Of course, you can practically design your own Firebird. Our option list is filled with magnificent suggestions. Those seat belts with pushbutton buckles are standard equipment at *all* passenger positions. They're just one of an impressive array of safety features which are standard on all 1968 Pontiacs.

Among the more notable are:
Energy absorbing steering column; Passenger-guard door locks with deflecting lock buttons—all doors; Four-way hazard warning flasher; Dual master cylinder brake system with warning light and corrosion-resistant brake lines; Folding seatback latches; Dual-speed windshield wipers and washers; Outside rearview mirror; Backup lights, new side marker lights and parking lamps that illuminate with headlamps; Padded instrument panel, sun visors; Reduced-glare instrument panel top, inside windshield moldings, horn buttons, steering wheel hub and windshield wiper arms and blades; Inside day-night mirror with deflecting base; Lane-change feature in direction signal control; Safety armrests; Thick laminate windshield; Soft, low-profile window control knobs and coat hooks; Padded front and intermediate seatback tops and lower structure; Yielding smooth-contoured door and window regulator handles.

1. Firebird 400's standard 400-cubic-inch V-8 comes with Quadra-jet carburetion and dual exhausts, and delivers 330 hp. Or you can order our extra-cost H.O. version with high-output cam and free-flowing exhaust.
2. The 400's scoops become functional when you add our Ram Air option. Which means that this induction system, combined with a higher output cam and valve springs, lifts both the horsepower and the horsepower peak. Which means the extra cost is money well spent.
3. The standard—but hardly ordinary—Firebird interior sports slimline buckets in expanded Morrokide, deep-pile carpeting, simulated burl wood grain dash and everything you see in the picture, except the shoulder belts. (And the model. Sorry about that.) A thin-profile front bench seat is available at extra cost.
4. Our mag-type Rally II wheels are all steel for extra strength and they'll cost you very little extra. The redlines (or whitelines) are standard on the 400, extra-cost on the other four Firebirds. Of course, wide-oval tires are standard on all five.
5. Order our special sports wheel for a continental touch. And if you're really the rally type, add our special gauge cluster and a hood-mounted tach (neither shown). If AM/FM radio isn't enough sound for you, order the stereo tape deck. All extra cost, but why not live a little?
6. Our revolutionary, 175-hp Overhead Cam Six performs like the sophisticated European sports machines it was inspired by. On regular fuel. A 4-BBL., premium-fuel, 215-hp version moves Firebird Sprint.

Picture this! You can get a magnificent 4-color reproduction of Firebird 400 and four other swinging Wide-Tracks, plus complete specs and decals by sending a mere 30¢ (50¢ outside U.S.A.) to: '68 Wide-Tracks, P.O. Box 888, 196 Wide-Track Blvd., Pontiac, Michigan 48056.

	Firebird	Firebird Sprint	Firebird 350	Firebird H.O.	Firebird 400		
					400	400 H.O.	400 Ram Air
Engine size (cu. in.)	250	250	350	350	400	400	400
Engine type	OHC 6, 1-BBL Regular fuel	OHC 6, 4-BBL Premium fuel	V-8, 2-BBL Regular fuel	V-8, 4-BBL Premium Fuel	V-8, 4-BBL Premium fuel	V-8, 4-BBL Premium fuel	V-8, 4-BBL Premium fuel
Std. transmission	3-speed Man. (column)	3-speed Man. (floor)	3-speed Man. (column)	3-speed Man. (column)	Heavy-duty 3-speed (floor)	Heavy-duty 3-speed (floor)	Heavy-duty 4-speed Man. (floor)
Opt. transmissions (extra cost)	4-speed Man., or 2-speed Auto.	4-speed Man., or 2-speed Auto.	H.O. 3-speed Man., 4-speed Man., or 2-speed Auto.	H.O. 3-speed Man., 4-speed Man., or 2-speed Auto.	4-speed Man. or 3-speed Turbo Hydra-Matic	4-speed Man. or 3-speed Turbo Hydra-Matic	4-speed Man. or 3-speed Turbo Hydra-Matic
Bore & stroke (inches)	3.88 x 3.53	3.88 x 3.53	3.88 x 3.75	3.88 x 3.75	4.12 x 3.75	4.12 x 3.75	4.12 x 3.75
Horsepower	175 @ 4800 rpm	215 @ 5200 rpm	265 @ 4600 rpm	320 @ 5100 rpm	330 @ 4800 rpm	335 @ 5000 rpm	335 @ 5300 rpm
Torque (lb.-ft.)	240 @ 2600 rpm	255 @ 3800 rpm	355 @ 2800 rpm	380 @ 3200 rpm	430 @ 3300 rpm	430 @ 3400 rpm	430 @ 3600 rpm
Compression ratio	9.0:1	10.5:1	9.2:1	10.5:1	10.75:1	10.75:1	10.75:1
Oil capacity (less filter)	5 Quarts	5 Quarts	5 Quarts	5 Quarts	5 Quarts	5 Quarts	5 Quarts
Camshaft duration, degrees—intake	240	244	269	273	273	228 (Man.) 273 (Auto.)	301 (Man.) 288 (Auto.)
exhaust	240	244	277	289 (Man.) 282 (Auto.)	289	302 (Man.) 289 (Auto.)	313 (Man.) 302 (Auto.)
overlap	28	25	47	54 (Man.) 55 (Auto.)	54	63 (Man.) 54 (Auto.)	76 (Man.) 63 (Auto.)
Camshaft lift @ zero lash—intake	.400	.438	.376	.410	.410	.414 (Man.) .410 (Auto.)	.414 (Man.) .410 (Auto.)
exhaust	.400	.438	.412	.413	.413	.413	.413
Valve head diameter—intake	1.92	1.92	1.96	1.96	2.11	2.11	2.11
exhaust	1.60	1.60	1.66	1.66	1.77	1.77	1.77
Carburetor, bore dia.—primary	1.75	1.38	1.69	1.38	1.38	1.38	1.38
secondary	.128	2.25		2.25	2.25	2.25	2.25
Spring rates, (lbs./in.) deflection, front wheel (a)	73 (92)	73 (92)	85 (92)	85 (92)	85 (92)	85 (92)	85 (92)
rear wheel (a)	83 (119)	90 (119)	90 (119)	90 (119)	90 (119)	90 (119)	90 (119)
Shipping weight (est.) (lbs./hp.) coupe	3032 (17.3)	3087 (14.4)	3188 (12.0)	3226 (10.1)	3303 (10.01)	3303 (9.9)	3303 (9.9)
convertible	3294 (18.8)	3346 (15.6)	3460 (13.1)	3498 (10.9)	3575 (10.8)	3375 (10.08)	3375 (10.08)
with 4-spd trans.	+9.0	+9.0	+6.0	+6.0	−13.0	−13.0	0
with auto trans.	−10.0	−10.0	−4.0	−4.0	+32.0	+32.0	+45.0
Radiator cap., (qts.)	12.1	12.1	18.6	18.6	17.8	17.8	17.8
Axle ratio#, (00)—mph/1000 rpm in high gear manual trans.	3.55:1 (20.9)	3.55:1* (21.4)	3.23:1 (23.5)	3.36:1* (22.6)	3.36:1* (22.1) (22.6)	3.36:1* (22.6)	3.90:1* (19.5)
auto trans.	3.23:1 (23.0)	3.23:1 (23.5)	2.56:1 (29.7)	3.23:1 (23.5)	3.08:1 (24.1) (24.7)	3.08:1 (24.7)	3.90:1* (19.5)
optional ratios	3.08:1 (24.1) 2.41:1** (29.0) 3.23:1† (23.0) Spec. ord. 3.55:1* (20.9)	2.78:1** (27.3) 3.55:1** (21.4)	3.08:1* (24.7) 2.93:1** (25.9) 2.78:1† (27.3)	2.78:1*† (27.3) Spec. ord. 3.55:1* (21.4) Spec. ord. 3.90:1 (19.5)	3.55:1* (21.4) 2.56:1*† (29.7) 3.23:1** (23.5) Spec. ord. 3.90:1** (19.5) Spec. ord. 4.33:1* (17.5)	3.55:1** (21.4) 2.56:1*† (29.7) Spec. ord. 3.90:1** (19.5) Spec. ord. 4.33:1* (17.5)	Spec. ord. 4.33:1* (17.5)

#Some ratios require extra-cost items like a h.d. cooling package, limited slip differential, etc. Special 4.11:1 ratio available, dealer-installed.
*w/automatic   †w/air conditioning   (a) Figure in ( ) indicates rate with firm ride and handling option—rate for rear spring on convertibles is increased to 123.
•Not available w/air conditioning (automatic transmission only)

Firebird General Specifications

Wheelbase		108.1
Tread: Front		60
Rear		60
Tire size*		E:70 x 14, wide-oval (a)
Luggage compartment		9.9 cubic feet, usable
Length, overall		188.8
Width, overall		72.8
Height, overall	Coupe	50.0
	Convertible	49.9
Headroom: front	Coupe	37.0
	Convertible	37.5
rear	Coupe	36.7
	Convertible	36.8

Leg room: front	Coupe	42.5
	Convertible	42.5
rear	Coupe	29.5
	Convertible	29.8
Fuel tank capacity		18.5 gallons
Steering gear ratio: manual		24:1 w/6 cyl.; 28:1 w/V-8
power		17.5:1

Brake, diameter: drums 9.5 inches; 269.2 sq. in. swept area (total, std. system) front, disc 11.12 inches; 323.6 sq. in. swept area (total, optional system)
*Space-Saver Spare is standard, conventional spare tire is a no-extra-cost option.
(a) F:70x14 std. with Firebird Sprint, 350, H.O. & 400 options.

In addition to the options and accessories noted on the previous pages, you can personalize your Firebird with these: Cruise control; Electric clock; Head restraints; Heavy-duty battery; Heavy-duty radiator; Limited slip differential; Luggage carriers; Power windows; Power brakes; Power steering; Safeguard speedometer; Soft-Ray glass (all around or windshield only); Rally I wheels (available only with disc brakes); Walnut shift knob and much, much more. Your Pontiac dealer will be happy to show you our entire accessory encyclopedia.

MARK OF EXCELLENCE

FIREBIRD 400 HARDTOP COUPE

Firebird

Hardtop Coupe (22337) Convertible (22367)
Strato Bucket Seats (Standard)

Hardtop Coupe (22337)
Strato Bench Seat with Center Armrest
(Optional at Extra Cost)

Firebird Custom Interior
(EXTRA-COST OPTION)

Hardtop Coupe (22337) Convertible (22367)
Strato Bucket Seats

Expanded Morrokide

Interior	Recommended Exterior Colors
250 TEAL	A, C, D, E, F, L
251 GOLD	A, C, G, Q, T
252 RED	A, C, N, R
253 BLACK	A, C, D, E, F, G, K, L N, P, Q, R, T, V, Y
261 TURQUOISE	A, C, K
262 PARCHMENT	A, C, D, E, F, G, K, L N, P, Q, R, T, V, Y

Expanded Morrokide

Interior	Recommended Exterior Colors
272 BLACK	A, C, D, E, F, G, K, L N, P, Q, R, T, V, Y
273 PARCHMENT	A, C, D, E, F, G, K, L N, P, Q, R, T, V, Y

Knit Vinyl & Expanded Morrokide

Interior	Recommended Exterior Colors
255 TEAL	A, C, D, E, F, L
256 TURQUOISE	A, C, K
257 GOLD	A, C, G, Q, T
258 RED	A, C, N, R
259 BLACK	A, C, D, E, F, G, K, L N, P, Q, R, T, V, Y
260 PARCHMENT	A, C, D, E, F, G, K, L N, P, Q, R, T, V, Y

Firebird Custom Interior
(EXTRA-COST OPTION)

Hardtop Coupe (22337)
Strato Bench Seat with Center Armrest
(Optional at Extra Cost)

Knit Vinyl & Expanded Morrokide

Interior	Recommended Exterior Colors
269 BLACK	A, C, D, E, F, G, K, L N, P, Q, R, T, V, Y
275 PARCHMENT	A, C, D, E, F, G, K, L N, P, Q, R, T, V, Y

Exterior Finishes

A Starlight Black
Two-tone
Combinations
C, F, P

C Cameo Ivory
Two-tone
Combinations
A, D, E, G, K, L

D Alpine Blue
Two-tone
Combinations
A*, C, E
(*upper only)

E Aegena Blue
Two-tone
Combinations
C, D

F Nordic Blue
Two-tone
Combinations
A, C*, L
(*upper only)

G April Gold
Two-tone
Combinations
A*, C,
(*upper only)

K Meridian Turquoise
Two-tone
Combinations
A*, C
(*upper only)

L Aleutian Blue
Two-tone
Combinations
A*, C, F
(*upper only)

N Flambeau Burgundy
Two-tone
Combinations
A*, C*
(*upper only)

P Springmist Green
Two-tone
Combinations
A, C*, V
(*upper only)

Q Verdoro Green
Two-tone
Combinations
A*, C*
(*upper only)

R Solar Red
Two-tone
Combinations
A*, C*
(*upper only)

T Primavera Beige
Two-tone
Combinations
A*, C*
(*upper only)

V Nightshade Green
Two-tone
Combinations
A*, C*, P
(*upper only)

Y Mayfair Maize
Two-tone
Combinations
A*, C*
(*upper only)

1968 Convertible Top Usage Chart

Firebird (22367), Tempest Custom (23567), Le Mans (23767), GTO (24267), Catalina (25267) and Bonneville (26267).

Top Color Code Number: 1 Ivory-White 2 Black 5 Teal 8 Gold

Black Interior Trim
Numbers 217, 223, 235, 253, 259, 520, 521, 567, 570, 572

A—1,2	N—1,2
C—1,2	P—1,2
D—1,2	Q—1,2
E—1,2	R—1,2
F—1,2,5	T—1,2,8
G—1,2,8	V—1,2
K—1,2	Y—1,2
L—1,2,5	

Parchment Interior
Trim Numbers 224, 236, 260, 262, 524, 568, 573

A—1,2	N—1,2
C—1,2,5	P—1,2
D—1,2	Q—1,2
E—1,2	R—1,2
F—1,2,5	T—1,2,8
G—1,2,8	V—1,2
K—1,2	Y—1,2
L—1,2,5	

Gold Interior Trim
Numbers 221, 251, 257, 518

A—1,2,8	Q—1,2
C—1,2,8	T—1,2,8
G—1,2,8	

Red Interior Trim
Numbers 218, 225, 252, 258, 519, 566

A—1,2	N—1,2
C—1,2	R—1,2

Teal Interior Trim
Numbers 219, 250, 255, 564

A—1,2,5	E—1,2
C—1,2,5	F—1,2,5
D—1,2	L—1,2,5

Blue Interior Trim
Numbers 213, 516

A—1,2,5	E—1,2
C—1,2,5	F—1,2,5
D—1,2	L—1,2,5

TRANS AM
400 CU. IN.
335 H.P.
400 CU IN
345 H.P.

1969

There was good news and bad news for Pontiac enthusiasts in 1969. The bad news was that sales took on disturbing downward momentum, giving a taste of grim times ahead for the division. The good news was a dramatically successful new Grand Prix, now on an intermediate body shell and featuring some of the best Pontiac styling in years. There was also a new Firebird, although whether it represented good news or bad depended on one's point of view and what development one was discussing.

The reskinning of the 1967-68 Firebird/Camaro body was not generally considered successful. It was hard to explain exactly why, but to most people the new models simply didn't look as nice as the old ones. Sales dropped precipitously and the all-new 1970 Firebirds (and Camaros) were delayed until early calendar year 1970 to allow for an extended 1969 model year-end cleanup campaign. The Camaro sold better than the Firebird, although the Firebird had the added problem of competing against the fabulous new Grand Prix. Total Firebird production for the seventeen-month 1969 model run was 87,708 units—down 19% from the normal 1968 model run. Of this number, 76,051 were coupes and 11,657 were convertibles.

The good news for Firebird in 1969—and it was very good news, indeed—was the advent of the first Trans Am. The Trans Am was not greeted by any sort of special fanfare upon its introduction; in fact, it was

years before it came to be appreciated. There was not even any customer sales literature issued on it that first year. It was a companion car to the GTO Judge, being basically a trim option on the Firebird 400 replete with spoilers, decals and hood scoops, much as the Judge was a cosmetic option for the high output Goats. In time, however, the Trans Am would become the high output Firebird itself and for that reason alone its birth would have been a special event for Firebird enthusiasts. Only 697 were built in 1969, including 689 coupes and 8 (that's right, 8) convertibles.

All 1969 Firebirds included the full compliment of government mandated safety items. Everything in the passenger compartment was padded or recessed. Head rests had been standard since the middle of the 1968 model run and now they were joined by shoulder belts and an anti-theft ignition lock. Prices were up by about 1%.

The 1969 Firebird literature consised of a spread in the full-line Pontiac catalogue saver (see pages 40-41), a spread in the Pontiac high performance catalogue (see page 42), and, as usual, a separate Firebird catalogue (see pages 43-44). There was no Trans Am literature, but there was a supplemental insert for the dealer data book (see page 45). There were two different post cards (see page 46) and the customary mention in the color and trim brochure (see page 48). A 1969 dealer order blank has also been included here, on page 47.

1969 Pontiac Colors & Interiors

FIREBIRD '69

PONTIAC '69

Four leading car experts report on Pontiac's Break Away Squad for '69—

22

FIREBIRD 400 CONVERTIBLE

FIREBIRD 350 CONVERTIBLE

FIREBIRD H.O. HARDTOP COUPE

FIREBIRD SPRINT HARDTOP COUPE

FIREBIRD HARDTOP COUPE

Firebirds

It doesn't take much figuring to understand why we call this year's 400 the Big Daddy of the Firebird aerie. 400 cubic inches of V-8. 330 hp at 4800 rpm. 10.75:1 compression ratio. Heavy-duty, fully synchronized 3-speed with Hurst shifter. Dual exhausts. Redline wide-ovals. You sure wouldn't name a machine like that "mom." Then there's our Firebird H.O. And that definitely doesn't stand for hands off. Not with a 350-cubic-inch, 325-hp V-8 in league with a fully synched 3-speed. Quadra-jet carb. High-lift cam. Heavy-rated front and rear springs. Heavy-duty clutch. And dual exhausts. Consider, also, our Firebird 350. It used to be that when dad passed out cigars he had to pass up sports cars. That day ended when we came up with this one. Take budgeting. It runs on regular. Yet with 265 hp, it moves when told. Versatility? We thought of that, too. Seats are upholstered in soft expanded Morrokide. A swipe with a sponge and they're clean. If you like, order the custom trim and they'll be done up in woven-vinyl upholstery that breathes (see right). Now about our Firebird Sprint. We get economy from a 250-cubic-inch Overhead Cam Six. Which just happens to have a high-output cam, 4-barrel carb, low-restriction exhaust system and 230 horses. So, you see, we get performance, too. Lastly, we offer you our Firebird. But it's hard to believe this is a basic anything. Not with those all-new looks; new camera-case-grain instrument panel; new wider, softer front buckets. And certainly not with our 175-hp OHC 6 that runs, not walks, on regular fuel. Make a believer out of you? They should. They're Firebirds. And from Pontiac.

23

Firebird plus all this plumbing equals grand touring.

Brand-new, larger buckets in '69.

See that redline? Don't fool with it.

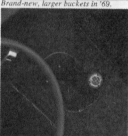

Dress-up Rally II wheels can be ordered with Polyglas cord tires and front discs.

4-speed plus Hurst. Worth every cent.

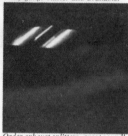

Rally gauge cluster also available.

You can add our sports steering wheel. Order exhaust splitters--great sound!

Talk about Dean Batchelor and you talk about one of the most knowledge-able automotive journalists in the western world. Editorial Director for Bond Publishing Company (Road & Track and Car Life Magazines), Dean adds our '69 Firebird 400 H.O. to an astounding list of machinery he's handled during his long writing career. Here are some of his impressions, noted during a series of super-secret test runs at the Waterford Hills road course outside Detroit.

If you like your styling bold, exciting and thoroughly contempo-rary, then you'll like Pontiac's '69 Firebird 400. Pontiac designers have purposely kept superfluous ornamentation to a minimum. The hood-mounted tach (which I consider a styling feature) took some getting used to, but it certainly is visible and in the direct line of sight. Admittedly, front-end styling follows the Pontiac family styling theme, but my own personal preference (not necessarily a typical reaction) would be to see less overhang at the front.

Put it all together, though, and the F-Bird is a handsome automobile, one of the most distinctive of the growing number of American Ponycars.

The general interior layout of the 400 suits me almost perfectly. Perfection could be achieved, for me anyway, by a slight relocation of the shift lever. The Hurst shifter for the 4-speed unit works beautifully. I couldn't ask for a smoother operating unit.

But, I found myself reaching for first and third. This probably has to do with my favorite driving position, which is "seat-all-the-way-back"— and should not necessarily be construed as representative of the average Firebird driver. That is why the Firebird comes so close to suiting me as an enthusiast driver.

The interior is one of the most pleasing of the contemporary American cars—luxurious without being gaudy.

As to performance, what can be said? The 400 H.O. represents nearly the top end of the Firebird series (the 400 Ram Air IV option being the ultimate). And, of course, the Pontiac philosophy of building to buyer specifications permits a bewildering array of equipment that can turn an "economy" model into a banker's delight.

Our driving was accomplished with a 400 H.O. 4-bbl. Quadra-jet V-8 driving through a 4-speed close-ratio gearbox. Such niceties as variable-

ratio power steering, tilting sports steering wheel, power brakes with discs at front and power windows are among the items specified when the customer wants his performance luxurious. My preference runs to high-speed touring rather than acceleration, so I like the 350 H.O. with a cruising axle (say, 3.08 to 1), 3-speed Turbo Hydra-matic and air conditioning. But that doesn't mean this setup would be perfect for every buyer.

Which brings me to a favorite topic . . . the American Grand Touring car. This is what Firebird really is. A domestic GT in the truest sense of the word. Fast. Quiet. Comfortable. Reliable. And serviceable. It's time to build an image for the American-style GT. And Firebird is one of the leaders in establishing that image.

PONTIAC FIREBIRD 400

ENGINE

Type	ohv V-8
Bore and stroke	4.12 x 3.75
Displacement	400 cubic inches
Compression ratio	10.75:1
Bhp @ rpm	330 @ 4800
Torque @ rpm	430 @ 3300 rpm
Carburetion	4-bbl
Type fuel required	premium

CHASSIS/BODY

Brakes	drums, 9.5 in; 269.2 sq. in., swept area. Front disc diameter, 11.12 in.; 323.6 sq. in., total opt. system
Wheels	steel 14 in. x 7 in.
Tires	Wide-oval Redline F70—14
Steering	ratio 28:1; power 17.5:1
Suspension	heavy-duty springs with wheel rates of 85.0 lbs. per in., front; 90 lbs. per in., rear

ACCOMMODATION

Seating capacity, persons	5
Seats	bucket-type, front

INSTRUMENTATION

Instruments: speedometer, odometer, fuel, oil-pressure, engine-temp. and ammeter light gauges and clock.
Warning lights: brake, turn indicator, high beam.

GENERAL

Wheelbase	108.1"
Track, front/rear	60/60
Overall length	191.1"
width	73.9"
height	49.6"
Ground clearance, in.	N.A.
Overhang, front/rear	40.7/42.3
Fuel tank capacity, gal.	18.5

Some of the equipment illustrated, described in copy or referred to above is available at extra cost. Consult your local Pontiac dealer for model availability and costs.

Firebird Specs.

Every Firebird we make this year will be outfitted with the following safety, anti-theft and convenience equipment:

Energy absorbing steering column

Seat belts with pushbutton buckle releases for *all* passenger positions

Shoulder belts with pushbutton buckle releases and special storage convenience provision for driver and right front passenger (except convertibles)

Two front-seat head restraints

Passenger-guard door locks—with forward-mounted lock buttons

Four-way hazard warning flasher

Dual master cylinder brake system, with warning light and corrosion-resistant brake lines

Folding seat back latches

Dual-speed windshield wipers and washers

Dual-action safety hood latches

Outside rearview mirror

Backup lights

Side marker lights and parking lamps that illuminate with headlamps

Energy absorbing instrument panel, padded sun visors

Reduced-glare instrument panel top, inside windshield moldings, horn buttons, steering wheel hub and windshield wiper arms and blades

Wide, inside day-night mirror with deflecting base

Lane-change feature in direction signal control

Safety armrests

Thick laminate windshield

Soft, low-profile window control knobs, coat hooks, dome lamp

Padded front seat back tops

Smooth contoured door and window regulator handles

Anti-theft ignition key warning buzzer

Anti-theft ignition, steering and transmission lock

Starter safety switch on all transmissions

Safety rim wheels

Safety door latches and hinges

Uniform automatic transmission quadrant (P R N D L and P R N D S L)

Snag-resistant steering wheel hardware

Door hinges, stamped steel (at least one assembly per door)

Nonprojecting wheel nuts, discs and caps

Improved fuel tank retention

Improved glove box door latches

10

Engine size (cu. in.)	Firebird 250	Firebird Sprint 250	Firebird 350 350	Firebird H.O. 350	400	Firebird 400 400 H.O.	400 Ram Air IV
Engine type	OHC 6, 1-BBL Regular fuel	OHC 6, 4-BBL Premium fuel	V-8, 2-BBL Regular fuel	V-8, 4-BBL Premium fuel	V-8, 4-BBL Premium fuel	V-8, 4-BBL Premium fuel	V-8, 4-BBL Premium fuel
Std. transmission	3-speed Man. (column)	3-speed Man. (floor)	3-speed Man. (column)	3-speed Man. (column)	Heavy-duty 3-speed (floor)	Heavy-duty 3-speed (floor)	Heavy-duty 4-speed Man. (floor)
Opt. transmissions (extra cost)	4-speed Man., 2-speed Auto., or Turbo Hydra-matic	4-speed Man., or Turbo Hydra-matic	H.D. 3-speed Man., 4-speed Man., Auto., or Turbo Hydra-matic	H.D. 3-speed Man., 4-speed Man., or Turbo Hydra-matic	4-speed Man. or 3-speed Turbo Hydra-matic	4-speed Man. or 3-speed Turbo Hydra-matic	4-speed Man. or 3-speed Turbo Hydra-matic
Bore & stroke (inches)	3.88 x 3.53	3.88 x 3.53	3.88 x 3.75	3.88 x 3.75	4.12 x 3.75	4.12 x 3.75	4.12 x 3.75
Horsepower	175 @ 4800 rpm	215 @ 5200 rpm	265 @ 4600 rpm	325 @ 5100 rpm	330 @ 4800 rpm	335 @ 5000 rpm	345 @ 5400 rpm
Torque (lb.-ft.)	240 @ 2600 rpm	255 @ 3800 rpm	355 @ 2800 rpm	380 @ 3200 rpm	430 @ 3300 rpm	430 @ 3400 rpm	430 @ 3700 rpm
Compression ratio	9.0:1	10.5:1	9.2:1	10.5:1	10.75:1	10.75:1	10.75:1
Oil capacity (less filter)	5 Quarts	5 Quarts	5 Quarts	5 Quarts	5 Quarts	5 Quarts	5 Quarts
Camshaft duration, degrees—intake	240	244	269	288	273	228 (Man.) 273 (Auto.)	301 (Man.) 288 (Auto.)
exhaust	240	244	277	302	289	302 (Man.) 289 (Auto.)	313 (Man.) 302 (Auto.)
overlap	28	26	47	63	54	63 (Man.) 54 (Auto.)	76 (Man.) 63 (Auto.)
Camshaft lift @ zero lash—intake	.400	.438	.376	.414	.410	.414 (Man.) .410 (Auto.)	.414 (Man.) .410 (Auto.)
exhaust	.400	.438	.412	.413	.413	.413	.413
Valve head diameter—intake	1.92	1.92	1.96	2.11	2.11	2.11	2.11
exhaust	1.60	1.60	1.66	1.77	1.77	1.77	1.77
Carburetor, bore dia.—primary	1.69	1.38	1.69	1.38	1.38	1.38	1.38
secondary		2.25		2.25	2.25	2.25	2.25
Spring rates, (lbs./in.) deflection, front wheel (a)	73 (92)	73 (92)	85 (92)	85 (92)	85 (92)	85 (92)	85 (92)
rear wheel (a)	83 (119)	90 (119)	90 (119)	90 (119)	90 (119)	90 (119)	90 (119)
Shipping weight (est.) (lbs./hp.) coupe	3084 (17.6)	3137 (14.6)	3239 (12.2)	3280 (10.1)	3319 (10.1)	3319 (9.9)	3319 (9.6)
convertible	3367 (19.2)	3420 (15.9)	3522 (13.3)	3563 (10.9)	3602 (10.9)	3602 (10.8)	3602 (10.4)
with 4-spd. trans.	+9.0	+9.0	+6.0	+6.0	−13.0	−13.0	−13.0
with auto. trans.	−10.0	−10.0	−4.0	−4.0	+32.0	+32.0	+45.0
Radiator cap. (qts.)	12.1	12.1	18.6	18.6	17.8	17.8	17.8
Axle ratio#, (00)—mph/1000 rpm in high gear manual trans.	3.55:1 (20.9)	3.55:1 (21.4)	3.23:1 (23.5)	3.36:1 (22.6)	3.36:1 (22.1) (22.6)	3.36:1 (22.6)	3.90:1* (19.5)
auto. trans.	3.23:1 (23.0)	3.23:1 (23.5)	2.56:1 (29.7)	3.23:1 (23.5)	3.08:1 (24.1) (24.7)	3.08:1 (24.7)	3.90:1* (19.5)
optional ratios	3.08:1 (24.1) 3.23:1 (23.0) Spec. ord. 3.55:1* (20.9)	2.78:1* (27.3) 3.55:1* (21.4)	3.08:1 (24.7) 2.93:1* (25.9) 2.78:1 (27.3)	2.78:1* (27.3) Spec. ord. 3.55:1* (21.4) Spec. ord. 3.90:1 (19.5)	3.55:1 (21.4) 3.23:1* (23.5) Spec. ord. 3.90:1* (19.5) Spec. ord. 4.33:1 (17.5)	3.55:1* (21.4) Spec. ord. 3.90:1* (19.5) Spec. ord. 4.33:1* (17.5)	

#Some ratios require extra-cost items like a heavy-duty cooling package, limited slip differential, etc. Special 4.11:1 ratio available, dealer-installed.
*w/automatic †w/air conditioning (a) Figure in ( ) indicates rate with firm ride and handling option—rate for rear spring on convertibles is increased to 123.
*Not available w/air conditioning (automatic transmission only).

Firebird General Specifications

Wheelbase		108.1
Tread: Front		60
Rear		60
Tire size*		E70 x 14, wide-oval (a)
Luggage compartment		9.9 cubic feet, usable
Length, overall		191.1
Width, overall		73.9
Height, overall	Coupe	49.6
	Convertible	49.5
Headroom: front	Coupe	37.0
	Convertible	37.5
rear	Coupe	36.7
	Convertible	36.8

Leg room:	front	Coupe	42.5
		Convertible	42.5
	rear	Coupe	29.5
		Convertible	29.5
Fuel tank capacity			18.5 gallons
Steering gear ratio:	manual		24:1 w/6-cyl.; 28:1 w/V-8
	power		fast ratio 16.2:1

Brakes, diameter: drums 9.5 inches; 269.2 sq. in. swept area (total, std. system) front, disc 11.12 inches; 323.6 sq. in. swept area (total, optional system)

*"Space-Saver Spare" is standard, conventional spare tire is a no-extra-cost option.

(a) F70 x 14 std. with Firebird Sprint, 350, H.O. & 400 options.

In addition to the options and accessories noted on the previous pages, you can personalize your Firebird with these: Cruise control; Electric clock; Underhood lamp; Variable-pitch, heavy-duty, 7-blade fan; Self-regulated 55-amp alternator; Spare wheel and tire cover package; Integrated rear-speaker control; Power convertible top; Luggage carriers; Power windows; Power brakes; Power steering; Safeguard speedometer; Soft-Ray glass (all around or windshield only); Walnut shift knob and much, much more. Your Pontiac dealer will be happy to show you our entire accessory encyclopedia.

11

PERFORMANCE OPTIONS

"Trans Am"—Firebird only (**Code 322 UPC WS4**)

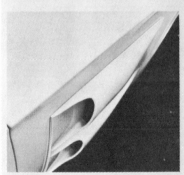

"Trans Am"—(Code 322 UPC WS4)
Performance and Appearance
Features:
- Special Hood with Functional, Driver-controlled, Air-intake Scoops

- Blacked-out Grille
- Special Sports-type Steering Wheel
- Quadra-jet Carburetor
- 3-speed, Heavy-duty, Manual Floor Shift
- Chromed Rocker Arm Covers, Oil Filler Cap and Air Cleaner Cover
- Free-flowing Dual Exhausts
- Full-width Rear Deck Airfoil
- Heavy-duty Springs and Shocks
- Heavy-duty 1"-diameter Stabilizer Bar
- Variable-pitch 5-blade Fan
- 400-Cu.-In. Ram Air V-8
- 3.55 ratio Safe-T-Track Rear Axle
- Full-length Body Stripes
- Special Power Brakes with Front Wheel Discs
- Special Variable-ratio Power Steering
- F70—14 Fiberglass Whitewall-belted Tires
- Functional Front Fender Engine Compartment Air Extractors

Performance and Convenience Options Available:
- Ram Air IV Engine
- 4-speed Stick Shift
- Rally Sports Shifter with Turbo Hydra-matic (4800 rpm shifts w/Ram Air) (5200 rpm w/Ram Air IV)
- Rally Gauge Cluster with Rally Clock
- Rally Gauge Cluster with Instrument Panel Tach
- Hood-mounted Tach
- Power Bucket Seat for Driver

Identification: Ram Air Decal on side of Hood Scoops; "Trans Am" on Front Fenders and Airfoil; Colored Vinyl Stripes along Hood, over Roof, Rear Deck and Airfoil. Rear-end Panel Same Color as Stripe.

Standard Tire Size:
F70—14

Standard Engine:
400-Cu.-In., 335 HP, 4-BBL Ram Air V-8

Available Engine:
400-Cu.-In., 345 HP, 4-BBL Ram Air IV V-8

Standard Transmission:
3-speed, Heavy-duty, Manual—Floor Shift

Available Transmissions:
4-speed Manual—Floor Shift, Close-ratio
Turbo Hydra-matic—Column Shift
Turbo Hydra-matic—Rally Sports Speed Shifter (console required)

For "Trans Am" standard equipment and general specifications, see page A-2 (Firebird section).

S-5

1969 Firebird. You can handle it for less than three grand. That's a Break Away.

1969 PONTIAC FIREBIRD

2337 Hardtop Coupe • 2367 Convertible

CUSTOMER OR TAG FOR	ZONE & DLR. CODE 14-18		ORDER DATE 3-5	ZONE USE 6-8
	DLR. NAME	DIST. 13		
DEALER SIGNATURE	STREET		ORDER NO. 19-23	
	DLR. TOWN	ZIP CODE		

FLEET CLASS CODE	C L P R S Z	GMAC	11A	TRUCK	123	CHECK MARK INDICATES SPEC. EQUIP. ORDER ATTACHED ☐

COLORS — *** SPEC. PAINTS** — **CORDOVA TOPS** — **CONV. TOPS**

SOLD 101	ODC * 11B	TRUCK-BOAT-TRUCK 124	
STOCK 102	CASH 11C	RAIL 129	
FLEET 103	ZONE STOCK 11J		

COLORS:
- A - Starlight Black
- B - Expresso Brown
- C - Cameo White
- D - Warwick Blue
- E - Liberty Blue
- *F - Windward Blue
- G - Antique Gold
- H - Limelight Green
- K - Crystal Turquoise
- M - Midnight Green
- N - Burgundy
- P - Palladium Silver
- Q - Verdoro Green
- R - Matador Red
- S - Champagne
- *T - Carousel Red
- *W - Goldenrod Yellow
- Y - Mayfair Maize

CORDOVA TOPS:
- 2 - Black
- 3 - Dark Blue
- 5 - Parchment
- 8 - Dark Fawn
- 9 - Dark Green

CONV. TOPS:
- 1 - White
- 2 - Black
- 3 - Dark Blue
- 9 - Dark Green

MODEL 24-27 / COLOR 28-29 / TRIM 30-31

FIREBIRD	CIRCLE MODEL TRIM & COLOR		CUSTOM													LOWER COLOR	UPPER COLOR	COR-DOVA TOPS	CONV. TOPS
		BLUE EXP. VINYL	GOLD EXP. VINYL	GREEN EXP. VINYL	PARCH. EXP. VINYL	BLACK EXP. VINYL	BLUE KNIT VINYL	GOLD KNIT VINYL	RED KNIT VINYL	GREEN KNIT VINYL	PARCH. KNIT VINYL	BLACK KNIT VINYL	PARCH. BENCH KNIT VINYL	BLACK BENCH KNIT VINYL	GOLD LEATHER	A G Q / B H R / C K S / D M *T / E N *W / *F P Y	A G Q / B H R / C K S / D M *T / E N *W / *F P Y	2 / 3 / 5 / 8 / 9	1 / 2 / 3 / 9
	2 DOOR HARDTOP 2337	00	02	06	07	08	10	12	14	16	17	18	27	28	93				
	CONV. COUPE 2367	00	02	06	07	08	10	12	14	16	17	18			93				

GROUPS

UPC	GROUPS	COL.
Y88	**BASIC GROUP**	
382	Radio—AM & Manual Antenna	
421	Mirror—Visor Vanity - R.H.	
424	Mirror—Outside Remote Control	32 1
474	Clock	
492	Deck Lid Release	
731	Air Cleaner, Dual Stage H.D.	
W54	**TRANS—AM PKG.**	32 2
	DECOR GROUP	
414	Dual Horns	
451	Deluxe Wheel Covers	
461	Deluxe Steering Wheel	32 4
464	Wheel Opening Mouldings & Roof Drip Mouldings	
514	Custom Pedal Trim Plates	
W56	**POWER ASSIST GROUP**	
351	Power Steering—Variable Ratio	
501	Power Steering—Variable Ratio	33 1
511	Power Disc Brakes, Front	
W55	**TURNPIKE CRUISE GROUP**	
441	Cruise Control	
504	Tilt Steering Wheel	33 2
564	Power Seat—L.H.	
W58	**RALLY GROUP**	
454	Rally II Wheels	
462	Custom Sports Steering Wheel	33 4
484	Rally Gauge Cluster & Clock	
621	Ride & Handling Pkg.	
	OTHER ACCESSORIES	

FIREBIRD

UPC	FIREBIRD	COL.
STD.	1 BBL. OHC 6 Cyl.—Reg. Fuel—250 Cubic Inch	34 1
	3 Speed Man.—Col. Shift, E70 x 14 Black Wide Oval	
W53	**FIREBIRD SPRINT**	
	4 BBL. OHC 6 Cyl.—Premium Fuel—250 Cubic Inch	34 2
	3 Speed Man.—Floor Shift—F70 x 14 Black Wide Oval	
L30	**FIREBIRD 350**	
	2 BBL. V8—Reg. Fuel—350 Cubic Inch	34 3
	3 Speed Man.—Col. Shift—F70 x 14 Black Wide Oval	
L76	**FIREBIRD 350 HO**	
	4 BBL. V8—High Output—Premium Fuel—350 Cu. In. Dual Exhausts	34 4
	3 Speed Man.—Col. Shift—F70 x 14 Black Wide Oval	
W66	**FIREBIRD 400**	
	4 BBL V8—Premium Fuel—400 Cubic Inch Chrome Air Cleaner, Rocker Covers & Oil Cap Dual Exhausts—Flexible Fan—3 Speed Man.— Floor Shift—F70 x 14 Red Wide Oval	34 5
L74	400 HO 4 BBL. V8—ENG. OPT. FOR FIREBIRD 400 ORDER IN PLACE OF 345	34 8

TRANSMISSIONS

UPC	TRANSMISSIONS	COL.
M38 M40	Turbo Hydra-Matic 3 Speed—AVAIL. W/ALL ENG. P	1
M31	Auto. 2 Speed—AVAIL. W/1 BBL. 6 CYL. OR 350 2 BBL. ONLY	2
STD.	3 Speed Man.—COL. SHIFT—1 BBL. 6 CYL. OR 350	3
M12	3 Speed Man.—FLOOR SHIFT—STD. SPRINT OPT. 1 BBL. 6 CYL.	35 6
M13	H.D. 3 Sp. Man.—FLOOR SHIFT—STD. 400— OPT. 350 & 350 HO T-A	5
M20	4 Speed Man.	4

AXLES

UPC	AXLES	COL.
G80	Safe-T-Track Rear Axle	1
G95 G97	Economy Axle	36 4
G90 G92	Performance Axle	8

OPTIONS & ACCESSORIES

UPC	OPTIONS & ACCESSORIES	COL.
U63 U75	Radio—AM & Manual Antenna B	2
U63 U75	Radio—AM & Elec. Antenna	3
U69	Radio—AM/FM & Man. Ant.	38 4
U69 U75	Radio—AM/FM & Elec. Ant.	5
U58	Radio, Stereo—AM/FM & Man. Ant.	8
U58 U75	Radio, Stereo—AM/FM & Elec. Ant.	9
U80	Rear Seat Speaker—N.A. W/388-394	39 3
U57	Stereo Tape Player	4
P17	Spare Tire Cover—N.A. W/708	40 2
C50	Defogger, Rear Window—N.A. CONV.	4
B93	Door Edge Guards	41 2
U05	Dual Horns D	4
D34	Mirror, Visor Vanity—R.H. B	42 1
DH5	Mirror, Visor Vanity—L.H.	2
D33	Mirror, Outside Remote Control—L.H. B	4
W51	Seat Belts, Cust.—INC. FRONT SHOULDER STRAPS	43 1
W52	Seat Belts, Cust.—INC. FRT & REAR SHOULDER STRAPS	2
A39	Seat Belts, Cust.—FRONT & REAR—CONV. ONLY DOES NOT INC. SHOULDER STRAPS	4
A51	Shoulder Straps, Front—CONV. ONLY	8
K30	Cruise Control—W/351-2 & V-8 ONLY T	44 1
U15	Safeguard Speedometer—N.A. 484	2
U30	Rally Gauge Cluster & I.P. Tach.—N.A. 442-471-474-484	4

OPTIONS & ACCESSORIES

UPC	OPTIONS & ACCESSORIES	COL.
P01	Deluxe Wheel Covers D	1
P02	Custom Wheel Covers	45 2
N95	Wire Wheel Covers	3
N98	Rally II Wheels R	4
N30	Deluxe Steering Wheel D	46 1
N34	Custom Sports Steering Wheel R	4
U85	Tachometer, Hood Mounted—N.A. W/322	47 1
D55	Console—W/BUCKET SEATS ONLY	2
U35	Clock, Electric—INC. W/484 B	48 1
N10	Dual Exhaust—ORD. W/343 ONLY—N.A. 6 CYL. T-A	2
W63	Rally Gauge Cluster & Clock—N.A. 442 R	49 2
A90	Deck Lid Release, Remote Control B	1
N41	Power Steering, Variable Ratio T-A P	50 2
J50	Power Brakes—N.A. 345-347-348	4
N33	Tilt Steering Wheel—N.A. WITH STD. STEERING / N.A. MAN. COL. SHIFT T	51 1
JL2	Power Disc Brakes, Front T-A P	2
JL1	Custom Pedal Trim Plates D	4
CD1	Windshield Wiper Blades, Arctic	52 1
PC1	6 Inch Wheels—REG. WHEN CHAINS ARE USED W/F 70 TIRES	2
A01	Soft Ray Glass—ALL WINDOWS	53 1
A02	Soft Ray Glass—WINDSHIELDS ONLY	2
M09	Custom Floor Shift Knob—MAN. TRANS. ONLY	4
C06	Power Top	54 4
A31	Power Windows	55 1
A46	Power Seat—BUCKET—L.H. ONLY T	56 4
C60	Air Conditioning, Custom—N.A. W/SPRINT OR RAM AIR	58 2
C57	Power Flow Ventilation—N.A. 582	8
A67	Rear Seat, Folding	60 4
T42	Hood Ram Air Inlet—OPT. 348 ONLY	61 1
Y96	Ride & Handling Pkg.—(SPRINGS & SHOCKS) T-A R	62 1
B32	Floor Mats—FRONT ONLY	63 1
B33	Floor Mats—REAR ONLY	2
U25	Lamp, Luggage	65 2
U29	Lamp, Instrument Panel Courtesy—STD. CONV. & 400	66 1
U27	Lamp, Glove Box—STD. 400	4
U26	Lamp, Underhood	67 1
UA1	Battery, H.D.—STD. WITH 344-345-347-348-582 T-A	2
V64	Instant-Aire Pump	69 4
N65	Space Saver Spare	70 8

TIRES — COLS. 71-72

UPC	TIRES	COLS. 71-72
P58	7.35 x 14 White—W/341 ONLY	BB
P65	7.35 x 14 Black—OPT. 341	CA
P62	7.75 x 14 White—W/342, 343, 344 ONLY	CB
PX5	F78 x 14 Black—Fiberglass—N.A. 400	GF
PX6	F78 x 14 White—Fiberglass—N.A. 400	GR
PX3	E78 x 14 Red—Wide Oval—W/341 ONLY	HC
PX2	E78 x 14 Black—Wide Oval—W/341 ONLY	HD
PL6	E70 x 14 Black—Wide Oval—W/341 ONLY	HE
PL2	E78 x 14 Black—Fiberglass—W/341 ONLY	HF
PL3	E78 x 14 White—Fiberglass—W/341 ONLY	HR
PY6	F70 x 14 Black—Wide Oval—OPT. 341	ME
PW8	F70 x 14 Red—Wide Oval	MC
PW7	F70 x 14 White—Wide Oval	MD
PY5	F70 x 14 Red—Wide Oval—FIBERGLASS	MT
PY4	F70 x 14 White—Wide Oval—FIBERGLASS T-A	MR
K45	Air Cleaner, Dual Stage H.D. B	73 1
B42	Floor Mat, Rear Compartment	2

1969 MODEL WHOLESALE CAR ORDER
PONTIAC MOTOR DIVISION GMC

FLEET ACCT. No. ☐ (ZONE USE ONLY)

ZONE COPY—White
DEALER COPY—Buff

Firebird

Hardtop Coupe 2337) Convertible (2367)
Strato Bucket Seats (Standard)

Expanded Morrokide

Interior	Recommended Exterior Colors
200 BLUE	C, D, E, F, P
202 GOLD	C, G, H, M, Q, S, W
206 GREEN	C, G, H, M, Q, S
207 PARCHMENT	C, D, E, F, G, H, K, M N, P, Q, R, S, T, W
208 BLACK	C, D, E, F, G, H, K, M N, P, Q, R, S, T, W

Firebird Custom Interior
(EXTRA-COST OPTION)

Hardtop Coupe (2337) Convertible (2367)
Strato Bucket Seats

Knit Vinyl and Expanded Morrokide

Interior	Recommended Exterior Colors
210 BLUE	C, D, E, F, P
212 GOLD	C, G, H, M, Q, S, W
214 RED	C, N, P, R, T
216 GREEN	C, G, H, M, Q, S
217 PARCHMENT	C, D, E, F, G, H, K, M N, P, Q, R, S, T, W
218 BLACK	C, D, E, F, G, H, K, M N, P, Q, R, S, T, W

Genuine leather option

293 GOLD	C, G, H, M, Q, S, W

(EXTRA-COST OPTION)

Hardtop Coupe (2337)
Notch Back Front Seat with Center Armrest

Knit Vinyl and Expanded Morrokide

Interior	Recommended Exterior Colors
227 PARCHMENT	C, D, E, F, G, H, K, M N, P, Q, R, S, T, W
228 BLACK	C, D, E, F, G, H, K, M N, P, Q, R, S, T, W

EFFECTIVE 9/26/68

The following 15 exterior colors are now classified as standard on all Pontiac series:

A Starlight Black	**M** Midnight Green
B Expresso Brown	**N** Burgundy
C Cameo White	**P** Palladium Silver
D Warwick Blue	**Q** Verdoro Green
E Liberty Blue	**R** Matador Red
G Antique Gold	**S** Champagne
H Limelight Green	**Y** Mayfair Maize
K Crystal Turquoise	

Please specifically note that (A) Starlight Black, (B) Expresso Brown and (Y) Mayfair Maize **are now standard** on Firebird and no longer Special Order

on Firebird at extra cost. These exterior colors are recommended with the following interior trim colors:

Exterior Colors	Firebird Interior Trim Colors
(A) Starlight Black	Blue, Gold, Green, Red, Parchment and Black
(B) Expresso Brown	Gold, Green, Parchment, Black
(C) Mayfair Maize	Gold, Parchment, Black

Also please note this change: (T) Carousel Red, (F) Windward Blue and (W) Goldenrod Yellow shown in this folder as standard Firebird colors only, are now available on Firebird on Special Order for **$12.64** Manufacturer's Suggested Retail Price.

1969 Convertible Top Usage Chart

Firebird (2367), Custom S (3567), LeMans (3767), GTO (4267), Catalina (5267) and Bonneville (6267).

Top Color Code Number:	1 Ivory-White	2 Black	3 Dark Blue	9 Dark Green

Black Interior Trim Numbers: 208‡, 218‡, 248, 258, 268, 538, 239, 568, 539, 569	Parchment Interior Trim Numbers: 207‡, 217‡, 257, 267, 567	Blue Interior Trim Numbers: 200‡, 210‡, 241, 250, 531, 560	Green Interior Trim Numbers: 206‡, 216‡, 256, 566	Gold Interior Trim Numbers: 202‡, 212‡, 252, 293‡, 532, 563
A—1,2 M—1,2,9	A—1,2 M—1,2,9	A—1,2,3 E—1,2,3	A—1,2 M—1,2,9	A—1,2 M—1,2,9
B—1,2 N—1,2	B—1,2 N—1,2	C—1,2,3 ‡F—1,2,3	B—1,2 S—1,2	B—1,2 Q—1,2,9
C—1,2 P—1,2	C—1,2 P—1,2	D—1,2,3 P—1,2	C—1,2 Q—1,2,9	C—1,2 S—1,2
D—1,2,3 Q—1,2,9	D—1,2,3 Q—1,2,9		G—1,2	G—1,2 ‡W—1,2
E—1,2,3 R—1,2	E—1,2,3 R—1,2	**Red Interior Trim** Numbers: 214‡, 254, 534, 564	H—1,2,9	H—1,2,9 Y—1,2
‡F—1,2,3 S—1,2	‡F—1,2,3 S—1,2	A—1,2 P—1,2		
G—1,2 ‡T—1,2	G—1,2 ‡T—1,2	C—1,2 R—1,2		‡*Firebird only.*
H—1,2,9 ‡W—1,2	H—1,2,9 ‡W—1,2	N—1,2 ‡T—1,2		
K—1,2 Y—1,2	K—1,2 Y—1,2			

Pontiac had a miserable year in 1970. Sales were down by over 20% and third place in industry ranking was lost for the first time since 1960. Further complicating the situation was the protracted year-end build-out, and sell-out, of the unpopular 1969 Firebirds. The division finally had to all but force dealers to take them and, meanwhile, the much anticipated arrival of the all-new 1970 Firebird was delayed. In order to avoid publicity about the situation, the leftover 1969 models were not referred to as 1969's. Indeed, they were not referred to as belonging to any model year. The catalogue was revised, with every reference to "1969" deleted, and it was no doubt hoped that car buyers wouldn't notice that these sporty little cars sharing showroom space with all the new 1970 Pontiacs weren't 1970 models, too. One can suppose that many salesmen became very adept at fudging the point.

The real 1970 Firebirds made their belated appearance on February 26, 1970, and they were well worth the wait. Unfortunately, their debut was timed to coincide almost perfectly with the collapse of the ponycar market. That somber fact notwithstanding, they were just about the most gorgeous cars on the road. The Camaros were lovely, too, but the Firebirds were clearly something special in terms of physical beauty. The new body seemed to be a piece of rolling sculpture. The front bumper/grille was molded out of Endura rubber painted body color, while the sides sported full wheel cut-outs and an absence of superfluous trim. They were knockouts.

The model designations were new for 1970. The base Firebird came as either a six or a V-8. The six was the Chevy 250 cid in-line sixbanger, the stupendous Pontiac ohc six having been dropped due to manufacturing costs. The two-barrel, 255 hp, 350 cid Pontiac V-8 was also listed. The next Firebird was the new Esprit. This model replaced the old custom interior trim option and came with either the 350 V-8 or a two-barrel, 265 hp version of the Pontiac 400 cid V-8. The Firebird Formula 400 came with either 330 or 345 hp, four-barrel editions of the 400 V-8. At the top of the list was the Trans Am. It came with the outside cosmetic details one by now associated with it, plus the 345 hp, 400 V-8.

Prices were up slightly, to $2,875 for the base Firebird, $3,241 for the Esprit, $3,370 for the Formula 400 and $4,305 for the Trans Am. Production, however, was down to 48,739 for the abbreviated model run. Of this number, 37,835 were Firebirds or Esprits, 7,708 were Formula 400's and 3,196 were Trans Ams. All of them were coupes since the convertible was no longer offered.

Firebird literature was pretty simple for 1970. The late intro made it impossible to include the Firebirds in the regular Pontiac literature. There was a nice Firebird catalogue, which was printed on a paper stock that has not held up well over time (see pages 50-59), and also a couple of post cards (see pages 50-51, upper). A Trans Am sheet exists, but it was probably intended for dealers only (see page 60). The Firebird was quite popular overseas by this time and some interesting foreign literature was issued. A Japanese Trans Am sheet is reproduced on page 61.

1. **The Basic Firebird.**
2. **The Firebird Esprit.**
3. **The Firebird Formula 400.**
4. **The Firebird Trans Am.**

Four separate and distinct automobiles. Each is endowed with its own personality. Each offers its own special set of advantages. Each makes its own special contribution to the future of driving.

But for all their individuality, there is something they all share. Call it honesty. Or practicality. Or any one of a hundred words. What it amounts to is a new approach to building the American automobile. An approach that stresses function over decoration. An approach that stresses the beauty of practicality and simplicity.

It came about simply because we take the fun of driving seriously.

SUBURBAN PONTIAC
17639 South Bellflower Boulevard
Bellflower, California
Torrey 6-1725

No stamped-on styling for Firebird. The lines are so clean, there isn't even a plain old outside radio antenna to get in the way. (It's in the windshield.)

That goes to show you what experts can do with the way economy looks. The significant achievement, however, is that our experts were able to put those looks to work.

Take the Endura front bumper for instance. It not only looks better... it *is* better. Because it's a hard rubber-like material that resists dings, pings and dents. And it won't rust, either.

The longer, sleeker doors enabled us to eliminate the rear quarter windows. So one long window covers the entire side area. This reduces noise and makes getting in and out of the rear seat a whole lot easier. That's pretty amazing in itself.

The taillights, too. Nice looking. But we spent considerable time and effort developing them to do a better job. So they produce an even, intense light free of "hot spots".

Too many people still cling to the notion that the inside of a sports car —especially a low-budget sports car —is a wind-in-the-face, knees-in-the-chest, pain-in-the-neck. Things will change. And this car will have a lot to do with it.

We took a long hard look at the problem of noise. And then turned the interior panel of the roof into a remarkably effective accoustical ceiling, by making the inner panel one solid piece and filling it with thousands of holes.

We also cut out a lot of noise by molding several body panels in the rear-seat area into one large panel. And by reducing the number of bolt-holes under the floor.

There used to be a lot of muttering about rear seats in sports cars. Three has always been a crowd. We decided it was better to make two people comfortable than to squeeze in three. So we put two bucket-type seats in the back.

Funny, that move ended up solving a rear-suspension problem. The space between the seats enabled us to increase the height of the drive tunnel, giving the suspension more room for vertical travel. This cushions the ride without sacrificing cornering ability. (Of course, it helps that there's a new front stabilizer bar to assist with the cornering chores.)

We weren't about to sink all that hard work with just any instrument panel. So we covered the panel face with a rich wood-grain vinyl. And we included handy toggle switches for the accessories.

But the clincher is the supreme common sense with which we designed the instrument panel as a whole.

The gauges are utter simplicity. Every switch and control is right *there* when you need it. And we engineered the panel so that any bulb in the instrument cluster can be replaced in 60 seconds. Usually less. Without your lying on the floor.

By now, you should have a pretty good idea of how we tackled everything else in the car. Using common sense to make Firebird work better, so we could keep the price down.

How far down that price stays is pretty much up to you. The standard 250-cubic-inch engine comes with a 3-speed manual transmission.

The standard brakes are manual front discs and rear drums.

Other standard equipment includes a pair of large-diameter, high-intensity single headlamps, long-wearing bias-belted tires, a front stabilizer bar and a stance that's wider this year. A wider Wide-Track. More than enough sports car look and feel to satisfy most people.

The rest might want to order a 350-cubic-inch, 255-hp V-8. With a wide-ratio, Hurst-shifted 4-speed. A vinyl-covered console. Variable-ratio power steering. Sports-styled mirrors. And any number of other adventurous options available.

Whether you add anything or not, you'll have a head start on tomorrow.

Because the things that make the basic Firebird such a revolutionary American car are all there to begin with.

WEIGHTS & MEASURES		
Overall Length		191.6"
Overall Width		73.4"
Overall Height		50.4"
Wheelbase		108.0"
Front Track		61.3"
Rear Track		60.0"
Est. Curb Weight (lbs.)		3270

	STANDARD	AVAILABLE
Engine Size (Cu.-In.)	250	350
Engine Type	Inline 6 OHV	V-8 OHV
Bore & Stroke (inches)	3.875 x 3.53	3.875 x 3.75
Horsepower	155 @ 4200	255 @ 4600
Torque (Lb.-Ft.)	235 @ 1600	355 @ 2800
Compression Ratio	8.5:1	8.8:1
Oil Capacity (Less Filter)	4 quarts	5 quarts
Camshaft Duration		
Degrees – Intake	244	266
Exhaust	244	277
Overlap	33.5	47
Camshaft Lift @		
Zero Lash – Intake	.398	.376 — .411
Exhaust	.395	.412 — .411
Valve Head		
Diameter – Intake	1.72	1.96
Exhaust	1.50	1.66
Carburetor Bore		
Diameter – Primary	1.69 (1-BBL)	1.69 (2-BBL)
Secondary	—	—
Spring Rates, (Lbs./In.)		
Deflection – Front	300	300
Rear	99	99
Stabilizer Bar (Front)	.938	.938
Tire Size (Rim Width)	E78-14 (6")	F78 or F70-14 (7")
Axle Ratios (Std. Engine)		
Manual Transmission	3.08:1 a	3.36:1 b
Automatic	3.08:1 a	2.73:1, 3.36:1 b
Turbo Hydra-matic	3.08:1 a	2.73:1, 3.36:1 b

a—Air conditioning not available.
b—Same ratios with air conditioning.

Exclusive soft-rimmed Formula wheel is available.

Vinyl-covered buckets are part of the deal.

Two bucket-type rear seats instead of one bench.

New longer doors have handy storage pockets.

1. The Basic Firebird.

Economy is what the basic Firebird is all about. But the beauty of the car is that the same economy that keeps its price down, also makes it a better sports car. That kind of beauty isn't easily accomplished. Even for Pontiac. But remember, we promised the beginning of tomorrow. And it starts here.

An honest luxury sports car should consist of a lot more than foam, chrome and gadgetry. So we took some basic measures.

Like a new method for constructing Firebird seats. Under the old method, a set of springs was tied together, padded with cloth and covered with a separate foam cushion.

We molded everything into one integral unit. So the wires are completely surrounded by foam padding.

The result is a seat that's much more uniformly comfortable. And because it's one solid and durable unit, it will stay more uniformly comfortable for the life of the car.

Esprit's upholstery is something special, too. Something called "knit vinyl." Since it "breathes," it doesn't feel hot and cold the way regular vinyl does. Cloth and vinyl is also available.

Esprit, like all Firebirds, seats four. But the driver's seat got most of our attention. Simply because this is where all the action takes place in a sports car, luxury or otherwise.

The instrument panel really looks like wood. And it was designed so that every switch and control is right at the driver's fingertips.

The available vinyl-covered console has two roomy storage compartments. The rear one is a glove compartment that opens, appropriately enough, toward the driver.

There's no groping for the shifter. It's positioned so that it seems to find your hand.

Same goes for the recessed, pull-type door handles. Below which are handy storage pockets built into each door.

The upper-level ventilation system is more comfortable this year because it moves more air.

Even the steering wheel adds comfort. It's covered with soft, squeezeable vinyl.

And, there's a lot more comfort you can order. Variable-ratio power steering. Air conditioning. An exclusive new 14" Formula steering wheel with a very heavily padded rim. Power front disc brakes (manual front discs are standard).

Outside. Esprit shows the same attention to detail. Thin, silvery strips of chrome along the roof edge. And around the twin scoop-like openings of the grille, as well as the wheel wells. The rocker panel moldings are cleanly executed. There's a distinctive wheel trim and Esprit nameplates.

There's nothing impractical about making concealed windshield wipers standard. So we did.

And those two outside mirrors are functional indeed. Because they're aerodynamically styled and endowed with a very broad field of view. Something more than good looks is going on here.

But that typifies the kind of "luxury" you'll find on Esprit. The standard engine is a special 350-cubic-inch V-8 that develops 255 hp and 355 lb.-ft. of torque.

The standard transmission is a floor-mounted, fully synchronized 3-speed.

And the standard suspension is a beautifully engineered blend of performance and comfort. It boasts a new front stabilizer bar to keep Esprit from leaning through corners. Which means the springs and shocks could be kept softer and more comfortable.

That, plus the increased suspension travel made possible by the rear seats, results in a ride you just don't expect from a tough-in-the-corners sports car.

In short, it looks like Firebird Esprit is going to change a lot of ideas about what a luxury sports car should be. But we kind of had to expect that. Because with Esprit, tomorrow begins today.

WEIGHTS & MEASURES		
Overall Length		191.6"
Overall Width		73.4"
Overall Height		50.4"
Wheelbase		108.0"
Front Track		61.3"
Rear Track		60.6"
Est. Curb Weight (Lbs.)		3610
	STANDARD	AVAILABLE
Engine Size (Cu.-In.)	350	400
Engine Type	V-8 OHV	V-8 OHV
Bore & Stroke (Inches)	3.875 x 3.75	4.12 x 3.75
Horsepower	255 @ 4600	265 @ 4800
Torque (Lb.-Ft.)	355 @ 2800	397 @ 2400
Compression Ratio	8.8:1	9.5:1
Oil Capacity (Less Filter)	5 quarts	5 quarts
Camshaft Duration, Degrees— Intake	.260	.269
Exhaust	.277	.277
Overlap	.47	.47
Camshaft Lift @ Zero Lash— Intake	.376 @ .011	.376 @ .011
Exhaust	.412 @ .011	.412 @ .011
Valve Head Diameter— Intake	1.96	1.95
Exhaust	1.66	1.66
Carburetor Bore Diameter— Primary	1.60 (2-BBL)	1.69 (2-BBL)
Secondary	—	—
Spring Rates, (Lbs./In.) Deflection—Front	300	300
Rear	.89	103
Stabilizer Bar (Front)	.938	.938
Tire Size (Trim Width)	E78-14 (6")	F78 or E70-14 (7")
Axle Ratios (Std. Engine) Manual Transmissions	3.36:1a	N.A.
Automatic	2.73:1, 3.36:1a	N.A.
Turbo Hydra-matic	2.73:1, 3.36:1a	3.07:1

A—Same ratios with air conditioning.

A new soft vinyl console is available.

Tasteful external trim sets Esprit apart.

Esprit's new 15/16" front stabilizer bar.

A pair of sports-type mirrors is standard.

2. The Firebird Esprit.

We've taken a great sports car. Made it luxurious. And managed to make it an even greater sports car in the process. Because we never let "luxury" get in the way of sport. We've stuck to the idea that how Esprit works is as important as how beautiful it looks. And feels. So you won't find anything frivolous or wasteful about Esprit's kind of luxury. Which is what makes Esprit tomorrow's kind of luxury sports car.

3. The Firebird Formula 400.

Formula 400 is a special breed of road car. What makes it special is the genuine practicality of its design . . . the appropriateness of its equipment . . . and the totality with which it performs. Formula 400 is a step apart. A step ahead. Which is why we rightfully declare it to be tomorrow's breed of road car.

Anybody can tell you that a road car needs a big engine under the hood. So Formula 400 has a 400-cubic-inch, 330-hp V-8 with 4-barrel carburetion. It turns out 430 lb.-ft. of torque at 3000 rpm. A heavy-duty, floor-mounted, Hurst-shifted 3-speed transmission is standard. A Hurst-shifted 4-speed is also available.

The fact is, however, that anybody can drop a power team like that into any car. What counts is what we did to make it efficient.

Take the simple matter of breathing. An engine that breathes better can work harder with less strain. So the air cleaner on our 400 V-8 has two snorkles instead of one.

Should you decide to order our 400 Ram Air V-8, you'll get another lesson on breathing. The scoops on that fiberglass hood are in a high-pressure area. So when the car is moving, cold air is literally rammed into the carburetor.

In keeping with the efficiency philosophy, Formula 400's 5-blade flex fan flattens out at high fan rpm to reduce drag on the engine. And the low-restriction dual exhaust removes gasses from the combustion chambers quickly to make way for incoming combustibles.

Our basic Firebird and our Esprit can boast of a big-car ride. Formula 400 doesn't have it quite as soft. But what, with the rear-seat configuration, the raised drive line tunnel and the resulting room for increased suspension travel, the ride's a whole lot smoother than what you're used to in a sports car.

And we didn't give up one iota of handling and cornering to get that ride.

Not one iota. In fact, handling and cornering are improved. Formula 400 has stabilizer bars front and rear (1-1/8" and 5/8" respectively). Special high-rate springs and a special wind-up control for the rear axle. Road-hugging F70-14 bias-belted tires. Front disc brakes. (A power assist is available.) And, of course, Pontiac's well-known Wide-Track.

We make variable-ratio power steering available, too. The steering gets faster the farther you turn the wheel. Ratio—16.0:1 to 12.1:1.

It should be obvious by now that Formula 400's styling is almost stark. No elaborate decoration. This automobile is all-business outside.

And inside. The instrument panel is most functional. If you order the gauge package (not a bad idea for a car of this sort), here's what you'll find staring back at you. A tachometer that red-lines straight up. A speedometer and oil and water gauges squarely in front of you. A fuel gauge and voltmeter off to one side.

Makes sense doesn't it?

So does the console you can order. It blends into the instrument panel, is covered with soft vinyl, has a place to hang seat belts when the car's bedded down for the night.

There's one piece of equipment you can order that we really can't explain in terms of function. The padded, vinyl-covered Formula steering wheel. It actually doesn't perform any better than our standard wheel. But our hats are off to anyone who can see it, grip it and not buy it.

Think of it this way. If Pontiac went to all the trouble to bring out tomorrow's road car so you can buy it a few years early, what's the harm in spending a few extra dollars to complete your image?

WEIGHTS & MEASURES		
Overall Length		191.6"
Overall Width		73.4"
Overall Height		50.4"
Wheelbase		108.0"
Front Track		61.6"
Rear Track		60.3"
Est. Curb Weight (Lbs.)		3545
	STANDARD	AVAILABLE
Engine Size (Cu. In.)	400	400
Engine Type	V-8 OHV Premium fuel	V-8 OHV Premium fuel
Bore & Stroke (Inches)	4.12 x 3.75	4.12 x 3.75
Horsepower	330 @ 4800	345 @ 5000
Torque (Lb.-Ft.)	430 @ 3000	430 @ 3400
Compression Ratio	10.25:1	10.5:1
Oil Capacity (Less Filter)	5 quarts	5 quarts
Camshaft Duration, Degrees— Intake	273	288
Exhaust	289	302
Overlap	54	63
Camshaft Lift @ Zero Lash— Intake	.410 ~ .203	.414 ~ .011
Exhaust	.413 ~ .011	.413 ~ .011
Valve Head Diameter— Intake	2.11	2.11
Exhaust	1.77	1.77
Carburetor Bore Diameter— Primary	1.38	1.38
Secondary	2.25	2.25
Spring Rates, (Lbs./In.) Deflection—Front	300	300
Rear	103	103
Stabilizer Front Bar—	1.125	1.125
Rear	.620	.620
Tire Size (Rim Width)	F70-14 (7")	H60-15 (7")
Axle Ratios (Std. Engine) Manual Transmissions	3.55:1, 3.73:1a	3.55:1, 3.73:1a
Turbo Hydra-matic	3.07:1, 3.31:1a	3.55:1, 3.73:1a
a—3.91:1 with air conditioning. b—Same ratios with air conditioning.		

A Hurst shifter is standard equipment.

Chrome exhaust extensions liven things up.

New rear stabilizer bar (5/8" diameter).

Rally II wheels and white-letter tires are available.

4. The Firebird Trans Am.

The ultimate Firebird. Like the other Firebirds, Trans Am is unique. And like the other Firebirds, it's not unique just because of the way it looks. You see, all the equipment that makes it look like something from the next decade is also making a definite contribution to performance. *That's* the ultimate achievement of Trans Am.

We've always suspected that a sports car could be as aerodynamic as it looked. Trans Am shows just how badly we wanted to prove it.

Look at the front end. There's an air dam under the bumper. A spoiler at each front wheel. Air extractors on each side of the engine compartment. And a shaker hood.

All that equipment works. *Really* works. In fact, the combination of the front air dam and the side air extractors is responsible for creating 50 pounds of downward pressure on the front end at expressway speeds. The spoilers at the wheels keep air pressure from building up in the wheel wells. Also at turnpike speeds.

The total effect is great front-end stability.

The shaker hood uses air differently, but just as effectively. Its rear-facing inlet is smack at the base of the windshield. Precisely where air-flow over the hood creates a maximum amount of pressure to feed Trans Am's standard Ram Air engine (more about the engine later).

Now look at the rear end. Another spoiler at each wheel. They function like the ones up front. And a rather spectacular spoiler in the rear. It creates a downward pressure of 50 pounds. Again, at expressway speeds. Again, more stability.

In keeping with Trans Am's aerodynamic integrity, the two outside mirrors are encased in aerodynamically styled shells (remote-controlled on the driver's side).

Naturally, part of Trans Am's stability comes from the suspension.

We beefed up the front stabilizer bar to 1-1/4". And we added a 7/8" rear stabilizer bar. Springs and shocks are heavy-duty. And the standard tires are white-letter, bias-belted F60–15's.

Here's the more we promised on the engine. It's a 400-cubic-inch Ram Air V-8. It has 4-barrel carburetion. A 10.5:1 compression ratio. And it develops 345 horsepower with 430 lb.-ft. of torque. For emphasis it comes with chrome accents. A most impressive piece of equipment.

Complemented by some equally impressive equipment. Like a wide-ratio 4-speed that's floor-mounted and Hurst-shifted. (Order a close-ratio if you prefer it.) Variable-ratio power steering with an extra-quick ratio. A special Safe-T-Track differential. Steel Rally II wheels. And Pontiac's exclusive new 14" Formula steering wheel.

That wheel is one reason Trans Am's interior is as exciting as the exterior. There are others.

The instrumentation is beautifully simple, accurate and appropriately set in a no-nonsense, engine-turned aluminum panel. Instruments include a voltmeter instead of an ammeter. An oil pressure gauge. A water-temperature gauge. And a tachometer that's turned on its side so it red-lines at 12 o'clock.

The available console makes just as much sense. It's integral with the dashboard this year, making tape decks or radios mounted in it a lot harder to "borrow." And it's covered with padded vinyl instead of molded plastic.

The all-new Firebird Trans Am is, in the final analysis, a brilliantly executed motor car. We're proud of it because we didn't build it the easy way. The right way is rarely easy.

Making all the right choices took inspiration as well as perspiration. But it brought about the beginning of a trend. The beginning of tomorrow.

Now you know what took so long.

WEIGHTS & MEASURES	
Overall Length	191.6"
Overall Width	72.4"
Overall Height	50.4"
Wheelbase	108.0"
Front Track	61.7"
Rear Track	60.4"
Est. Curb Weight (Lbs.)	3666

	STANDARD
Engine Size (Cu. In.)	400
Engine Type	V-8 OHV, 4-BBL Premium Fuel
Bore & Stroke (Inches)	4.12 x 3.75
Horsepower	345 @ 5000
Torque (Lb.-Ft.)	430 @ 3400
Compression Ratio	10.5:1
Oil Capacity (Less Filter)	5 quarts
Camshaft Duration	
Degrees — Intake	288
Exhaust	302
Overlap	63
Camshaft Lift @	
Zero Lash — Intake	.414 ÷ .011
Exhaust	.413 ÷ .011
Valve Head	
Diameter — Intake	2.11
Exhaust	1.77
Carburetor Bore	
Diameter — Primary	1.38
Secondary	2.25
Spring Rates (Lbs./In.)	
Deflection — Front	100
Rear	126
Stabilizer Front	1.250
Bar — Rear	.875
Tire Size (Rim Width)	F60-15 (7")
Axle Ratios (Std. Engine)	
Manual Transmission	3.55:1, 3.73:1
Turbo Hydra-matic	3.55:1

Gauges are set in an engine-turned aluminum panel.

A front air dam that really works.

The shaker hood's rear-facing inlet literally "rams" air.

Our rear spoiler works at turnpike speeds.

TRANS AM

F-LUCERNE BLUE WITH WHITE STRIPES

C-POLAR WHITE WITH BLUE STRIPES

FIREBIRD Trans-Am

Firebird TRANS-AM
1970 PONTIAC

圧倒的な量感、エネルギッシュな風ぼう………
空気抵抗を巧にとらえたスタイリングはポンテアックの誇るラムエアー皿エンジンとの結合により、するどい性能を発揮します。高速走行に"ずっしり"と手ごたえのあるハイフィーリングは乗る方の喜びに変わります。もちろん、ワイドな性能を安心して発揮できるよう充実した安全装備でいっぱいです。

造形美・安全性
冷却効率の高いマグネシウムホイールと、耐久性・フィーリングが大幅に向上した"アイバーグラスベルテッドタイヤ"の採用により信頼度の高い走行を可能にしました。

本格派のハートをとらえるインストルーメントパネル………
豪華でスポーティな計器盤にはフォミュラータイプの皮巻ステアリングを中心にメタ類が機能的にレイアウトされています。

SPECIFICATION

全 長 (mm)	全 巾 (mm)	全 高 (mm)	ホイルベース (mm)	トレッド(F) (mm)	トレッド(R) (mm)	総排気量 (cc)	ボア×ストローク (mm)	馬 力 (HP/rpm.)	トルク (kg・m/rpm.)	圧 縮 比
4,870	1,865	1,280	2,745	1,565	1,535	6,560	104.6×95.3	345/5,000	59.3/3,400	10.5:1

Nichiei JIDOSHA　日英自動車株式會社　東京都千代田区永田町2－11－2　TEL (03) 581－6731〜5番

Pontiac had a mixed year in 1971. Sales were down, even from 1970's depressed levels, but that was due primarily to national economic conditions. Pontiac's market penetration was actually up a bit and third place in the national rankings was regained. The standard size Pontiacs were all-new and there was a compact Ventura II series later in the year (based on the Chevy Nova), but other Pontiac lines were more or less revised from the 1970 models.

The 1971 Firebird was one of the "less" revised. In fact, the 1971 Firebirds were almost indistinguishable from their predecessors. There were minor trim changes, but these cars were simply too new to warrant even normal model year changes.

The most significant changes were in the engine compartment. The Formula Firebird was now available with a choice of 350, 400 and 455 cid powerplants. The top-of-the-line Trans Am still came with the top-rated 455 engine, but, thanks to a lower (8.4:1, instead of 10.5:1) compression ratios, horsepower was down to 335 at 4800 rpm.

Prices rose noticeably in 1971. The base Firebird cost $3,047. The Esprit cost $3,416. The Formula cost $3,445. And, finally, the Trans Am listed out at $4,595. Production, however, was down to half the 1968 level, the last normal model run. A grand total of 53,124 were produced, including 23,021 base models, 20,185 Esprits, 7,802 Formulas and 2,116 Trans Ams.

In 1971, for the first time in its brief history, there was no Firebird sales literature, as such. The Firebirds were included in the regular Pontiac full-line catalogue (see the montage below), the Pontiac high performance catalogue (see pages 64-69) and in the color and trim brochure (see page 70). The 1971 Firebird post card is included in the montage below.

The Firebird

19

The Firebird Esprit

The Firebird Trans Am

The Firebirds

Four of them. Because one sports car can't fill the needs of all sports car drivers. So every Firebird has an assigned task. An assigned spot to fill in Pontiac's specialty car scheme.

Take the basic Firebird. Its appeal is to the driver who wants a good sports car. But simply has economic priorities that preclude going whole hog on one.

So the basic Firebird is economical. In the way it's priced. And in the way it operates.

A 250-CID six is standard. 145 gross horsepower (110 net).[†] If you'd prefer a V-8, the available 350-CID 2-bbl. will give you additional power without a frightening leap in your gas bills.

The economy of a 3-speed manual transmission is standard. But you can get a floor-mounted, Hurst-shifted 3-speed, or the snick-snick-snick of the Hurst-shifted 4-speed that's available. To let your left foot rest, automatic or Turbo Hydra-matic should be checked on the available list.

We weren't about to give up our reputation of innovation for the sake of economy. So the basic Firebird has many of the features that make all Firebirds a bench mark for cars to come.

The doors are long. For two good reasons: One, they make it easier to get in and out of the rear seats. Two, they eliminate the need for rear-quarter windows. That, when combined with a new, soft foam window seal, means far less wind noise.

Firebird's roof is quite an innovation. It has a special double-shell construction for added strength.

The inner shell is an acoustical ceiling. Thousands of little holes in it reduce interior noise.

The instrument panel face is covered with wood grain vinyl. And it's laid out in a very straightforward manner. Every gauge, every control, is easy to see.

Easy to reach.

And the instruments are as easy to service as they are to see. The panel is designed so that any bulb can be replaced—by the owner—in less than 60 seconds. And without having to crawl under the dash to do it.

Every sports car has bucket seats. But Firebird has four. True buckets up front. Bucket-type seats in the rear. The front seats are high-back. Headrests are integral.

Under the rugged vinyl upholstery, there's an innovation in the construction of the seats. All the components are molded into one unit. Foam padding completely surrounds the springs. The result is a seat that's more comfortable to start with. And one that will stay more comfortable for years to come.

One final bit of innovation. The Endura front end. Endura is a rubber-like material that resists dents and dings and won't ever rust. And the entire front section of every Firebird has it.

The basic Firebird. It is, simply, a clean-cut, well-proportioned, economical automobile.

The Firebird Esprit is kind of a sports-car-sized Grand Prix. It handles. But it's luxurious.

Esprit is set apart from the other Firebirds on the outside. With tasteful strips of chrome. And wheel trim rings.

Esprit's custom interior has distinctive door panels with pull straps. Soft full-length armrests. An instrument panel assist strap above the glove box door. More sound insulation in the roof.

The seats are upholstered in knit vinyl and expanded Morrokide. It breathes. Keeps you cooler in the summer, warmer in the winter.

Our custom cushion steering wheel is also standard. It's covered with a soft vinyl that squeezes. And

while it's luxurious, it also gives you an excellent grip on the wheel.

Firebird's bucket-style rear seats helped us develop the first big-car ride ever in a sports car.

A raised drive tunnel between the seats gives the rear suspension more vertical travel. So we can use softer springs without bottoming out or hurting handling potential.

As a matter of fact, the handling potential is considerable. Due, in part, to the front stabilizer bar. And the wide, wide Wide-Track stance.

Standard power comes from a 350-CID V-8. Or order the 400-CID 2-bbl. V-8.

To help that power breathe, every new Firebird has front-fender extractors for venting underhood air. They help supply the engine with cooler outside air, and reduce air pressure buildup.

So if you want a sports car with a luxury ride, get yourself a Firebird Esprit.

Some drivers want a firmer ride. They love roads. And they want to feel an occasional expansion joint. The Formula Firebirds are built for just that kind of driver. They're special road cars. In three special setups.

Special power setups. The Formula 350 has a 350-CID 2-bbl. V-8. The Formula 400 boasts a 400-CID 4-bbl. V-8. And the Formula 455 is powered by a 455-CID 4-bbl. V-8 or the new 455 H.O. LS5 V-8 you can order.

We use a process called select-fit to assemble our engines. It's almost like custom-building every engine that comes down the line.

Take the pistons for example. After the block has been bored, a precise measurement of bore diameter is taken and fed to a computer. The computer then selects one of six different piston sizes. The piston that perfectly fits the bore diameter. The piston sizes vary by a mere four ten-thousandths of an inch. Not much. But it compensates for any bore size variation due to the block

†Gross horsepower/torque figures represent maximum output of the bare engine without fan, air cleaner or exhaust system *before* engine is installed. Net figures are derived from engine after installation in the car.

metallurgy, tooling wear, etc.

The result of select-fitting pistons is a constant compression ratio through all eight cylinders. Equalized compression pressures through all eight cylinders. And an inherently well-balanced engine.

The select-fit process is also used to come up with camshaft bearings, main bearings and connecting rod bearings. All to give you the most carefully assembled production engines in the business.

There's more to the Formula formula. We laid a fiberglass hood over the precision-balanced engine. Its twin scoops will gobble cold, dense air if you order them functional with the 455 H.O. LS5 engine. The scoop openings are located in a high-pressure area. So you also get a slight supercharging effect when you're rolling.

The Formula Firebirds get firmer springs. And a rear stabilizer bar to go with the front one. So the ride's more stable. The cornering a lot flatter. Especially with the standard F70—14 tires holding onto the asphalt.

Since most roads have corners, our Formula road cars can be ordered with power for the front disc brakes and variable-ratio power steering. So much for handling the corners.

From the long list of Pontiac availables, you might want to get the vinyl-covered console for your Formula. Or the new rear-seat console. It holds an ashtray and

places to keep the rear lap belts when they're not in use.

It's hard to stay calm about a car like Pontiac's Firebird Trans Am. Because we got it all together for this one. Everything that makes an enthusiast enthusiastic is standard equipment.

Start with the most obvious. A front air dam. Side air extractors. A spoiler at each wheel. And a rear-deck spoiler. They all work. Providing 50 lbs. of downward pressure, both front and rear. At turnpike speeds.

The shaker hood works, too. When you punch the throttle, a rear-facing inlet door allows cold air to be rammed directly to the Quadra-jet carb.

Hungrily waiting for the fuel-air mixture is our pride and joy. The new 455-CID H.O. LS5 V-8. For all its virtues, check the GTO section.

Checking the operation of the LS5 is easy. The Trans Am's engine-turned aluminum-style instrument panel holds all the gauges you'll ever need. Oil, water, fuel and volt gauges. A big round speedometer. A clock. And an accurate tach that's turned on its side. So it redlines straight up.

While your right hand is busy with the standard floor-mounted, Hurst-shifted, heavy-duty 3-speed transmission, your left hand will be gripping a special steering wheel. It's our 14" Formula wheel. Very thick, very black, heavily padded vinyl, molded around a black anodized aluminum frame. It's linked to the extra-quick variable-ratio power steering that's standard.

Every Trans Am comes standard with power-assisted front disc brakes, F60—15 white-lettered tires and the beefiest suspension this side of the Golden Gate Bridge.

The front springs are as firm as those in the Formula Firebirds. The rear springs are even firmer. There's a super-thick (1-1/4") front stabilizer bar. A huge 7/8" rear stabilizer bar. And very firm shocks.

The result of this suspension and the air dams and spoilers is an incredibly stable car. One you'll have to drive to appreciate.

The Trans Am is, in conclusion, a finely tuned performer in the purest sense of the word. It is, frankly, not for every driver. But if you want to experience the ultimate—the state of the art—in enthusiast driving, there is no other choice. Firebird Trans Am. Pure Pontiac!

Dimensions	Basic	Esprit	Formulas	Trans Am
Overall Length (in.)	191.6	191.6	191.6	191.6
Overall Width (in.)	73.4	73.4	73.4	73.4
Overall Height (in.)	50.4	50.4	50.4	50.4
Wheelbase (in.)	108.0	108.0	108.0	108.0
Track, Front/Rear (in.)	61.3/60.0	61.3/60.0	61.6/60.3*	61.7/60.4
Turning Diameter (curb-to-curb—ft.)	36.5	36.5	36.5	36.5
Head Room, Front/Rear (in.)	37.4/36.1	37.4/36.1	37.4/36.1	37.4/36.1
Leg Room, Front/Rear (in.)	43.8/29.6	43.8/29.6	43.8/29.6	43.8/29.6
Shoulder Room, Front/Rear (in.)	57.4/54.4	57.4/54.4	57.4/54.4	57.4/54.4
Hip Room, Front/Rear (in.)	56.7/47.3	56.7/47.3	56.7/47.3	56.7/47.3
Trunk Capacity (cu. ft.)	7.24	7.24	7.24	7.24

*With 7"-wide rims

Engines	250 L-6 1-bbl.	350 V-8 2-bbl.	400 V-8 2-bbl.	400 V-8 4-bbl.	455 V-8 4-bbl.	455 HO V-8 4-bbl.
Standard on	Basic	Esprit Formula 350	—	Formula 400	Formula 455	Trans Am
Available on	—	Basic	Esprit	—	—	Formula 455
Gross Horsepower @ rpm†	145@4200	250@4400	265@4400	300@4800	325@4400	335@4800
Net Horsepower @ rpm	110@3800	185@4200‡	185@3800	250@4400	255@4000	305@4400
Gross Torque @ rpm (lb.-ft.)	230@1600	350@2400	400@2400	400@3600	455@3200	480@3600
Net Torque @ rpm (lb.-ft.)†	185@1600	275@2200‡	320@2200	340@3200	380@2800	410@3200
Displacement (cu. in.)	250	350	400	400	455	455
Bore and Stroke (in.)	3.88 x 3.53	3.88 x 3.75	4.12 x 3.75	4.12 x 3.75	4.15 x 4.21	4.15 x 4.21
Compression Ratio	8.5:1	8.0:1	8.2:1	8.2:1	8.2:1	8.4:1
Carburetor Barrels (no.)	1	2	2	4	4	4
Carburetor Bore Diameter Primary	1.69	1.69	1.69	1.38	1.38	1.38
Secondary	—	—	—	2.25	2.25	2.25
Camshaft Duration, Degrees—Intake	244	269	269	273	273	288
—Exhaust	244	277	277	289	289	302
—Overlap	33.5	51	51	54	54	63
Camshaft Lift @ Zero Lash Intake	.388	.377 ± .011	.377 ± .011	.410 ± .011	.410 ± .011	.410 ± .011
Exhaust	.388	.413 ± .011	.411 ± .011	.413 ± .011	.414 ± .011	.413 ± .011
Valve Head Diameter Intake	1.72	1.96	1.96	2.11	2.11	2.11
Exhaust	1.50	1.66	1.66	1.77	1.77	1.77
Exhaust System	Single	Dual (Formula)	Single	Dual	Dual	Dual
Fuel Tank Capacity (gal.)	17.0	17.0	17.0	17.0	17.0	17.0
Cooling System Capacity (qt.)	12.0	19.4	18.6	18.6	17.9	17.9
Crankcase Oil Capacity (qt.)	5	5	5	5	5	5
Spring Rates, (lbs./in.) Deflection—Front	300	300	300	300	300	300
—Rear	90 (104 H.D.)	90 (104 H.D.)	90 (104 H.D.)	104 (125 H.D.)	104 (125 H.D.)	125
Axle Ratios Manual Transmission	3.08:1	3.42:1	N.A.	3.42:1	N.A.	3.42:1
Turbo Hydra-matic	3.08:1	2.73:1	2.73:1	3.08:1	3.42:1	3.42:1

*Std. on Formula 350   †150 @ 4400 (hp); 285 @ 2600 (torque) on Formula 350

27

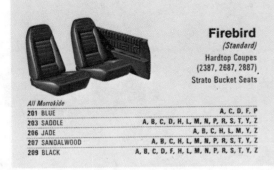

Firebird
(Standard)
Hardtop Coupes
(2387, 2687, 2887)
Strato Bucket Seats

All Morrokide

201 BLUE	A, C, D, F, P
203 SADDLE	A, B, C, D, H, L, M, N, P, R, S, T, Y, Z
206 JADE	A, B, C, H, L, M, Y, Z
207 SANDALWOOD	A, B, C, H, L, M, N, P, R, S, T, Y, Z
209 BLACK	A, B, C, D, F, H, L, M, N, P, R, S, T, Y, Z

Firebird
Custom Interior
(Available at Extra Cost)
Hardtops Coupes
(2487,* 2687, 2887)
Strato Bucket Seats

Knit Vinyl and Morrokide

211 BLUE	A, C, D, F, P
212 IVORY	A, B, C, D, F, H, L, M, N, P, R, S, T, Y, Z
213 SADDLE	A, B, C, D, H, L, M, N, P, R, S, T, Y, Z
214 SIENNA	A, B, C, H, S, T, Y, Z
216 JADE	A, B, C, H, L, M, Y, Z
217 SANDALWOOD	A, B, C, H, L, M, N, P, R, S, T, Y, Z
219 BLACK	A, B, C, D, F, H, L, M, N, P, R, S, T, Y, Z

Standard on Esprit (2487)

Firebird
Custom Interior
(Available At Extra Cost)
Hardtop Coupes
(2487,* 2687, 2887)
Strato Bucket Seats

Pinehurst Pattern Cloth and Morrokide

227 SANDALWOOD	A, B, C, H, L, M, N, P, R, S, T, Y, Z
229 BLACK	A, B, C, D, F, H, L, M, N, P, R, S, T, Y, Z

Standard on Esprit (2487)

2

1971 Pontiac Exterior Finishes

A - Starlight Black

B - Sandalwood

C - Cameo White

D - Adriatic Blue

E - Regency Blue

F - Lucerne Blue

H - Limekist Green

L - Tropical Lime

M - Laurentian Green

N - Rosewood

P - Nordic Silver

R - Cardinal Red

S - Castillian Bronze

T - Canyon Copper

W - Bronzini Gold

Y - Quezal Gold

Z - Aztec Gold

Pontiac sales were up in 1972, but not enough to regain third position in national sales rankings. There was nothing much that was new with any of the Pontiac lines, and that was certainly the case with the Firebirds. Even the sales catalogue couldn't find any trumped up "new" features to herald. The only notable change was in the way horsepower ratings were figured—they were now "SAE" ratings that were thought to be more demonstrative of the actual power delivered to the rear wheels (i.e., lower than the old quotes).

Prices actually dropped in 1972. The base Firebird was down almost 7% to $2,838. Other models dropped similarly: the Esprit to $3,194, the Formula to $3,221 and the mighty Trans Am to $4,256. If Pontiac officialdom thought this would spur sales, they must have been profoundly disappointed. The customers greeted the 1972 'Birds with an overwhelming display of apathy and production plummeted to 29,951 units. Of these, 12,000 were base models, 11,415 were Esprits, 5,250 were Formulas and a pathetic 1,286 were Trans Ams.

As in 1971, there was no specific Firebird literature for 1972 except for a color post card (reproduced in the montage below). Firebird models were included in the regular Pontiac full-line catalogue (see pages 72-73) and in the color and trim brochure (see page 76). The spread from the fleet ordering guide is also included here (see pages 74-75).

Firebirds

FIREBIRD ESPRIT HARDTOP COUPE

FIREBIRD HARDTOP COUPE

Firebird

Pontiac's got quite a reputation for thinking ahead.

But we should make it clear that we don't change just for the sake of change. We looked to the future in designing our Firebirds, for example, just to give you better cars right now.

Take the basic 'Bird. You don't have to be a designer to see that the styling is futuristic. And futuristic styling is merely the beginning.

The roof of a Firebird is really two roofs—a double-shell construction. It does quite a job of absorbing sound, so the car rides quieter.

Firebird's Endura bumper doesn't even look like a bumper. Because it matches the color of the car. It covers the entire front end. It shrugs off dents, dings and chips. And it won't ever rust.

Firebird's foam-constructed seats never lump. Anybody who has to put up with less has our sympathy.

And the ride. Boulevard smooth. Without sacrificing any handling characteristics whatsoever. All because we put in four

bucket-type seats, raised the drive tunnel and gave the suspension more room to travel. Bring on your gravel roads if you don't believe it.

No question, Firebird's full of innovation. But we really got the spirit when we became aware of the need for different types of Firebirds. Which is where we got Firebird Esprit.

FIREBIRD ESPRIT CLOTH AND VINYL INTERIOR

Firebird Esprit

What we needed was a luxurious Firebird with a reasonable price.

So on the outside, Esprit is set apart by some pretty nice chrome accents, emblems and wheel trim rings.

Inside, there's an assist strap on the dash. Thick loop-pile carpeting. A squeezably soft Custom Cushion steering wheel. Special, perforated-vinyl upholstery on the

FIREBIRD ALL-VINYL INTERIOR

high-back bucket seats. And an extra measure of sound insulation to help make Esprit the quietest of all the Firebirds.

There's a standard 350-CID V-8 under the hood for quick response.

Even a luxurious Firebird has to get up and go.

Formula Firebirds

We talked about Pontiac recognizing the need for different types of Firebirds. All right, these are our performing Firebirds. Compared to Esprit they're not as smooth-riding. Depending on your idea of luxury, they're not as luxurious. But they're unexcelled when it comes to roadwork.

19

FIREBIRD TRANS AM HARDTOP COUPE

Engines make the Formula Firebirds different. A Formula 350 has a 350-CID V-8. A Formula 400 gets a 400 V-8. The Formula 455 gets its name from its 455 H.O. V-8.

Every Formula Firebird is a showcase for Pontiac performance know-how. Each has hood scoops. (Functional scoops can be ordered with the available 455 H.O. V-8.) Thick front and rear stabilizer bars. Firm springs and shocks. Special low-restriction performance dual exhausts. F70 — 14 wide-tread tires. A Custom Cushion steering wheel.

If you'd like to see, first-hand, what all this does for you, pick your Formula. And put in some time on the road. One drive is worth all our words.

FIREBIRD FORMULA 400 HARDTOP COUPE

20

Firebird Trans Am

Lots of cars aspire to the stature of Pontiac's Trans Am. But they'll never make it. Because everything Pontiac knows about enthusiast driving is standard.

A shaker hood with rear-facing inlet allows cold, dense air to be rammed into the 455-CID H.O. V-8. Torque is fed to the rear wheels through a 4-speed, Hurst-shifted Muncie transmission or Turbo Hydra-matic. Power front disc brakes and tough springs, shocks and stabilizer bars are

A front air dam, side air extractors, spoilers at each wheel and on the rear deck all work together to give Trans Am exceptional stability. And they work at everyday expressway speeds.

A 14" thickly padded Formula steering wheel is linked to variable-ratio power steering. And a unitized ignition system is available.

In short, the works. Standard. Because Trans Am was built to be the ultimate Firebird.

designed to keep the F60 — 15 white-lettered tires firmly on track.

Oil, water, fuel, voltage, rpm, time and speed information shows up on an engine-turned dash. A 14" thickly padded Formula steering wheel is linked to variable-ratio power steering. And a unitized ignition system is available.

Dimensions	Hardtop Coupe
Wheelbase	108.0"
Overall Length	191.6"
Overall Width	73.4"
Overall Height	50.4"
Front-seat Leg Room (1)	43.9"
Rear-seat Leg Room (2)	29.6"
Front Head Room (3)	37.4"
Rear Head Room (3)	36.1"

(1) Maximum effective (2) Minimum effective (3) Seat depressed

Firebird

Standard Engine	Available Transmissions	Standard Axle Ratios	Available Axle Ratios
6-cyl., 250-cu.-in. 1-bbl. Compression ratio: 8.5:1	3-speed column shift (standard)	3.08:1 (1)	
	3-speed floor-shift		
	Automatic		
	Turbo Hydra-matic		
Available Engine			
V-8, 350-cu.-in. 2-bbl. Compression ratio: 8.0:1	3-speed floor shift (standard)	3.42:1	
	4-speed manual		
	Automatic	2.73:1	3.08:1
	Turbo Hydra-matic		

(1) Not available with air conditioning

Dimensions	Hardtop Coupe
Front Tread	61.3"
Rear Tread	60.0"

Esprit

Standard Engine	Available Transmissions	Standard Axle Ratios	Available Axle Ratios
V-8, 350-cu.-in. 2-bbl. Compression ratio: 8.0:1	3-speed floor shift (standard)	3.42:1	
	4-speed manual		
	Automatic	2.73:1	3.08:1
	Turbo Hydra-matic		
Available Engine			
V-8, 400-cu.-in. 2-bbl. Compression ratio: 8.2:1	Turbo Hydra-matic	2.73:1	3.08:1

Dimensions	Hardtop Coupe
Front Tread	61.3"
Rear Tread	60.0"

Formula Firebirds

Standard Engine	Available Transmissions	Standard Axle Ratios	Available Axle Ratios
V-8, 350-cu.-in. 2-bbl. Compression ratio: 8.0:1	3-speed floor shift (standard)	3.42:1	
	4-speed manual		
	Automatic	2.73:1	3.08:1
	Turbo Hydra-matic		
Available Engines			
V-8, 400-cu.-in. 4-bbl. Compression ratio: 8.2:1	4-speed manual	3.42:1	
	4-speed close-ratio		
	Turbo Hydra-matic	3.08:1	3.42:1
V-8, 455-cu.-in. H.O. 4-bbl. Compression ratio: 8.4:1	4-speed close-ratio	3.42:1	
	Turbo Hydra-matic	3.42:1 3.08:1 (1)	

(1) Standard with air conditioning

Dimensions	Hardtop Coupe
Front Tread	61.6"
Rear Tread	60.3"

Trans Am

Standard Engine	Available Transmissions	Standard Axle Ratios	Available Axle Ratios
V-8, 455-cu.-in. H.O. 4-bbl. Compression ratio: 8.4:1	4-speed close-ratio (standard)	3.42:1	
	Turbo Hydra-matic	3.42:1 3.08:1 (1)	

(1) Standard with air conditioning

Dimensions	Hardtop Coupe
Front Tread	61.7"
Rear Tread	60.4"

1972 PONTIAC—FIREBIRD SERIES

	Model No.
FIREBIRD HARDTOP COUPE	S87X
ESPRIT HARDTOP COUPE	T87X
FORMULA HARDTOP COUPE	U87X
TRANS AM HARDTOP COUPE	V87X

STANDARD EQUIPMENT— FIREBIRD, ESPRIT

INTERIOR
Firebird and Esprit
- Ashtray Lamp
- Deluxe Steering Wheel (Firebird)
- Door-operated Dome Light Switches
- Flame Chestnut Wood Grain Appearance Instrument Panel Applique
- Integral Molded-foam, Front Bucket Seats with Solid Foam Backs
- Nylon-blend, Loop-pile Carpet
- Storage Pockets in each Door
- Upper-level Ventilation

Esprit only
- Custom Cushion Steering Wheel
- Custom Interior Trim Includes:
  - All-Morrokide or Cloth and Morrokide Bucket Seats
  - Formed-rubber Trunk Mat
  - Instrument Panel Assist Strap

EXTERIOR
Firebird and Esprit
- Endura Front Bumper
- Lift-type Door Handles
- Windshield Radio Antenna

Esprit only
- Body-colored Inserts in Outside Door Handles
- Concealed Windshield Wipers, Left Arm Articulated
- Dual Horns

- "Esprit" Nameplates on Roof Side Panels
- Right- and Left-hand, Body-colored Outside Mirrors— Left-hand, Remote-controlled
- Roof Drip Moldings
- Windowsill Moldings and Hood Rear-edge Moldings
- Wheel Opening Moldings
- Wheel Trim Rings with Hubcaps
- Wide Rocker Panel Moldings

POWER TRAIN & CHASSIS

Standard Engine:
250-cu.-in., 6-cyl., 1-bbl. (Firebird)
350-cu.-in., V-8, 2-bbl. (Esprit)

Available Engine:
350-cu.-in., V-8, 2-bbl. (Firebird)
400-cu.-in., V-8, 2-bbl. (Esprit)

Standard Transmission:
3-speed Manual, Floor Shift

Available Transmissions:
4-speed Manual
Automatic (with 350-cu.-in., V-8 engine only)
Turbo Hydra-matic

Standard Axle Ratio:
3.42:1

Standard Tires:
E78—14 Black

Standard Steering:
Manual

Brakes:
Front Disc

Capacities
Fuel Tank (gals.)	18.6
Cooling System (qts.)	19.4
Oil, less filter refill (qts.)	5.0

Exterior Dimensions (inches)
Overall Length	191.6
Wheelbase	108.0
Height	50.4
Overall Width	73.4
Front Tread (Wide-Track)	61.3
Rear Tread (Wide-Track)	60.0

Interior Dimensions (inches)
FRONT:
Hip Room	56.7
Shoulder Room	57.4
Head Room (effective)	37.4
Leg Room (max. effective)	43.8

REAR:
Hip Room	47.3
Shoulder Room	54.4
Head Room (effective)	36.1
Leg Room (min. effective)	29.6
Trunk Capacity (usable luggage, cu. ft. w/conventional spare)	7.24

Fold out page 7 for listing of standard equipment on all 1972 Pontiacs

30

Wide, horizontal split taillamps have lenses, which act like large reflectors. The wraparound bumper accentuates the tapered rear end. Rear side markers are lighted when parking lights or headlamps are on.

High-back bucket seats with integral head restraints are standard on all Fire-birds. The interior trim on the basic Firebird is all-Morrokide. Pull-type inside door handles are flush-designed for a smooth appearance.

FACTORY-INSTALLED OPTIONS & ACCESSORIES

Order
Code

331 Basic Group—includes Turbo Hydra-matic Transmission, Standard Size Whitewall Tires, (White-lettered U87-V87), AM Radio, Chrome Wheel Trim Rings and Power Steering
422 Air Cleaner, Dual-stage, Heavy-duty—N.A. V87
582 Air Conditioning, Custom—N.A. with 6-cyl. Engine
361 Axle, Safe-T-Track, Rear, Std. V87
368 Axle, Performance
691 Battery, Maintenance-free w/455 Engine only
692 Battery, Heavy-duty
502 Brakes, Power, Front Disc—Std. V87
732 Bumper Guards, Rear
722 Clock, Electric—Std V87X—Inc. w/714-718
431 Console (with floor shift only)
424 Console, Rear
— Cordova Top—available in White, Black, Pewter, Beige (Covert), Tan
541 Defogger, Rear-window—N.A. 534
534 Defroster, Rear-window, Electric—N.A. with 6-cyl. Engine & 541

Engines
34D Engine, 250-cu.-in. 6-cyl. 1-bbl. Carburetor—N.A. T87-U87-V87
Engine, 350 cu.-in. V-8, 2-bbl. Std. T87-U87, N.A. V87
34R Engine, 400-cu.-in. V-8, 2-bbl. Carburetor (with Turbo Hydra-matic Transmission only—Esprit only)

34S Engine, 400-cu.-in. V-8, 4-bbl. Turbo Hydra-matic or 4-spd. only—N.A. S87-T87-V87
34X Engine, 455-cu.-in. V-8, 4-bbl. H.O. Std.—N.A. S87, T87
531 Glass, Soft-Ray—all windows
532 Glass, Soft-Ray—windshield only
492 Guards, Door-edge
332 Handling Package Formula—Includes F60—15 White-lettered tires, Trans Am Rear Springs, Trans Am Front & Rear Stabilizer Bars
681 Horns, Dual (Std. T87-U87-V87)
664 Lamps, Convenience
554 Locks, Door, Electric
521 Mats, Floor, Front—available in Black, Dark Blue, Dark Jade, Dark Beige, Dark Saddle, Dark Sienna and Ivory
522 Mats, Floor, Rear—available in Black, Dark Blue, Dark Jade, Dark Beige, Dark Saddle, Dark Sienna and Ivory
524 Mats, Floor, Rear Compartment (std. on Esprit)
441 Mirror, Vanity, Right-hand
434 Mirrors, Body Color, R.H. & L.H. (L.H. Remote-control) Std. on T87-U87-V87
484 Moldings, Windowsill (std. on Esprit)
494 Moldings, Body Side, Vinyl—Black only—N.A. V87
481 Moldings, Roof Drip (std. on Esprit)
491 Moldings, Wheel Opening, Front & Rear (std. on Esprit—N.A. on V87)
401 Radio, AM, Pushbutton
403 Radio, AM/FM
405 Radio, AM/FM, Stereo—N.A. w/411

718 Rally Gauge Cluster & Clock—N.A. V87
714 Rally Gauge Cluster & Instrument Panel Tachometer—N.A. w/712-718—Std. V87
451 Seat Belts, Custom, Front & Rear and Shoulder Straps, Front
684 "Space-Saver Spare" Tire
411 Speaker Rear—N.A. w/405, 412, 414
614 Spoiler, Rear Air—U87, Std. V87, N.A. S87 and T87
501 Steering, Power, Variable-ratio—Std. V87
461 Steering Wheel, Custom Cushion—Std. T87-U87-V87
464 Steering Wheel, Formula—with Variable-ratio Power Steering only—Std. V87
504 Steering Wheel, Tilt—N.A. with Standard Steering or Column-shift Transmission
614 Stripes, Vinyl—N.A. V87
414 Tape Player, Cassette—N.A. w/411-412
412 Tape Player, Stereo, 8-track—N.A. w/411-414
Tires, Bias-belted
HR E78—14 Whitewall—N.A. U87-V87
GR F78—14 Whitewall—N.A. U87-V87
MF F70—14 Blackwall—Std. U87—N.A. V87
ML F70—14 White Lettered—N.A. V87
Transmissions
35A Transmission, 3-speed Manual Floor Shift—N.A. V87
35J Transmission, Automatic, 2-speed (with non air-conditioned 1-bbl., 6-cyl. Engine or with 2-bbl. 350-cu.-in. Engine) N.A. V87
35L Transmission, Turbo Hydra-matic, 3-speed
35C Transmission, Manual, 3-speed, Heavy-duty, Floor Shift, N.A. with 6-cyl. Engine or with 400-cu.-in. V-8, 2-bbl. Engine
35B Transmission, Manual, 3-speed, Floor Shift—N.A. T87-V87
35E Transmission, Manual, 4-speed—N.A. 34D-R-X
35G Transmission, 4-speed Manual—Close-ratio—N.A. S87-T87
471 Trim Rings, Wheel, Chrome—Std. T87-V87
472 Wheel Covers, Finned—N.A. 332, N.A. V87
476 Wheel Covers, Deluxe—N.A. 332
474 Wheels, Rally II—Std. V87
478 Wheels, Honeycomb
551 Windows, Power (with console only)
432 Windshield Wipers, Concealed—Std. T87-V87

See sample order forms at rear of binder.

31

Firebird, Esprit, Formula, Trans Am: Hardtop Coupes

This *standard* Bucket-seat style
is available in Madrid Morrokide (1)

This *extra-cost* Custom Bucket-seat style
is available in Perforated Roulet Morrokide(2)
or Potomac Pattern Cloth and Madrid Morrokide(3)

Style	Material	(STD.) FIREBIRD, FORMULA, TRANS AM	(STD.) ESPRIT, (EXTRA COST) FORMULA, TRANS AM
(1) Bucket Seat (standard)	Morrokide	121 Ivory, 131 Saddle, 141 Green, 161 Black	
(2) Bucket Seat (extra cost)	Morrokide		211 Blue, 221 Ivory, 231 Saddle, 241 Green, 251 Beige (Covert), 261 Black
(3) Bucket Seat (extra cost)	Cloth and Morrokide		351 Beige (Covert), 361 Black

Note: Trans Am exterior colors available are: C—Cameo White
with Blue striping or F—Lucerne Blue with White striping only.

3

EXTERIOR COLORS
A— Starlight Black
C— Cameo White
D— Adriatic Blue
E— Quezal Gold
F— Lucerne Blue
G— Brittany Beige
H— Shadow Gold
J— Brasilia Gold
K— Julep Green
L— Springfield Green
M— Wilderness Green
N— Revere Silver
P— Antique Pewter
R— Cardinal Red
S— Anaconda Gold
T— Cinnamon Bronze
U— Cumberland Blue
V— Spice Beige
W— Arizona Gold
Y— Monarch Yellow
Z— Sundance Orange

This year was the calm before the storm. The industry as a whole experienced its best year ever as 11,000,000 cars were sold. Pontiac, too, chalked up a record with its 919,872 units. It wasn't good enough to regain third place in national rankings, but it was very good news, nonetheless. All this would grind to a halt in the latter weeks of the year with the Arab Oil Embargo and the ensuing recession, but it was fun while it lasted.

The big event at Pontiac was the completely revised intermediate line, including the Grand Prix. The styling of the standard intermediates was not greeted with much favor by the public, but the Grand Prix was beautifully done. Better still, the Grand Prix sported the most deluxe interior ever. Real mahogany veneer was featured, but the detailing was superb throughout and Grand Prix sales took off as a result. The Grand Prix interior was shared in large part with the new Grand Am series, an attempt at a European-style sport sedan, and the lovely bucket seats showed up in the Firebird, as well.

The Firebirds were not greatly altered for 1973. Indeed, they very nearly got the axe after their miserable showing of the previous season. Fortunately, the powers that were gave them a reprieve and, in 1973, sales at last began to improve. In addition to the Grand Prix/Grand Am seats, the "screaming chicken" hood decal made its first appearance on Trans Ams (as an option) this year. Firebirds were all being detuned en masse as a result of government regulations. The small Esprit V-8 now batted out a mere 150 hp. Horsepower on the standard Trans Am 455 V-8 was down to 250 with an 8.0:1 compression ratio. The optional Trans Am engine still put out 310 hp with an 8.4:1 compression ratio, but these models were clearly not as fast as their recent predecessors.

Prices remained fairly stable, rising a shade on some models and declining a bit on others. The base Firebird now listed at $2,895. The Esprit listed at $3,249. The Formula listed at $3,276. Finally, the Trans Am topped the chart at $4,204.

Production was up dramatically to 46,313 units. Of this number, 14,096 were base units, 17,249 were Esprits, 10,166 were Formulas and 4,802 were Trans Ams.

The Firebird had its own brochure again for the first time since 1970. It is pictured in the montage below, as is the post card. The Firebird was still included in the full-line Pontiac catalogue (see pages 78-79) and in the regular color and trim brochure (see page 84). Information from the fleet/dealer ordering guide is included on pages 80-83, including a copy of the order blank (see page 83).

Firebird
Pontiac's sports cars.

Pontiac 1973

1973 PONTIAC INTERIOR TRIMS AND EXTERIOR COLORS

Grand Prix · Grand Ville · Bonneville · Catalina · Grand Am · Luxury LeMans
LeMans Sport Coupe · LeMans · Ventura · Firebird · Safari Station Wagons

Firebird

Pontiac's sports cars.

Trans Am in Buccaneer Red.

Formula Firebird in Ascot Silver.

You obviously take the excitement of driving pretty seriously. Or you wouldn't even be considering one of our four 1973 Firebirds. The question is . . . just how serious do you want to get?

Trans Am is as serious as they come. A 455-cu.-in., 4-bbl. V-8 with a 4-speed manual transmission is standard. And there's a new Super Duty 455 V-8 available. Whichever engine you go with, the spoilers spoil and the air dams dam. That's why a lot of folks rank Trans Am as the best performing American on the road.

The big bird on the hood you can order. It's a Firebird, isn't it?

Those scoops on the Formula Firebirds look tough. But the toughest part of any Firebird is the front bumper. It's been reinforced this year to make it stronger. And it's made of Endura to fight dents and dings.

The new interior is all business. So are the front disc brakes. And the 455 4-bbl. V-8 you can order.

Can a sports car really be luxurious? Esprit wipes out all doubt. The new bucket seats, the new cloth or all-vinyl upholstery, the new instrument panel and door trim are as plush as you'll find in many a luxury car.

The ride's almost that plush, too. What's interesting about our basic Bird is how much we didn't have to sacrifice for price. You see, this is our most affordable Firebird. You still get molded foam bucket seats, loop-pile carpeting, High-Low ventilation, the Endura bumper, a strong, double-shell roof that absorbs sound, Firebird's futuristic styling and sensational handling.

That's our way with sports cars. Now . . . are you ready to get serious?

Custom Interior—available on Formula and Trans Am, standard on Esprit.
Shown in burgundy—also available in white, saddle and black.

Standard Firebird, Formula and Trans Am interior. Shown
in black—also available in saddle and white.

Available Honeycomb wheels.

Firebird Esprit in Navajo Orange.

Firebird Coupe in Admiralty Blue.

Dimensions (inches)	Esprit Firebird	Formula	Trans Am
Overall length	192.1	192.1	192.1
Overall width	73.4	73.4	73.4
Overall height	50.4	50.4	50.4
Wheelbase	108.0	108.0	108.0
Track, front/rear	61.3/60.0	61.6/60.3	61.7/60.4
Head room, front/rear	37.5/35.9	37.5/35.9	37.5/35.9
Leg room, front/rear	43.9/28.5	43.9/28.5	43.9/28.5
Shoulder room, front/rear	56.4/54.4	56.4/54.4	56.4/54.4
Trunk capacity (cu. ft.)	8.6	8.6	8.6

TRANSMISSIONS	ENGINES					
	250-cu.-in. 1-bbl. L6	350-cu.-in. 2-bbl. V-8	400-cu.-in. 2-bbl. V-8	400-cu.-in. 4-bbl. V-8	455-cu.-in. 4-bbl. V-8	SD 455-cu.-in. 4-bbl. V-8
3-speed Manual	Standard on FIREBIRD with 3.08:1 axle	Standard on ESPRIT and FORMULA, available on FIREBIRD, all with 3.08:1 axle(1)				
4-speed Manual		Available on FIREBIRD, ESPRIT, and FORMULA, all with 3.08:1 axle(1)		Available on FORMULA with 3.42:1 axle		Available on TRANS AM and FORMULA, both with 3.42:1 axle
4-speed Close-ratio Manual				Available on FORMULA with 3.42:1 axle	Standard on TRANS AM with 3.42:1 Limited-slip axle(3)	Available on TRANS AM and FORMULA, both with 3.42:1 axle
Turbo Hydra-matic	Available on FIREBIRD with 3.08:1 axle	Available on FIREBIRD, ESPRIT and FORMULA, all with 2.73:1 axle(2)	Available on ESPRIT with 2.73:1 axle(2)	Available on FORMULA with 3.08:1 axle(1)	Available on TRANS AM and FORMULA, both with 3.08:1 axle(1)	Available on TRANS AM and FORMULA, both with 3.42:1 axle

(1) 3.42:1 Performance ratio available (2) 3.08:1 Performance ratio available (3) Available on Formula with 3.42:1 axle

1973 PONTIAC—ESPRIT & FIREBIRD

ESPRIT HARDTOP COUPE (T87X)

**STANDARD EQUIPMENT—
ESPRIT HARDTOP COUPE**

INTERIOR
- Ash Tray Lamp
- High-low Level Body Ventilation
- Nylon-blend, Loop-pile Carpeting
- Single-buckle Seat and Shoulder Belt and Warning System
  —Driver and Right Front Passenger

Distinctive from Firebird
- Custom Cushion Steering Wheel
- Custom Interior Trim Includes:
  - All Knit Morrokide or Cloth and Morrokide Bucket Seats
  - Rear-quarter Ash Tray
  - Formed-rubber Trunk Mat
  - Instrument Panel Assist Strap
  - Roof Insulator Pads
  - Lateral Restraint Bucket Seat Design

EXTERIOR
- Endura Front Bumper
- Windshield Radio Antenna

Distinctive from Firebird
- Body-colored Inserts in Outside Door Handles
- Concealed Windshield Wipers, Left Arm Articulated
- Deluxe Wheel Covers
- Dual Horns
- Esprit Nameplate on Sail Panel
- Right- and Left-hand, Body-colored Outside Mirrors, Left-hand, Remote Controlled

STANDARD MOLDINGS
(Also Distinctive from Firebird)
- Roof Drip Moldings
- Wheel Opening Moldings
- Wide Rocker Panel Moldings
- Windowsill Moldings and Hood Rear-edge Moldings

POWER TRAIN & CHASSIS

Standard Engine
350-cu.-in., V-8, 2-bbl.

Available Engine
400-cu.-in., V-8, 2-bbl.

Standard Transmission
3-speed Manual, Floor Shift (350 only)

Available Transmissions
4-speed Manual (350 only)
Turbo Hydra-matic (all engines)

Standard Axle Ratio
3.42:1

Standard Tires
E78—14 Black

Standard Steering
Manual

Brakes
Front Disc, Rear Drum

Capacities
Fuel Tank (gals). 18.0
Cooling System (qts.). 22.4
Oil, less filter refill (qts.). 5.0

FIREBIRD HARDTOP COUPE (S87X)

**STANDARD EQUIPMENT—
FIREBIRD HARDTOP COUPE**

INTERIOR
- Ash Tray Lamp
- Deluxe 2-spoke Steering Wheel
- Nylon-blend, Loop-pile Carpeting
- Single-buckle Seat & Shoulder Belt System
- High-low Level Body Ventilation

EXTERIOR
- Endura Front Bumper
- Narrow Rocker Panel Moldings
- Standard Hubcaps
- Windshield Radio Antenna

POWER TRAIN & CHASSIS

Standard Engine
250-cu.-in., Overhead-valve, 6-cyl., 1-bbl.

Available Engine
350-cu.-in., V-8, 2-bbl.

Standard Transmission
3-speed Manual, Floor Shift

Available Transmissions
4-speed Manual (with 350-cu.-in., V-8 engine)
Turbo Hydra-matic (all engines)

Standard Axle Ratio
3.08:1

Standard Tires
E78—14 Black

Standard Steering
Manual

Brakes
Front Disc, Rear Drum Manual

Capacities
Fuel Tank (gals.). 18.0
Cooling System (qts.). 12.5
Oil, less filter refill (qts.). 4.0

EXTERIOR DIMENSIONS (inches)	
Overall Length.	192.1
Wheelbase.	108.0
Height (Preliminary).	50.4
Overall Width.	73.4
Front Tread (Wide-Track).	61.3
Rear Tread (Wide-Track).	60.0

HANDLING PACKAGE
ORDER CODE 342—UPC CODE Y99

(Std. on Trans Am, Available on Formula.
Not Available on basic Firebird or Esprit)
- Heavy-duty Front and Rear Stabilizer Bars
- Heavy-duty Rear Springs and Shocks
- F60—15 White Letter Tires
- 15 x 7 Steel Wheels

BASIC GROUP
ORDER CODE 331—UPC CODE Y88

- Turbo Hydra-matic Transmission
- Whitewall Tires—White Letter Tires on Formula and Trans Am
- AM Radio
- Wheel Trim Rings—(n/a Esprit—std. Trans Am)
- Power Steering—(std. Trans Am)
- Dual Horns (std. Trans Am, Formula and Esprit)

PROTECTION GROUP (New)
ORDER CODE 344—UPC CODE Y95
(N/A Trans Am)
- Vinyl Body Side Moldings
- Door Edge Guards
- Rear Bumper Guards

LAMP GROUP
ORDER CODE 344—UPC CODE Y92

- Luggage Compartment Lamp
- Glove Box Lamp
- I.P. Courtesy Lamp

15

1973 PONTIAC—TRANS AM & FORMULA

TRANS AM HARDTOP COUPE (V87X)

STANDARD EQUIPMENT— TRANS AM HARDTOP COUPE

INTERIOR
- Ash Tray Lamp
- Nylon-blend, Loop-pile Carpeting
- Single-buckle Seat and Shoulder Belt and Warning System —Driver and Right Front Passenger
- High-low Level Body Ventilation

Distinctive Interior from Firebird
- Formula Steering Wheel
- Rally Gauges with Clock & Instrument Panel Tachometer
- Swirl-finish Instrument Panel Trim Plate

EXTERIOR
- Endura Front Bumper
- Windshield Radio Antenna

Distinctive Exterior from Firebird
- Black Textured Grille
- Concealed Windshield Wipers, Left Arm Articulated
- Full-width Rear, Deck-lid Spoiler
- Right- and Left-hand, Body-colored Outside Mirrors— Left-hand Remote Controlled
- Special Air Cleaner & Rear-facing, Cold Air Intake through Hood (throttle controlled)
- Wheel Opening Air Deflectors
- Front Fender Air Extractors

OTHER FEATURES DISTINCTIVE FROM FIREBIRD
- Dual Horns
- Lower Restriction Performance Dual Exhausts with Chrome Extensions
- Rally II Wheels with Trim Rings
- Special Suspension Includes:
  - 1¼" Front Stabilizer Bar
  - ⅞" Rear Stabilizer Bar
  - Firm Control Springs & Shocks (same as Formula except higher rear spring rate)

POWER TRAIN & CHASSIS

Standard Engine
455-cu.-in., V-8, 4-bbl.

Available Engine
455-cu.-in., V-8, S.D. 4-bbl.

Standard Transmission
4-speed Manual with Floor-mounted Shifter

Available Transmission
Turbo Hydra-matic

Standard Axle Ratio
3.42:1 (Safe-T-Track) (limited slip) std.

Standard Tires
F60—15 White-lettered

Standard Steering
Fast-ratio, High-effort, Variable-ratio Power

Brakes
Power, Front Disc, Rear Drum

Capacities
Fuel Tank (gals.)............................ 18.0
Cooling System (qts.)....................... 20.9
Oil, less filter refill (qts.).................. 5.0

NOTE: Trans Am Exterior Colors are: Cameo White, Buccaneer Red, Brewster Green.

FORMULA HARDTOP COUPE (U87X)

STANDARD EQUIPMENT— FORMULA HARDTOP COUPE

INTERIOR
- Ash Tray Lamp
- Nylon-blend, Loop-pile Carpeting
- Single-buckle Seat and Shoulder Belt and Warning System —Driver and Right Front Passenger
- High-low Level Body Ventilation

Distinctive Interior from Firebird
- Custom Cushion Steering Wheel

EXTERIOR
- Endura Front Bumper
- Standard Hubcaps
- Windshield Radio Antenna

Distinctive Exterior from Firebird
- Fiberglass Hood with Dual Air Scoops
- Formula "350," "400" or "445" emblem on Front Fenders
- Right- and Left-hand, Body-colored Outside Mirrors— Left-hand, Remote Controlled

OTHER FEATURES DISTINCTIVE FROM FIREBIRD
- Dual Horns
- Lower Restriction Performance Dual Exhausts with Chrome Extensions
- Special Suspension Includes:
  - Firm Springs and Shocks
  - 1⅛" Front Stabilizer Bar
  - ⅝" Rear Stabilizer Bar
  - Black Textured Grille

POWER TRAIN & CHASSIS

Standard Engine
350-cu.-in., V-8, 2-bbl.

Available Engines
400-cu.-in., V-8, 4-bbl.
455-cu.-in., V-8, 4-bbl.
455-cu.-in., V-8, S.D. 4-bbl. (with Trans Am Hood and Rear Facing Cold Air Intake)

Standard Transmission
3-speed Manual, Floor Shift (with 350-cu.-in., V-8 engine only)

Available Transmissions
4-speed Manual with Floor Shift (all engines)
4-speed Manual, Close Ratio (with 400-cu.-in., V-8, 4-bbl.)
Turbo Hydra-matic

Standard Axle Ratio
3.42:1

Standard Tires
F70—14 Black

Standard Steering
Manual

Brakes
Front Disc, Rear Drum (Manual)

Capacities
Fuel Tank (gals.)............................ 18.0
Cooling System (qts.)....................... 22.4
Oil, less filter refill (qts.).................. 5.0

NOTE: When Power Steering is ordered on Formula, steering ratio is faster (same as Trans Am).

EXTERIOR DIMENSIONS (inches)		
Overall Length		192.1
Wheelbase		108.0
Height (Preliminary)		50.4
Overall Width		73.4
	Formula	Trans Am
Front Tread (Wide-Track)	61.6	61.7
Rear Tread (Wide-Track)	60.3	60.4

14

1973 WHEELS, WHEEL COVERS

**WHEELS AND
WHEEL COVERS**

HUBCAPS
Standard: Catalina, Safari, LeMans Sport Coupe, LeMans and LeMans Safari.

MOON HUBCAPS
Standard: GTO Option, Formula, Firebird and Ventura.

WHEEL TRIM RINGS
ORDER CODE 471—UPC P06
Standard: Trans Am.
Available: GTO Option, LeMans Sport Coupe, LeMans, Lemans Safari, Formula, Firebird and Ventura.

DELUXE WHEEL COVERS—14"
ORDER CODE 476—UPC P01
Standard: Luxury LeMans, Esprit, and Ventura Custom.
Available: LeMans Sport Coupe, LeMans, LeMans Safari, Formula, Firebird and Ventura.

DELUXE WHEEL COVERS—15"
ORDER CODE 476—UPC P01
Standard: Grand Prix Model J, Grand Ville, Bonneville, and Grand Safari.
Available: Catalina and Safari.

FINNED WHEEL COVERS
ORDER CODE 472—UPC P02
Standard: Grand Prix Model SJ and Grand Am.
Available: Grand Prix Model J, Grand Ville, Bonneville, Catalina, Grand Safari, Safari, LeMans Sport Coupe, LeMans, Formula, Esprit and Firebird.

RALLY II WHEELS
ORDER CODE 474—UPC N98
Standard: Trans Am.
Available: All others including all series Safaris.

HONEYCOMB WHEELS
ORDER CODE 478—UPC P05
Available: Grand Prix, Grand Am, GTO Option, LeMans Sport Coupe, LeMans, LeMans Safari, Trans Am, Formula, Esprit and Firebird.

22

1973 PONTIAC FIREBIRD
Hardtop Coupe

5-1-72

CUSTOMER OR TAG FOR	ZONE & DLR. CODE 13-17		ORDER DATE 4-6	ZONE USE 7-9
	DLR. NAME	DIST. 18		
DEALER SIGNATURE	STREET		ORDER NO. 18-23	
	DLR. TOWN	ZIP CODE	SAMPLE	

FLEET CLASS CODE	C L P	GMAC	11A
	R S Z	ODC †	11B
SOLD	031	CASH	11C
STOCK	032	ZONE STOCK	11J
FLEET	033		

CHECK MARK INDICATES SPEC. EQUIP. ORDER ATTACHED

COLORS

C - CAMEO WHITE	H - DESERT SAND	M - BREWSTER GREEN	U - NAVAJO ORANGE
D - PORCELAIN BLUE	J - GOLDEN OLIVE	R - BUCCANEER RED	V - ASCOT SILVER
E - ADMIRALTY BLUE	K - VERDANT GREEN	S - FLORENTINE RED	Y - VALENCIA GOLD
F - REGATTA BLUE	L - SLATE GREEN	T - SUNLIGHT YELLOW	Z - BURMA BROWN

CORDOVA TOPS
1 - WHITE
2 - BLACK
3 - BEIGE
4 - CHAMOIS
5 - GREEN
6 - DARK BURGUNDY
7 - BLUE

Model 24-27 /Color 28-29 /Trim 30-31-32

CIRCLE MODEL TRIM & COLOR		BUCKET			CUSTOM BUCKET					TWO-TONE PAINT NOT AVAILABLE		
		WHITE VINYL	SADDLE VINYL	BLACK VINYL	WHITE VINYL	SADDLE VINYL	BLACK VINYL	BURGUNDY VINYL	BEIGE CLOTH	LOWER COLOR 28	CORDOVA TOPS (N.A. V87) 29	SOLID PAINT (CIRCLE BOTH LETTERS) 28-29
STANDARD AVAIL. IN ALL COLORS	S87X	321	331	361						C K T	1	CC KK TT
ESPRIT AVAIL. IN ALL COLORS	T87X				421	431	461	471	551	D L U / E M V / F R Y / H S Z / J	2 3 4 5 6 7	DD LL UU / EE MM VV / FF RR YY / HH SS ZZ / JJ
FORMULA AVAIL. IN ALL COLORS	U87X	321	331	361	*421	*431	*461	*471	*551			
TRANS AM AVAIL. IN C.M.R ONLY	V87X	321	331	361	*421	*431	*461	*471	*551			

OTHER ACCESSORIES

UPC	GROUPS	COL.	S	T	U	V
Y88	BASIC GROUP (INC. 411,421,681, N.A. T87 STD. V87, 501 STD. V87, HYD. TRANS., M/SW TIRES (S87-T87), WHITE LETTER TIRES (U87-V87)	33	1			
Y95	BODY PROTECTION GROUP P (INC. 492, 494, 732		4			0
Y99	HANDLING PKG. (INC. F78X15 WHITE LETTER TIRES, H.D. STABILIZER BARS, H.D. REAR SPRINGS & SHOCKS, 15X7 WHEELS	34	2	0	0	S
Y92	LAMP GROUP INC. LUGGAGE LAMP, GLOVE BOX LAMP, I.P. COURTESY LAMP		4			

ENGINES

			COL.	S	T	U	V
STD.	250 1 Barrel 6 Cyl.—N.A. S82		D	0	0	0	
L30	350 2 Barrel V-8 STD. ESPRIT & FORMULA		M				
L65	400 2 Barrel V-8—HYD. ONLY	35	R	0		0	0
L78	400 4 Barrel V-8 HYD. OR 4 SPD. ONLY		S	0	0		0
L75	455 4 Barrel V-8 HYD. OR SPD. ONLY STD. TRANS AM		W	0	0		0
LS2	455 4 Barrel V-8—S.D. HYD. OR 4 SPD ONLY		X	0			0

TRANSMISSIONS

M38 M40	Turbo Hydro-Matic 3 Speed B		L				
M12	3 Speed Manual—FLOOR SHIFT—W/350 W ONLY	36	U			0	
M20	4 Speed Man.—N.A. 350-R		E				
M21	4 Spd. Man.—CLOSE RATIO W/ 355 ONLY		H	0	0		0

AXLES

G80	Safe-T-Track Rear Axle	37	U	1			S
G92	Performance Axle Ratio		U				

TIRE OPTIONS (COLS. 39-40)

PL3	F78x14 White—N.A. S82	HR			0	0
PX5	F78x14 Black—STD. S82	GF			0	0
PX6	F78x14 White	GR			0	0
PY6	F78x14 Black	MF		S	0	
PL4	F78x14 White Letter	ML			0	
P85	GR70x15 White—STEEL BELTED W/361 OR RADIAL PLY TRANS AM	VJ	0	0		

UPC	OPTIONS & ACCESSORIES		COL.	S	T	U	V
U63	Radio, AM	B		1			
U69	Radio, AM/FM		41	3			
U58	Radio, Stereo AM/FM—N.A. W/421			5			
U80	Rear Seat Speaker—N.A. WITH 415-422			1			
U57	Stereo 8 Tape Player—N.A. W/421 W/431 ONLY		42	2			
D50	Rear Console			4			
D55	Console			1			
C24	Concealed Windshield Wipers		43	2	S		S
D35	R.H.&L.H. Body Color Mirrors—L.H. REMOTE CONTROL			4	S	S	S
D34	Mirror—Visor Vanity-R.H.		44	1			
AK1	Seat Belts, Custom—INC. FRONT SHOULDER STRAPS		45	1			
N30	Custom Cushion Steering Wheel		46	1	S	S	0
NK3	Formula Steering Wheel—w/501 ONLY			4			
P06	Wheel Trim Rings	B		1	0		S
P02	Custom Finned Wheel Covers—N.A. 542			2			0
N98	Rally II Wheels—INC. 471		47	4			S
P01	Deluxe Wheel Covers—N.A. 542			4	S		S
P05	Honeycomb Wheels			8			
B80	Roof Drip Scalp Moulding		48	1		S	
B85	Window Sill & Hood Edge Mouldings			4			S
B96	Mouldings, Wheel Opening			1		S	0
B93	Door Edge Guards	P	49	2			
B84	Vinyl Body Side Mldgs.—BLACK INSERT	P		4			0
N41	Power Steering, Variable Ratio	B		1			S
JL2	Power Disc Brakes, Front		50	2			S
N33	Tilt Steering Wheel—N.A. W/STD. STEER. N.A. COL. SHIFT HYD			4			
WW7	Trans AM Hood Decal		51	2	0	0	0

UPC	OPTIONS & ACCESSORIES		COL.	S	T	U	V
A01	Glass—Soft Ray—ALL WINDOWS			1			
A02	Glass—Soft Ray—WINDSHIELD ONLY		53	2			
C49	Rear Wind. Defroster, Electric—N.A. 350 541			4			
C50	Rear Window Defogger—N.A. 534		54	1			
K45	Air Cleaner, Dual Stage H.D.—N.A. 35X			2			0
A31	Power Windows—w/431 ONLY		55	1			
AU3	Electric Door Locks			4			
C60	Air Cond., Cust.—N.A. 350		58	2			
B42	Floor Mat—REAR COMPARTMENT STD. W/CUSTOM BUCKETS		60	4	S		
75F	Red Carpet—W/TRIMS 321-361-421-461			1			
97F	Orange Carpet—W/TRIMS 321-421		61	2			
24F	Bright Blue Carpet—w/TRIMS 321-421			4			
B32	Floor Mats—FRONT ONLY		62	1			
B33	Floor Mats—REAR ONLY			2			
D98	Vinyl Accent Stripes			1			0
D80	Rear Air Spoiler		63	2	1	0	S
WU3	Hood Ram Air—W/355-W ONLY INC. W/35X			4	0	0	S
U05	Dual Horns	B		1	S	S	S
N65	Spare Tire, Space Saver		68	4			
TP1	Maintenance Free Battery—N.A. W/692			1			
UA1	Battery—Heavy Duty—N.A. W/691		69	2			
K65	Unitized Ignition System—w/355-W ONLY			4	0	0	
U35	Clock, Electric—INC. W/732, 714			1			S
W63	Rally Gauge Cluster & Clock—N.A.W/714, 711		71	2			0
WW8	Rally Ga. Clu. Clock & I.P. Tach.—N.A.W/732, 711			4			S
Y32	Rear Bumper Guards	P	72	2			
	Color & Trim Incompatibility Skip Punch		77				

† DEALER CERTIFIES THAT HE HAS CURRENT ARRANGEMENTS WITH AN ODC FINANCER AND THAT SETTLEMENT SHOULD BE MADE THROUGH SUCH ODC FINANCER.

FORM 516-S 5-1-72

1973 MODEL WHOLESALE CAR ORDER PONTIAC MOTOR DIVISION GMC

0 = Not Available S = Standard * EXTRA COST

FLEET ACCT. No. (ZONE USE ONLY)

ZONE COPY—White
DEALER COPY—Buff

FIREBIRD, FORMULA, TRANS AM
(Standard Interiors)

BUCKET SEATS
Madrid Morrokide

STANDARD—ALL MORROKIDE

Models	Interior Trims	Exterior Colors
HARDTOP COUPE	321 (WHITE)	C, D, E, F, H, J, K, L, M, R, S, T, U, V, Y, Z
	331 (SADDLE)	C, H, J, L, M, T, U, V, Y, Z
	361 (BLACK)	C, D, E, F, H, J, K, L, M, R, S, T, U, V, Y, Z

ESPRIT (Standard Interiors)
FORMULA, TRANS AM
(Extra-cost Custom Interiors)

BUCKET SEATS
Perforated and Madrid Morrokides or
Prado Cloth with Bravo Bolster Cloth and Madrid Morrokide

STANDARD OR EXTRA COST—ALL MORROKIDE

Models	Interior Trims	Exterior Colors
HARDTOP COUPE	421 (WHITE)	C, D, E, F, H, J, K, L, M, R, S, T, U, V, Y, Z
	431 (SADDLE)	C, H, J, L, M, T, U, V, Y, Z
	461 (BLACK)	C, D, E, F, H, J, K, L, M, R, S, T, U, V, Y, Z
	471 (BURGUNDY)	C, E, S

STANDARD OR EXTRA COST—CLOTH AND MORROKIDE

Models	Interior Trims	Exterior Colors
HARDTOP COUPE	551 (BEIGE)	C, E, H, J, K, L, M, R, S, T, U, V, Y, Z

Extra-cost custom interior available on Formula and Trans Am (standard on Esprit) includes Trunk-fitted Floor Mat, Roof Insulation Pads, Rear-quarter Ash Tray, Door and Quarter Panel Interior Trim, Exterior Door Handle Trim and Assist Grip on Instrument Panel.

4

Body Colors
R — Buccaneer Red
T — Sunlight Yellow
U — Navajo Orange
C — Cameo White
D — Porcelain Blue
E — Admiralty Blue
F — Regatta Blue
H — Desert Sand
J — Golden Olive
K — Verdant Green
L — Slate Green
M — Brewster Green
S — Florentine Red
V — Ascot Silver
Y — Valencia Gold
Z — Burma Brown
A — Starlight Black
G — Mesa Tan
W — Burnished Umber

Sales plummeted throughout the industry in 1974 and Pontiac was no exception. Wide track production was off by a startling 36%. The public, at least that part of it that was still in the market, was buying small econoboxes and that was a type of car for which Pontiac was not known. Curiously, the all-out sporty machines, such as the Trans Am, also spurted in sales. This was hard to explain other than to speculate that there was a get-a-real-car-while-you-still-can feeling among the muscle car crowd that prompted them to buy cars dramatically out of temper with the mass mood of the market.

The Firebird received its first facelift since the introduction of the 1970 body. The new frontal design was much more massive in appearance than before and the horizontal, louvred rear tail lamps made their debut. That was the good news. The not-so-good news was further detuning of the Firebird engines. This was most notable in the Trans Am, where the standard engine was now a 400 cid V-8 rated at 225 hp. The standard 455 V-8 from 1973 was now optional and the top rated 455 V-8 was quoted at 290 hp, down from the old 310.

Prices were moving in inverse ratio to horsepower (it seemed) and were up significantly in 1974. The base Firebird now listed at $3,335, compared to $3,687 for the Esprit, $3,659 for the Formula and $4,446 for the Trans Am.

Production climbed to 73,729, the highest total since 1969. This included 26,372 base 'Birds, 22,583 Esprits, 14,519 Formulas and a starting 10,255 Trans Ams. The Trans Am total was up 113% since 1973 and up a whopping 697% since 1972!

The literature situation was roughly the same as in the previous year. There was a separate Firebird folder (see the montage below and page 86) and the Firebird line was inlcuded in the regular Pontiac full-line catalogue, although in abbreviated form, and in the color and trim brochure (see page 90). There were two different Firebird post cards (see page 87). The Firebird spread from the fleet ordering guide is reproduced on pages 88-89.

FIREBIRD SERIES FACTS AND FIGURES
MODELS
Hardtop Coupe, offered under four names: Firebird, Firebird Esprit, Formula Firebird and Firebird Trans Am.

POWER TEAMS (SEE CHART INSIDE)
STANDARD INTERIOR FEATURES
Standard Firebird Features
Front bucket seats and bucket-type rear seats with all-Morrokide trim. Front seat cushions of solid foam with integral springs. Black Deluxe 2-spoke steering wheel. Nylon-blend, cut-pile carpeting. High-Low ventilation. Ash tray lamp.

Special Firebird Esprit Features
Custom trim of cloth and Morrokide or perforated Morrokide on deep contour bucket seats. Distinctive door trim panels. Custom Cushion steering wheel. Pedal trim plates. Door and instrument panel assist straps. Rear quarter ash tray. Formed rubber trunk mat.

Special Formula Firebird Features
Color-coordinated Custom Cushion steering wheel.

Special Firebird Trans Am Features
14" Formula steering wheel. Rally gauges, electric clock and instrument panel tach. Aluminum swirl-finish instrument panel trim plate.

STANDARD EXTERIOR FEATURES
Standard Firebird Features
Endura front and rear bumpers with integral bumper guards. Windshield radio antenna. Moon hubcaps. Narrow rocker panel moldings. Bright headlight bezels and windshield, rear window and grille moldings. Firebird emblems on grille panel and rear deck lid.

Special Firebird Esprit Features
Esprit identification. Body-colored sport wheel.

Available Super Duty 455-cubic-inch 4-bbl. V-8.

mirrors, left-hand remote control. Concealed wipers. Body-colored door handle inserts. Deluxe wheel covers. Bright moldings on roof, windowsills, hood, rocker panels and wheel openings.

Special Formula Firebird Features
Formula "350", "400", or "455" emblem on front fender. Body-colored sport mirrors, left-hand remote control. Blacked-out grille. Fiberglass hood with twin simulated air scoops.

Special Firebird Trans Am Features
Trans Am decal on front fenders and on wrap-around rear deck spoiler. Front air dam. Wheel opening air deflectors. Front fender air extractors. Body-colored sport mirrors, left-hand remote control. Concealed wipers. Blacked-out grille. 15x7" Rally II wheels with trim rings. Shaker hood.

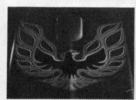

Available Firebird Trans Am hood decal.

STANDARD CHASSIS FEATURES
Standard Firebird and Firebird Esprit Features
Front disc brakes. Coil-spring front and leaf-spring rear suspension. E78—14 belted blackwall tires.

Special Formula Firebird Features
Front and rear stabilizer bars. Computer-selected springs. Lower restriction, performance dual exhausts (in California, available only with 455 V-8). Power-flex fan (400, 455 and SD-455 V-8s).

Special Firebird Trans Am Features
Fast-rate, variable-ratio power steering. Power brakes with front discs and rear drums. 1.25" front and .812" rear stabilizer bars. Computer-selected springs. Safe-T-Track limited-slip differential. Lower restriction, performance dual exhausts. Power-Flex fan.

Dimensions (inches)	Firebird, Esprit	Formula	Trans Am
Overall length	196.0	196.0	196.0
Overall width	73.4*	73.0	73.2
Wheelbase	108.0	108.0	108.0
Track, front/rear	61.3/60.0	61.5/60.3	61.7/60.4
Head room, front/rear	37.5/35.9	37.5/35.9	37.5/35.9
Leg room, front/rear	43.9/29.6	43.9/29.6	43.9/29.6
Shoulder room, front/rear	57.4/54.4	57.4/54.4	57.4/54.4
Hip room, front/rear	56.7/47.3	56.7/47.3	56.7/47.3

*Firebird—73.0

Capacities	Firebird	Esprit, Formula	Trans Am
Fuel tank (gals.)	20.2	20.2	20.2
Cooling system (qts.)	13.2	22.1	21.9
Oil, less filter refill (qts.)	4.0	5.0	5.0

POPULAR EQUIPMENT AVAILABLE
Super Duty 455-cu.-in. 4-bbl. V-8 (Formula and Trans Am only). Turbo Hydra-matic transmission. Radial Tuned Suspension, which includes: steel-belted radial tires, Plia-cell shock absorbers, jounce restrictors and more. Honeycomb wheels. Custom interior trim (std. on Esprit, available on Formula and Trans Am). Front and rear consoles.

Available Honeycomb wheels.

Rally gauge instrument cluster (V-8s only). 8-track stereo tape player. Wrap-around rear deck spoiler on Firebird and Formula Firebird. Hood ram air for Formula Firebird. Dual exhausts for Firebird and Firebird Esprit.

Radial Tuned Suspension—available on Firebird, Firebird Esprit, Formula Firebird and Firebird Trans Am.

FIREBIRD SAFETY FEATURES
OCCUPANT PROTECTION
Seat belts with pushbutton buckles for all passenger positions. Two front combination seat and shoulder belts for driver and right front passenger (with reminder light and buzzer, inertia reel and starter interlock). Two front-seat head restraints. Energy-absorbing steering column. Passenger-guard door locks. Safety door latches and hinges. Folding seat-back latches. Energy-absorbing padded instrument panel and front seat-back tops. Contoured windshield header. Thick laminate windshield. Padded sun visors. Safety armrests. Safety steering wheel. Cargo-Guard. Side-Guard beams. Contoured full roof inner panel.

ACCIDENT PREVENTION
Side marker lights and reflectors (front side marker lights flash with direction signal). Parking lamps that illuminate with headlamps. Four-way hazard warning flasher. Backup lights. Lane-change feature in direction signal control. Windshield defrosters, washers and dual-speed wipers. Wide-view inside day/night mirror (vinyl edged, shatter-resistant glass and deflecting support). Outside rearview mirror. Dual master cylinder brake system with warning light. Starter Safety Switch. Dual-action safety hood latches. Improved bumper systems.

ANTI-THEFT
Anti-theft ignition key warning buzzer. Anti-theft steering column lock.

Shown on the cars and described in this catalog are some of the many options and accessories offered by Pontiac. They're available at extra cost, and well worth it in driving comfort and convenience. Pontiac Motor Division of General Motors Corporation reserves the right to make changes at any time, without notice, in colors, equipment, specifications, prices and models—and also to discontinue models. The right is also reserved to change any specifications, parts or equipment at any time without incurring any obligation to equip same on cars built prior to date of such change.

Pontiac Motor Division, General Motors Corporation, One Pontiac Plaza, Pontiac, Michigan 48053.

PONTIAC GM

Litho in U.S.A. 300M

1974 Pontiac Firebird

1974 PONTIAC—FIREBIRDS

FIREBIRD HARDTOP COUPE (S874) ··· FIREBIRD ESPRIT HARDTOP COUPE (T874)
FIREBIRD FORMULA HARDTOP COUPE (U874) ··· FIREBIRD TRANS AM HARDTOP COUPE (V874)

STANDARD EQUIPMENT—
FIREBIRD ESPRIT and FIREBIRD SERIES

INTERIOR
- Ash Tray Lamp
- High-Low Level Body Ventilation
- Nylon-blend, Cut-pile Carpeting
- Single-buckle Seat and Shoulder Belt System with Starter Interlock

Distinctive from Firebird
- Custom Cushion Steering Wheel
- Custom Interior Trim
  Includes
  - All-Morrokide or Cloth-and-Morrokide Bucket Seats
  - Assist Straps on Doors
  - Rear Quarter Ash Tray
  - Trunk Mat
  - Instrument Panel Assist Strap
  - Lateral Support Bucket Seat Design
  - Custom Pedal Trim Plates

EXTERIOR
- Dual Horns
- Endura Front and Rear Bumpers
- Integral Front and Rear Bumper Guards
- Windshield Radio Antenna

Distinctive from Firebird
- Body-color Inserts in Outside Door Handles
- Concealed Windshield Wipers
- Deluxe Wheel Covers
- Esprit Nameplate on Sail Panel
- Outside Sport Mirrors, L.H. Remote Control

STANDARD MOLDINGS
- Windshield Moldings
- Rear Window Moldings

Moldings Distinctive from Firebird
- Roof Drip Moldings
- Wheel Opening Moldings
- Wide Rocker Panel Moldings
- Windowsill and Hood Rear Edge Molding

POWER TRAIN & CHASSIS

Standard Engines
250-cu.-in., 6 cyl. OHV, 1-bbl. (Firebird)
350-cu.-in., V-8, 2-bbl. (Firebird Esprit)

Available Engines
350-cu.-in., V-8, 2-bbl. (Firebird)
400-cu.-in., V-8, 2-bbl. (Turbo Hydra-matic Firebird Esprit only)

Standard Transmission
3-speed Manual, Floor Shift

Available Transmissions
4-speed Manual, Floor Shift (350 V-8 only)
Turbo Hydra-matic

Standard Axle Ratio
3.08:1

Standard Tires
E78—14 Black

Standard Steering
Variable-ratio Power Steering

Standard Brakes
Manual, Disc Front, Rear Drum

Capacities
Fuel Tank (gals.)	21.5
Cooling System (qts.)	22.1
Oil, less filter refill (qts.)	6 cyl. 4.0; V-8, 5.0

Exterior Dimensions
(inches)
Overall Length	196.0
Wheelbase	108.0
Overall Width	73.4
Front Tread (Wide-Track)	61.3
Rear Tread (Wide-Track)	60.0

Interior Dimensions
(inches)

FRONT:
Hip Room	56.7
Shoulder Room	57.4
Head Room (effective)	37.5
Leg Room (max. effective)	43.9

REAR:
Hip Room	47.3
Shoulder Room	54.4
Head Room (effective)	35.9
Leg Room (min. effective)	29.6
Trunk Capacity (usable luggage space, cu. ft. est. w/conventional spare)	N.A.

Fold out page 7 for listing of standard equipment on all 1974 Pontiacs.

30

The rear styling for the 1974 Firebird is no less dramatic. The tail lamp treatment is all-new and the bumper system features the same type protection method as the front, with bumpers and guards of Endura. Great engineering attention has been paid to the need for added strength against minor impact.

High-back bucket seats with integral head restraints in Madrid Morrokide, are standard on the Firebird, Firebird Formula and Firebird Trans Am. Front seat cushions are of solid foam with integral springs. Cut-pile carpeting is standard.

The rally gauge cluster with instrument panel tachometer standard on the Firebird Trans Am is also available on the Firebird, Firebird Esprit and Firebird Formula. A similar cluster without the tachometer also is available on the Firebird, Firebird Esprit and Firebird Formula.

Right- and left-hand body-colored outside sport mirrors are standard on the Firebird Esprit, Firebird Formula and Firebird Trans Am. The left-hand mirror is remote controlled.

FACTORY-INSTALLED OPTIONS & ACCESSORIES

Order Code

Accessories

604	Air Cleaner, Dual-stage, Heavy-duty—N.A. V87, 35X
582	Air Conditioning, Custom—N.A. 35D
371	Axle, Safe-T-Track, Rear, Std. V87
378	Axle, Performance, Req. 682 w/Man. Trans.
574	Battery, Delco Maintenance-Free—N.A. w/591
591	Battery, Heavy-duty—N.A. 574
502	Brakes, Power, Front Disc—Std. V87 Req. w/35X-W Engines, Air Cond. Code 582 & GR70x15 Radial Tires
711	Clock, Electric—Std. V87—Incl. w/712, 714
431	Console
424	Console, Rear
—	Cordova Top—Available in White, Black, Beige, Russet, Green, Burgundy, Blue, Brown, Saddle, Taupe
594	Defogger, Rear Window—N.A. 592
592	Defroster, Rear Window, Electric—N.A. 35D, 594
682	Exhaust, Dual—N.A. 35D—Std. U87 & V87
571	Glass, Soft-Ray—All Windows
572	Glass, Soft-Ray—Windshield only
492	Guards, Door Edge
601	Heater, Engine Block—N.A. 35D
512	Horns, Dual, Trans Am, N.A. S87, T87, U87
694	Horns, Dual (Std. T87, U87, V87)
602	Ignition System, Unitized, w/35S-W only, N.A. S87, T87
654	Lamp Pkg.—Inc. Luggage, Glove Box and I.P. Courtesy Lamps
554	Locks, Door, Electric
622	Mats, Floor, Front
624	Mats, Floor, Rear

614	Mats, Floor, Rear Compartment (Std. w/Custom Buckets & T87)
441	Mirror, Vanity, Right-hand
434	Mirrors, Body-colored, R.H. & L.H. (L.H. Remote Control) Std. on T87, U87, V87
494	Moldings, Body Side, Vinyl—Black only—N.A. V87
481	Moldings, Roof Drip (Std. T87)
491	Moldings, Wheel Opening (Std. on T87—N.A. on V87
484	Moldings, Windowsill & Hood Rear Edge (Std. on T87)
511	Pedal Trim Plates, Custom—Std. T87
411	Radio, AM, Pushbutton
413	Radio, AM/FM
415	Radio, AM/FM, Stereo
712	Rally Gauge Cluster & Clock—N.A. 714, 711, V87
714	Rally Gauge Cluster, Instrument Panel Tach & Clock— N.A. w/711, 712—Std. V87
514	Ram Air, Hood w/35S-W only, Incl. w/35X—Std. U87 —N.A. S87, T87, V87
691	Seat Belts, Custom, Front & Rear and Shoulder Straps, Front
421	Speaker, Rear—N.A. w/415, 422.
681	Spoiler, Rear Air—Std. V87—N.A. T87
461	Steering Wheel, Custom Cushion—Std. T87, U87— N.A. V87
464	Steering Wheel, Formula—Std. V87
504	Steering Wheel, Tilt—N.A. Col. Shift Hyd.
638	Stripes, Vinyl—N.A. V87
422	Tape Player, Stereo 8—w/431 only
684	Tire, Spare, Space-saver
472	Wheel Covers, Custom Finned—N.A. V87
476	Wheel Covers, Deluxe—Std. T87—N.A. V87
471	Wheel Trim Rings, Chrome—Std. V87—N.A. T87
474	Wheels, Rally II—Std. V87, Incl. 471
478	Wheels, Honeycomb
551	Windows, Power w/431 only

432	Windshield Wipers, Concealed—Std. T87-V87

Engines

35M	Engine, 350-cu.-in. V-8, 2-bbl. Std. T87-U87, N.A. V87
35R	Engine, 400-cu.-in. V-8, 2-bbl. Turbo Hydra-matic only—N.A. S87 & V87
35S	Engine, 400-cu.-in. V-8, 4-bbl. Turbo Hydra-matic or 4-speed only. N.A. S87 & T87
35W	Engine, 455-cu.-in. V-8, 4-bbl. Turbo Hydra-matic only. N.A. S87 & T87
35X	Engine, 455-cu.-in. V-8, 4-bbl. S.D. Turbo Hydra-matic or 4-speed only. N.A. S87 & T87

Transmissions

36B	Transmission, 3-speed Manual Floor Shift w/35D-M only—N.A. V87
36L	Transmission, Turbo Hydra-matic 3-speed
36E	Transmission, 4-speed Manual—N.A. 35D-R-W

Tires, Bias-belted

H8	E78—14 Whitewall—N.A. U87-V87, 582
GF	F78—14 Blackwall—N.A. U87-V87, Std. 582
GR	F78—14 Whitewall—N.A. U87-V87
ML	F70—14 White-letter—N.A. U87-V87
*GJ	FR78—14 Whitewall—Steel-belted Radial—N.A. V87
*GK	FR78—14 White-letter—Steel-belted Radial—N.A. V87
*VH	GR70—15 Blackwall—Steel-belted Radial—N.A. S87, T87—Std. V87
*VK	GR70—15 White-letter—Steel-belted Radial—N.A. S87, T87.

*Tire options include R.T.S.

See sample order forms at rear of binder.

31

Pontiac

FIREBIRD Standard Interiors (Firebird, Formula and Trans Am Models)

BUCKET SEATS

Madrid Morrokide

STANDARD—ALL MORROKIDE

Model	Interior Trims	Exterior Colors
HARDTOP COUPE	721 (White)	C, E, F, G, H, J, K, M, N, R, S, T, V, W, Y, Z
	731 (Saddle)	C, G, H, J, S, T, V, W, Z
	761 (Black)	C, E, F, G, H, J, K, M, N, R, S, T, V, W, Y, Z

AVAILABLE—COLORED INTERIOR WITH WHITE SEATS

Model	Interior Trim	Seat Color
HARDTOP COUPE	761 (Black)	White (Order Code 331)

AVAILABLE—COLORED APPOINTMENTS* WITH COMPATIBLE SEATS

Model	Interior Trim	Seat Color
HARDTOP COUPE	721 (White)	Blue (Order Code 335)
		Green (Order Code 336)
		Red (Order Code 338)
	761 (Black)	Red (Order Code 338)

Pontiac

FIREBIRD Custom Interiors (Standard on Esprit. Extra-cost on Formula and Trans Am Models)

BUCKET SEATS

Prado Corduroy and Bravado Bolster Cloths with Madrid Morrokide or Perforated and Madrid Morrokides

STANDARD OR EXTRA COST—CLOTH AND MORROKIDE

Model	Interior Trims	Exterior Colors
HARDTOP COUPE	831 (Saddle)	C, G, H, J, S, T, V, W, Z
	861 (Black)	C, E, F, G, H, J, K, M, N, R, S, T, V, W, Y, Z

STANDARD OR EXTRA COST—ALL MORROKIDE

Model	Interior Trims	Exterior Colors
HARDTOP COUPE	811 (Blue)	C, E, F
	901 (Red)	C, E, R, V
	921 (White)	C, E, F, G, H, J, K, M, N, R, S, T, V, W, Y, Z
	931 (Saddle)	C, G, H, J, S, T, V, W, Z
	941 (Green)	C, J, M, N
	961 (Black)	C, E, F, G, H, J, K, M, N, R, S, T, V, W, Y, Z

AVAILABLE—COLORED INTERIOR WITH COMPATIBLE SEATS

Model	Interior Trims	Seat Colors
HARDTOP COUPE	811 (Blue)	White (Order Code 331)
	901 (Red)	
	941 (Green)	
	961 (Black)	
	901 (Red)	Black (Order Code 332)
	961 (Black)	Red (Order Code 333)

AVAILABLE—COLORED APPOINTMENTS* WITH COMPATIBLE SEATS

Model	Interior Trims	Appointment Colors
HARDTOP COUPE	921 (White)	Blue (Order Code 335)
		Green (Order Code 336)
		Red (Order Code 338)
	861 (Black)	Red (Order Code 338)
	961 (Black)	Red (Order Code 338)

*Carpeting, Instrument Panel, Steering Column, Package Shelf.

6

EXTERIOR COLORS

H — Denver Gold	
M — Fernmist Green	
R — Buccaneer Red	
T — Sunstorm Yellow	
C — Cameo White	
E — Admiralty Blue	
F — Regatta Blue	
G — Carmel Beige	
J — Limefire Green	
K — Gulfmist Aqua	
N — Pinemist Green	
S — Honduras Maroon	
V — Ascot Silver	
W — Fire Coral Bronze	
Y — Colonial Gold	
Z — Crestwood Brown	
A — Starlight Black	
D — Porcelain Blue	
L — Lakemist Green	
U — Shadowmist Brown	

Industry conditions grew even worse in 1975 as the recession deepened. The only thing that saved Pontiac from the ignominy of slipping below the half-million mark in sales was the introduction of the sub-compact Astre (a.k.a. Vega) line. The only traditional Pontiac line that was still healthy was the Firebird.

There were only minor styling alterations in the Firebirds for 1975. The most noticeable was the new wrap-around rear window. The drive-train was, however, further downgraded by the deletion from the catalogue of the 455 cid V-8. This year, the only engine available in a Trans Am was the 400 cid V-8 with a 7.6:1 compression ratio rated at 185 hp. The base 'Bird's Chevy stovebolt six was actually increased in rated horsepower (to 105 from 100), but that engine was now standard on the Esprit, too.

Prices jumped again, to $3,713 for the base Firebird, $3,431 for the Esprit, $4,349 for the Formula and $4,740 for the Trans Am. Production rose to 84,063 units, of which 22,293 were base models, 20,826 were Esprits, 13,670 were Formulas and 27,274 were Trans Ams. The Trans Am total was up 165% from 1974.

The Firebird literature was much the same as in the two previous years. There was a separate Firebird folder as well as a post card (both are in the montage below). The Firebird was also included in the full-line Pontiac catalogue and in an interesting mailer catalogue (see page 92), as well as in the regular color and trim brochure (see page 95). The Firebird spread from the fleet ordering guide appears on pages 93-94.

Firebird. Our basic Firebird has the styling you'd expect in a sports car. And a lot you wouldn't. Including features like rich, full-foam bucket seats. Cut-pile carpeting. Radial Tuned Suspension with steel-belted radial tires. Power steering. Pontiac's Maximum Mileage System. And a thrifty 250-cu.-in. Six. Whoever thought basic could be so beautiful? And affordable.

Firebird Esprit. Because of Esprit, you don't have to give up Firebird styling and handling to get pampered.

Right off, you'll notice body colored sport mirrors, deluxe wheel covers and attractive accent trim on the outside.

But Esprit's personality runs a lot deeper. To a plush custom interior and added sound insulation. Now you know why it's one of our most popular Firebirds.

Formula Firebird. There are two Formula Firebirds to choose from.

Go with the Firebird Formula 350. Or up your order to a Formula 400. There's a V-8 to match both numbers. And a long list of standard performance equipment that includes a 4-speed, front disc brakes, front and rear stabilizer bars.

The standard twin hood scoops

will tell the world you drive a Formula Firebird. We leave it to you to let them know which one.

Firebird Trans Am. This is our ultimate 'Bird.

It's equipped with a standard 400 4-bbl. A 4-speed transmission. A shaker hood. And enough functional air dams, extractors, deflectors and spoilers to help keep this 'Bird hugging the road.

Economy, luxurious appointments, a little performance or a lot. Whatever it is you want in a sports car, chances are there's a '75 Pontiac Firebird that's got it.

Firebird Esprit.

(Left) Formula Firebird. (Right) Firebird Trans Am.

Pontiac's Sporty Cars

FIREBIRD SERIES 2-DOOR HARDTOP COUPE (S875)
FIREBIRD ESPRIT SERIES 2-DOOR HARDTOP COUPE (T875)
FIREBIRD FORMULA SERIES 2-DOOR HARDTOP COUPE (U875)
FIREBIRD TRANS AM SERIES 2-DOOR HARDTOP COUPE (V875)

STANDARD EQUIPMENT

EXTERIOR
- New Wraparound Rear Window
- Endura Front and Rear Bumpers
- Integral Front and Rear Bumper Guards
- Front and Rear Protective Rubber Bumper Strips
- Moon Hubcaps
- Fluid-on-demand Windshield Washer
- Windshield Radio Antenna
- Dual Horns

In Addition, Firebird Esprit Includes:
- Body Color Inserts in Outside Door Handles
- Concealed Windshield Wipers
- Deluxe Wheel Covers
- Esprit Identification
- Outside Sport Mirrors, LH Remote Control

INTERIOR
- Ash Tray Lamp
- Deluxe 2-spoke Steering Wheel with Soft Covered Center in Interior Matching Colors
- Nylon-blend, Cut-pile Carpeting
- Front Bucket Seats in All-Morrokide
- High-low Level Body Ventilation
- Crossfire Mahogany Applique on Instrument Panel Trim Plate

In Addition, Firebird Esprit Includes:
- Custom Cushion Steering Wheel

- Custom Interior Trim Including:
  All-Morrokide Bucket Seats
  Assist Straps on Doors
  Rear Quarter Ash Trays
  Custom Pedal Trim Plates
  Luggage Compartment Mat
  Instrument Panel Assist Strap
- Lateral Support Bucket Seat Design
- Extra Body Insulation

POWER TRAIN & CHASSIS
(Includes: High Energy Ignition & Catalytic Converter)
Standard Engines
Firebird—250-cu.-in., Overhead Valve, 6-cyl., 1-bbl.—Federal and California
Firebird Esprit—250-cu.-in., 6-cyl., 1-bbl. —Federal and California

Available Engines
Firebird and Firebird Esprit—350-cu.-in., V-8, 2-bbl.—Federal
Firebird and Firebird Esprit—350-cu.-in., V-8, 4-bbl.—Federal and California

Standard Transmissions
Firebird and Firebird Esprit—3-speed Manual Floor Shift—Federal
Firebird and Firebird Esprit—Turbo Hydra-matic—California

Available Transmission
Firebird and Firebird Esprit—Turbo Hydra-matic—Federal

Standard Axle Ratio
2.73:1—Federal

Standard Tires
FR78-15 Black Steel-belted Radials with Radial Tuned Suspension

Standard Steering
Variable Ratio, Power

Standard Brakes
Manual, Front Disc, Rear Drum

Capacities	Firebird	Firebird Esprit
Fuel Tank (gals.)	20.2	20.2
Oil, Less Filter Refill (qts.)	4.0	5.0

STANDARD MOLDINGS
- Narrow Rocker Panel Moldings
- Windshield and Rear Window Moldings

In Addition, Firebird Esprit Includes:
- Wide Rocker Panel Moldings
- Windowsill and Hood Rear Edge Moldings
- Roof Drip Moldings
- Wheel Opening Moldings

AVAILABLE MOLDINGS
- Windowsill and Hood Rear Edge Moldings (std. Firebird Esprit)
- Body Side Moldings
- Door Edge Guards
- Roof Drip Moldings (std. Firebird Esprit)
- Wheel Opening Moldings (std. Firebird Esprit)

DIMENSIONS

Exterior Dimensions (inches)	Firebird & Firebird Esprit 2-door Hardtop Coupes	Firebird Formula 2-door Hardtop Coupe	Firebird Trans Am 2-door Hardtop Coupe
Overall			
Length....	196.0	196.0	196.0
Wheelbase..	108.1	108.1	108.1
	73.0	73.0	73.0
Overall Width..			
Front Tread.	60.9	61.3	61.2
Rear Tread.	60.0	60.4	60.3
Interior Dimensions (inches)			
FRONT:			
Hip Room...	52.4	52.4	52.4
Shoulder Room.....	57.4	57.4	57.4
Head Room (effective).	37.3	37.3	37.3
Leg Room (max. effective)..	44.1	44.1	44.1
REAR:			
Hip Room...	45.8	45.8	45.8
Shoulder Room.....	54.4	54.4	54.4
Head Room (effective)	36.0	36.0	36.0
Leg Room (min. effective)..	29.6	29.6	29.6

See fold out page at front of binder for standard equipment on all 1975 Pontiacs.

14

Here's looking at Firebird's dramatic new wraparound rear window. It's standard this year on all models. The European look increases visibility while giving a completely integrated look to the entire car.

Custom bucket seats in Perforated and Madrid Morrokides are part of a trim package standard on Firebird Esprit, extra cost on Firebird Formula and Firebird Trans Am. Lateral seat design features integral head restraints and springs with solid foam seat cushions for enduring support. Assist straps on doors and instrument panel, custom pedal trim plates and extra body and underhood insulation are included in package. Nylon-blend, cut-pile carpeting is standard on all models.

The standard instrument panel for Firebird, Firebird Esprit, and Firebird Formula is trimmed in woodgrain textured Crossfire Mahogany. The new speedometer follows a European motif offering kilometre readings as well as miles per hour. Other standard instruments include a fuel gauge; indicator lights for oil, water and alternator, and warning lights for brakes and seat belts. A deluxe 2-spoke steering wheel comes standard on Firebird. The Custom Cushion steering wheel is standard on Firebird Esprit and Firebird Formula.

Right- and left-hand body colored outside sport mirrors are standard on Firebird Esprit, Firebird Formula and Firebird Trans Am. The left-hand mirror is remote controlled.

FACTORY-INSTALLED OPTIONS & ACCESSORIES

Order Code

Accessories

602	Air Cleaner, Dual-stage, Heavy-duty—N.A. Trans Am
582	Air Conditioning, Custom—N.A. 350
381	Axle, Safe-T-Track, Rear
591	Battery, Heavy-duty—N.A. 574
502	Brakes, Power, Front Disc—Req. w/V-8 Engines
711	Clock, Electric—Inc w/712, 714
431	Console
424	Console, Rear
—	Cordova Top—Available in White, Black, Sandstone, Cordovan, Green, Burgundy, Blue, Red, Silver.
594	Defogger, Rear Window—N.A. 592
592	Defroster, Rear Window, Electric—N.A. 360, 594
584	Extra Sound Insulation Pkg.—Std. T87
571	Glass, Soft-Ray—All Windows
572	Glass, Soft-Ray—Windshield only
492	Guards, Door Edge
444	Headlamp On Warning System
601	Heater, Engine Block—N.A. 360
512	Hood Decal, Trans Am (Trans Am only)
704	Indicator, Fuel Economy—w/712 only
654	Lamp Pkg.—Inc. Luggage, Glove Box and I.P. Courtesy Lamps
554	Locks, Door, Electric
622	Mats, Floor, Front
624	Mats, Floor, Rear

614	Mats, Floor, Rear Compartment (Std. w/Custom Buckets)
432	Mirror, Vanity, Right-hand
422	Mirrors, Body-colored, R.H. & L.H. (L.H. Remote Control)—Std. on T87, U87, W87
494	Moldings, Body Side, Vinyl—Color-keyed—N.A. W87
481	Moldings, Roof Drip (Std. T87)
491	Moldings, Wheel Opening (Std. on T87—N.A. on W87
484	Moldings, Windowsill & Hood Rear Edge (Std. on T87)
511	Pedal Trim Plates, Custom—Std. T87
401	Radio, AM, Pushbutton
403	Radio, AM/FM
405	Radio, AM/FM, Stereo
712	Rally Gauge Cluster & Clock—N.A. 711, 714, W87
714	Rally Gauge Cluster, Instrument Panel Tach & Clock—N.A. w/711, 712, 704—Std. W87
441	Seat Belts, Custom, Inc. Front Shoulder Straps and Soft Tone Warning System
411	Speaker, Rear—N.A. w/405,412
681	Spoiler, Rear Air—Std. W87, N.A. T87
461	Steering Wheel, Custom Cushion—Std. T87, U87—N.A. W87
464	Steering Wheel, Formula—Std. W87
504	Steering Wheel, Tilt—N.A. Col. Shift Hyd.
638	Stripes, Vinyl—N.A. W87
412	Tape Player, Stereo 8-track—w/431 only
684	Tire, Spare, Space-saver
472	Wheel Covers, Custom Finned—N.A. W87
476	Wheel Covers, Deluxe—Std. T87—N.A. W87
471	Wheel Trim Rings—Std. W87—N.A.T87
478	Wheels, Honeycomb

474	Wheels, Rally II—Inc. 471, Std. W87
551	Windows, Power—w/431 only
414	Windshield Wipers, Concealed—Std. T87, W87

Engines

36M	Engine, 350-cu.-in., V-8, 2-bbl. Hyd. only—N.A. U87 & W87
36E	Engine, 350-cu.-in., V-8, 4-bbl.—N.A. W87
36S	Engine, 400-cu.-in., V-8, 4-bbl. Turbo Hydra-matic or 4-speed only. N.A. S87 & T87—Std. W87

Transmissions

37B	Transmission, 3-speed Manual Floor Shift w/36D only—N.A. U87 & W87
37L	Transmission, Turbo Hydra-matic 3-speed
36E	Transmission, 4-speed Manual—36E only—N.A. W87
37F	Transmission, 4-speed Manual—Close-ratio—w/36S only. N.A. S87 & T87

Tires

39Y	E78—14 Whitewall—N.A. U87, W87
39Z	F78—14 Blackwall—N.A. U87, W87
*39W	FR78—15 Whitewall—Steel-belted Radial—N.A. W87
*39L	FR78—15 White-letter—Steel-belted Radial—N.A. W87
*39B	GR70—15 Blackwall—Steel-belted Radial—N.A. S87, T87—Std. W87
*39M	GR70—15 White-letter—Steel-belted Radial—N.A. S87, T87

*Tire options include Radial Tuned Suspension

15

PONTIAC FIREBIRD Standard Interiors
(Firebird, Formula and Trans Am Models)

BUCKET SEATS
Madrid Morrokide

Model	Interior Trims	Exterior Colors
STANDARD—ALL MORROKIDE		
2-DR. HARDTOP COUPE	19V1 (Black)	C,D,E,F,G,H,J,L,M,P,R,T,V,W,Y,Z
	11V1 (White)	C,D,E,F,G,H,J,L,M,P,R,T,V,W,Y,Z
	63V1 (Saddle)	C,G,H,J,L,M,T,W,Y,Z
AVAILABLE—COLORED INTERIOR WITH WHITE SEATS		
2-DR. HARDTOP COUPE	91V1 (Black w/Wht)	C,D,E,F,G,H,J,L,M,P,R,T,V,W,Y,Z
	96V1 (Saddle w/Wht)	C,G,H,J,L,M,T,W,Y,Z
AVAILABLE—SPECIAL INTERIOR APPOINTMENTS*		
2-DR. HARDTOP COUPE	11V1/346 (White/Blue)	C,D,E,F,V
	11V1/347 (White/Burgundy)	C,P,V,W
	19V1/347 (Black/Burgundy)	C,P,V,W
	11V1/343 (White/Saddle)	C,G,H,J,L,M,T,W,Y,Z

Carpeting, Instrument Panel, Steering Column, Package Shelf

PONTIAC FIREBIRD Custom Interiors
(Standard on Esprit, Extra Cost on Formula and Trans Am Models)

BUCKET SEATS
Perforated and Madrid Morrokides

Model	Interior Trims	Exterior Colors
STANDARD OR EXTRA COST—ALL MORROKIDE		
2-DR. HARDTOP COUPE	19W1 (Black)	C,D,E,F,G,H,J,L,M,P,R,T,V,W,Y,Z
	11W1 (White)	C,D,E,F,G,H,J,L,M,P,R,T,V,W,Y,Z
	63W1 (Saddle)	C,G,H,J,L,M,T,W,Y,Z
	26W1 (Blue)	C,D,E,F,V
	73W1 (Burgundy)	C,P,V,W
AVAILABLE—COLORED INTERIOR WITH WHITE SEATS		
2-DR. HARDTOP COUPE	92W1 (Blue w/Wht)	C,D,E,F,V
	91W1 (Black w/Wht)	C,D,E,F,G,H,J,L,M,P,R,T,V,W,Y,Z
	97W1 (Burgundy w/Wht)	C,P,V,W
	96W1 (Saddle w/Wht)	C,G,H,J,L,M,T,W,Y,Z
AVAILABLE—SPECIAL INTERIOR APPOINTMENTS*		
2-DR. HARDTOP COUPE	11W1/347 (White/Burgundy)	C,P,V,W
	11W1/346 (White/Blue)	C,D,E,F,V
	11W1/343 (White/Saddle)	C,G,H,J,L,M,T,W,Y,Z
	73W1/349 (Burgundy/Black)	C,P,V,W
	19W1/347 (Black/Burgundy)	C,P,V,W

Carpeting, Instrument Panel, Steering Column, Package Shelf

EXTERIOR COLORS AND COLOR CODES

C - Cameo White

D - Arctic Blue

E - Stellar Blue

F - Bimini Blue

G - Carmel Beige

H - Sandstone

J - Ginger Brown

L - Lakemist Green

M - Alpine Green

P - Honduras Maroon

R - Buccaneer Red

T - Sunstorm Yellow

V - Sterling Silver

W - Graystone

Y - Copper Mist

Z - Persimmon

This was the fiftieth anniversary of the Pontiac car. Fortunately, that was not the only piece of good news for Pontiac—sales, too, were back up to mentionable levels and the fast moving (both on the roads and on the showroom floors) Firebirds were pacing the revival of the division's fortunes.

The Firebird line received another facelift in 1976, the second since that body was announced in 1970. Front and rear ends were redone and now sported matching, body-color bumpers. Other performance changes included a Formula Appearance Package for Formula Firebirds and a new canopy top. The Formula Appearance Package essentially consisted of a full length blacked out strip along the side of the car with the name "Formula" in bold, reversed white on black) letters. The canopy top consisted of a front half vinyl roof with a wide multi-layered stripe beginning at the front fenders and running back up over the top of the roof. It was available on all Firebirds except the Trans Am. The Trans Am was offered in a limited edition T-top, of which 643 were sold.

There was some good news (for once) on the engine front: the 455 cid V-8 returned as an option on the Trans Am and was now rated at 200 hp. The 350 cid V-8 was, however, now standard on the Formula, although the 400 cid V-8 was available as an option.

Prices continued their inexorable climb in 1976 as the base 'Bird was now listed at $3,906. The Esprit listed at $4,302, the Formula listed at $4,566 and the Trans Am topped out at $4,987.

Production, as if trying to keep pace with prices, also soared to new record levels. A grand total of 110,775 Firebirds were produced, including 21,209 base Firebirds, 22,252 Esprits, 20,613 Formulas and 46,701 Trans Ams. The Trans Am total was now up 3,531% since 1971!

The 1976 Firebird literature followed the program of the last few years. The Firebirds were included in the full-line Pontiac catalogue as well as in the color brochure (see the montage below). There was, once again, a nice Firebird folder (see pages 98-102) and a post card (see the montage). The Firebird spread from the dealer ordering guide appears on pages 103-104.

Our basic 'Bird is the easiest way to get into the Firebird family. Because it's the most affordable Firebird of them all.

Affordable driving, too. A 250-cu.-in. Six is standard. As is a 3-speed manual transmission (Turbo Hydra-matic in California.)

But the new front and rear ends with their integral body-colored bumpers look so fantastic, people will think you laid out a bundle.

Slip behind the wheel and it's the same story. The cut-pile carpeting. The Morrokide upholstery. It's all very upper class.

Not as upper class as our new Firebird Esprit. Because if you really want to be coddled with luxury, Esprit is the sports car you were born to drive.

The running gear is like our basic 'Bird. Pontiac's High Energy Electronic Ignition and catalytic converter help you go a long time between scheduled maintenance.

Esprit has a custom interior plush enough to make a chauffeur feel at home. With added sound insulation and a custom cushion steering wheel.

Esprit gets the treatment on the outside, too. Body-colored sport mirrors. Deluxe wheel covers. And special moldings.

You can even order an available new over-the-roof stripe option and a canopy vinyl top.

Obviously, Esprit is the plushest Firebird you can buy.

A.

B.

C.

D.

A. Information Central. Firebird's standard instrument panel with available Formula steering wheel, rally and fuel economy gauges.
B. Sit down and let the performance begin. Standard Firebird, Formula Firebird and Firebird Trans Am interior. Shown in buckskin—also available in white and black.
C. Firebird Hardtop Coupe.
D. Want an even sportier Firebird? Order the available new canopy vinyl top and over-the-roof stripe job.
E. Get ready for some grand touring. This custom interior is standard on Firebird Esprit, available on Formula and Trans Am. Shown in firethorn—also available in white, black, blue and buckskin.

E.

Shown on the cars on these pages are some of the options and accessories offered by Pontiac at extra cost.

The driver's door seems to open almost eagerly.

The seat wraps around you and says "Welcome."

You insert the key, light the engine and put it into gear.

And suddenly you know something special's about to happen.

You're about to take off. In a new 1976 Pontiac Firebird.

There are four ways to do it this year. Because this year, there are four different versions of Pontiac's sports machine.

They all share the same basic styling. The kind that always deserves a second glance.

They all share the same basic interior. Contoured buckets, easy-to-reach controls and a cockpit-like instrument panel.

And they all share Pontiac's own Radial Tuned Suspension. Designed for agility in corners. And a certain nonchalance over some of the nastiest roads.

So what makes these four Firebirds different? You're about to find out.

Firebird Esprit Hardtop Coupe.

If you've read this far, you're pretty serious about getting into a Firebird of your very own.

That's terrific. Because the next two Firebirds are the ones serious 'Bird watchers flock to.

Like the new 1976 Formula Firebird. It's not exactly your Driver's Training Special.

A 5.7 liter 2-bbl. V-8 and Turbo Hydra-matic are standard. Californians get four barrels and Turbo Hydra-matic.

The spent gasses are piped through new dual splitter chromed exhausts.

Variable-ratio power steering and Pontiac's own Radial Tuned Suspension will help you 'round the corners.

There's even a blacked-out grille and a new steel hood with dual scoops.

If you're really looking for attention, order the available new Formula Appearance Package.

Firebird Trans Am Hardtop Coupe.

The whole lower perimeter of the body gets blacked out, with multi-colored stripes above.

"Formula" supergraphics are emblazoned on the sides. Even the scoops get the black-with-stripes treatment.

Now imagine what you'd have if you took everything the Formula Firebird has and added a shaker hood, functional air dams, extractors, deflectors, spoilers, etc.

Stop imagining. This is it. The ultimate Firebird. Known to the world as the 1976 Trans Am.

The etc. includes things like GR70-15 radials on Rally II wheels. A thickly padded 14" Formula steering wheel. And an instrument panel with tach, clock and a full set of rally gauges.

Trans Am is powered by a 6.5 liter 4-bbl. V-8 bolted to a floor-shifted 4-speed and a limited-slip differential. California Trans Ams come with Turbo Hydra-matic.

And this year, unless you live in California, you can even order an available 7.5 liter V-8 under Trans Am's hood.

For the top of Trans Am's hood, you can order the available giant Firebird decal.

Firebird. Firebird Esprit. Formula Firebird. Or Trans Am. Pick one...and drive it.

A. Trans Am's available hood decal.
B. The look of engine-turned aluminum. Full rally instrumentation. Formula steering wheel. Trans Am is ready when you are.
C. Even Firebird's wheels are colorful. If you order the available new body-colored Rally II wheels.
D. Back by popular demand. Pontiac's 455 V-8 is available on the 1976 Trans Am (except in California).

FACTS AND FIGURES

FIREBIRD

MODELS

Hardtop Coupe, offered in four versions: Firebird, Firebird Esprit, Formula Firebird and Firebird Trans Am.

POWER TEAMS*

Engines: 250-cu.-in. 1-bbl. 6-cyl. standard on Firebird and Esprit. 350-cu.-in. 2-bbl. V-8 standard on Formula, available on Firebird and Esprit. 350-cu.-in. 4-bbl. V-8 available on Firebird, Esprit and Formula (Calif. only). 400-cu.-in. 4-bbl. V-8 standard on Trans Am, available on Firebird, Esprit and Formula. 455-cu.-in. 4-bbl. V-8 available on Trans Am. Transmissions: 3-speed manual standard on Firebird and Esprit. 4-speed manual standard on Trans Am, available on Firebird, Esprit and Formula. Turbo Hydra-matic standard on Formula, available on all others.

*Manual transmissions and certain engines are not available in California.

Ask your Pontiac dealer for full details on engine/transmission combinations.

STANDARD INTERIOR FEATURES

Standard Firebird Features

Front bucket seats and bucket-type rear seats with all-Morrokide trim. Front seat cushions of solid foam with integral springs. Deluxe 2-spoke steering wheel in matching interior colors. Nylon-blend, cut-pile carpeting. Trunk floor mat. Fluid-on-demand windshield washer. Ash tray lamp.

Special Firebird Esprit Features

Custom all-Morrokide deep contour bucket seats. Distinctive door trim panels. Custom cushion steering wheel in matching interior colors. Pedal trim plates. Door and instrument panel assist straps. Rear ash tray. Added acoustical insulation.

Special Formula Firebird Features

Custom cushion steering wheel in matching interior colors. New full-length front console.

Special Firebird Trans Am Features

Formula steering wheel. Rally gauges, electric clock and instrument panel tach. Aluminum swirl-finish instrument panel trim plate.

STANDARD EXTERIOR FEATURES

Standard Firebird Features

New front and rear styling with integral body-colored bumpers. Hubcaps. Bright headlight bezels and windshield, rear window and grille moldings. Firebird emblems on grille panel, sail panel and rear deck lid.

Special Firebird Esprit Features

Esprit identification. Body-colored sport mirrors, left-hand remote control. Body-colored door handle inserts. Concealed wipers. Deluxe wheel covers. Bright moldings on roof, windowsills, hood, rocker panels and wheel openings.

Special Formula Firebird Features

Formula identification. New steel hood with twin simulated air scoops. Body-colored sport mirrors, left-hand remote control. Blacked-out grille. Dual chrome splitter tailpipe extensions.

Special Firebird Trans Am Features

Trans Am decal on front fenders and on wraparound rear deck spoiler. New front air dam. Wheel opening air deflectors. Front fender air extractors. Body-colored sport mirrors, left-hand remote control. Concealed wipers. Blacked-out grille. 15" x 7" Rally II wheels with trim rings. Shaker hood. Dual chrome splitter tailpipe extensions.

STANDARD CHASSIS FEATURES

Standard Firebird and Esprit Features

Radial Tuned Suspension, which includes: FR78-15 GM specification steel-belted radial tires, firm shock absorbers, jounce restrictors, computer-selected springs, front stabilizer bar. Front disc brakes. Variable-ratio power steering. Coil-spring front and leaf-spring rear suspension. High Energy Electronic Ignition and catalytic converter which requires unleaded fuel.

Special Formula Firebird Features

Power-flex fan with 400 V-8. Heavy front and rear stabilizer bars.

Special Firebird Trans Am Features

Safe-T-Track limited-slip differential. Power brakes. Power-flex fan. GR70-15 steel-belted radial tires.

DIMENSIONS (Inches)	Firebird, Esprit	Formula	Trans Am
Overall length	196.8	196.8	196.8
Overall width	73.0	73.0	73.0
Wheelbase	108.1	108.1	108.1
Track, front/rear	60.3/60.0	61.3/60.4	61.2/60.3
Head room, front/rear	37.5/35.9	37.5/35.9	37.5/35.9
Leg room, front/rear	44.1/29.6	44.1/29.6	44.1/29.6
Shoulder room, front/rear	57.4/54.4	57.4/54.4	57.4/54.4
Hip room, front/rear	52.4/45.8	52.4/45.8	52.4/45.8

CAPACITIES	Firebird, Esprit	Formula, Trans Am
Fuel tank (gals.)	20.2	20.2
Cooling system (qts.)	14.6	21.3*
Oil, less filter refill (qts.)	4.0	5.0

*Trans Am—22.3 with 455 V-8.

POPULAR EQUIPMENT AVAILABLE

New Formula Appearance Package including special striping and super-graphics. New over-the-roof accent stripes. New canopy vinyl top. New body-colored Rally II wheels. Custom interior trim package (std. on Esprit). Air conditioning with new idle stop solenoid for improved fuel economy. New 455 V-8 with 4-speed manual transmission (Trans Am only). Front and rear consoles. Electric rear window defroster. Rally gauge instrument cluster. Fuel economy gauge. Turbo Hydra-matic transmission (std. on Formula) AM, AM/FM and AM/FM stereo radios. 8-track stereo tape player. Honeycomb wheels. Formula steering wheel (std. on Trans Am). Added acoustical insulation (std. on Esprit).

FIREBIRD SAFETY FEATURES

Occupant Protection

Seat belts with pushbutton buckles for all passenger positions. Two front combination seat and inertia reel shoulder belts for driver and right front passenger (with reminder light and buzzer). Energy-absorbing steering column. Passenger-guard door locks. Safety door latches and hinges. Folding seat-back latches. Energy-absorbing padded instrument panel and front seat-back tops. Contoured windshield header. Thick laminate windshield. Cargo-Guard. Contoured roof inner panel. Safety armrests.

Accident Prevention

Side marker lights and reflectors. Parking lamps that illuminate with headlamps. Four-way hazard warning flasher. Backup lights. Lane-change feature in direction signal control. Windshield defrosters, washers and dual-speed wipers. Wide-view inside day/night mirror (vinyl-edged, shatter-resistant glass and deflecting support). Outside rearview mirror. Dual master cylinder brake system with warning light. Starter Safety Switch. Dual-action safety hood latches.

Anti-theft

Anti-theft ignition key reminder buzzer. Anti-theft steering column lock.

Shown on the cars and described in this catalog are some of the many options and accessories offered by Pontiac. They're available at extra cost and well worth it in driving comfort and convenience. Pontiac Motor Division of General Motors Corporation reserves the right to make changes at any time, without notice, in colors, equipment, specifications, prices and models—and also to discontinue models. The right is also reserved to change any specifications, parts or equipment at any time without incurring any obligation to equip same on cars built prior to date of such change.

Pontiac Motor Division, General Motors Corporation, One Pontiac Plaza, Pontiac, Michigan 48053.

Formula and Trans Am Firebirds sport these new dual splitter chromed exhausts.

Firebird's High Energy Electronic Ignition zaps up to 35,000 volts of power to the plugs.

Pontiac's own Radial Tuned Suspension and steel-belted radials are standard on every 1976 Firebird.

Firebird Series 2-DOOR HARDTOP COUPE (S876)
Firebird Esprit Series 2-DOOR HARDTOP COUPE (T876)

Firebird Formula Series 2-DOOR HARDTOP COUPE (U876)
Firebird Trans Am Series 2-DOOR HARDTOP COUPE (W876)

Firebird Esprit 2-door hardtop coupe (T876)

STANDARD EQUIPMENT

EXTERIOR
- New Front and Rear End Styling
- Endura Front and Rear Bumpers in Body Color
- New Parking Lights Located in Front Bumpers
- Standard Hubcaps
- Wraparound Rear Window
- Fluid-on-demand Windshield Washer
- Dual Horns

In Addition to Firebird Features, Firebird Esprit Includes:
- Body Color Inserts in Outside Door Handles
- Deluxe Wheel Covers
- Esprit Identification
- Outside Sport Mirrors, L.H. Remote Controlled
- Concealed Windshield Wipers

In Addition to Firebird Features, Firebird Formula Includes:
- New All-steel Hood with Simulated Dual Air Scoops
- Formula Identification
- Outside Sport Mirrors, L.H. Remote Controlled
- Black Grille
- Chrome Side Splitter Tailpipe Extensions

In Addition to Firebird Features, Firebird Trans Am Includes:
- New Front Center Air Dam
- New

- Black Grille
- Rear Deck-lid Spoiler
- Outside Sport Mirrors, L.H. Remote Controlled
- Rear Wheel Opening Air Deflectors
- Front Fender Air Extractors
- Chrome Side Splitter Tailpipe Extensions
- Rally II Wheels with Trim Rings
- Shaker Hood and Air Cleaner

INTERIOR
- Ash Tray Lamp
- Deluxe 2-spoke Steering Wheel
- Nylon-blend, Cut-pile Carpeting
- Simulated Rosewood Applique on Instrument Panel Trim Plate
- Front Bucket Seats in All-Morrokide
- Speedometer Graduated in Kilometres per Hour as well as Miles per Hour (odometer registers miles)
- Single-buckle Seat and Shoulder Belt System
- High-low Level Body Ventilation

In Addition to Firebird Features, Firebird Esprit Includes:
- Custom Cushion Steering Wheel
- Custom Interior Trim
Includes:
— All-Morrokide Bucket Seats
— Assist Straps on Doors
— Rear Quarter Ash Trays
— Luggage Compartment Mat
— Instrument Panel Assist Strap
— Lateral Support Bucket Seat Design
— Custom Pedal Trim Plates
— Extra Body and Underhood Insulation

In Addition to Firebird Features, Firebird Formula Includes:
- Custom Cushion Steering Wheel
- Full-length Front Console

In Addition to Firebird Features, Firebird Trans Am Includes:
- Formula Steering Wheel
- Rally Gauges with Clock and Instrument Panel Tachometer
- Engine-turned Instrument Panel Trim Plate

POWER TRAIN & CHASSIS
(Includes: High Energy Ignition & Catalytic Converter)

Standard Engines
Firebird—250-cu.-in., Overhead Valve, 6-cyl., 1-bbl.—Federal & Calif.
Firebird Esprit—250-cu.-in., 6-cyl., 1-bbl.—Federal & Calif.
Firebird Formula—350-cu.-in., V-8, 2-bbl.—Federal
— 350-cu.-in., V-8, 4-bbl.—Calif.
Firebird Trans Am—400-cu.-in., V-8, 4-bbl.—Federal & Calif.

Available Engines
Firebird—350-cu.-in., V-8, 2-bbl.—Federal
Firebird—350-cu.-in., V-8, 4-bbl.—Calif.
Firebird Esprit—350-cu.-in., V-8, 4-bbl.—Calif.
Firebird Formula—400-cu.-in., V-8, 4-bbl.—Federal & Calif.
- Firebird Trans Am—455-cu.-in., V-8, 4-bbl.—Federal

Standard Transmissions
Firebird & Esprit—3-speed Manual Floor Shift—Federal
Turbo Hydra-matic—Calif.
Firebird Formula—Turbo Hydra-matic—Federal & Calif.
Firebird Trans Am—4-speed Manual Floor Shift—Federal
Firebird Trans Am—Turbo Hydra-matic—Calif.

Available Transmissions
Firebird (ALL)—4-speed Manual Floor Shift—Federal
Firebird (ALL)—Turbo Hydra-matic—Federal & Calif.

Standard Axle Ratios
Firebird—3.08:1
Firebird Esprit—3.08:1
Firebird Formula—2.41:1
Firebird Trans Am—3.08:1 (Safe-T-Track)

Standard Tires
Firebird—FR78-15 Black Steel-belted Radials with Radial Tuned Suspension
Firebird Esprit—FR78-15 Black Steel-belted Radials with Radial Tuned Suspension
Firebird Formula—FR78-15 Black Steel-belted Radials with Radial Tuned Suspension
Firebird Trans Am—GR70-15 Black Steel-belted Radials with Radial Tuned Suspension

Standard Steering
Variable-ratio, Power

Standard Brakes
Manual, Front Disc, Rear Drum
Firebird Trans Am—Power, Front Disc, Rear Drum

Capacities

	Firebird	Firebird Esprit
Fuel Tank (gals.)	20.2	20.2
Oil, Less Filter Refill (qts.)	4.0	5.0

	Firebird Formula	Firebird Trans Am
Fuel Tank (gals.)	20.2	20.2
Oil, Less Filter Refill (qts.)	5.0	5.0

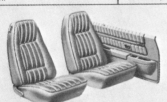

Firebird, Formula, Trans Am Models—Standard Bucket Seats

Morrokide Interiors: White, Black, Buckskin
Seat Mixes: Black with White
Appointment Mixes: White with Blue, White with Firethorn, White with Lime

Esprit—Firebird Custom Interiors—Standard Bucket Seats

Formula and Trans Am Models—Extra Cost Bucket Seats

Morrokide Interiors: White, Black, Blue, Buckskin, Firethorn
Seat Mixes: Black with White, Blue with White, Firethorn with White
Appointment Mixes: White with Blue, White with Firethorn, White with Lime

16

Interior. Instrument panel trim has a simulated rosewood applique on the Firebird, Firebird Esprit and Firebird Formula. The Firebird Trans Am is "engine-turned." Additional interior features on the Firebird Esprit are the custom cushion steering wheel; Custom interior trim including all-Morrokide, lateral support bucket seats; door assist straps; rear quarter ash trays; luggage compartment mat. The Firebird Formula has a full-length front console. The Firebird Trans Am has rally gauges with clock and instrument panel tachometer.

Canopy/cordova top. Newly available on all Firebird models. Colors are White, Black, Buckskin, Mahogany, Firethorn, Blue, Silver.

Stowaway tire. Standard Trans Am. Available on all other Firebird models. Adds more storage space. Inflator included.

FACTORY-INSTALLED OPTIONS & ACCESSORIES

Order Code

492	Air Conditioning, Custom	
582	Appearance Package, Formula, Includes Black Lower Body Paint & Special Striping	
391	Axle, Safe-T-Track	
681	Battery, Heavy-duty	
452	Brakes, Power Disc	
474	Clock, Electric	
581	Console	
—	Canopy Top—Available in White, Black, Buckskin, Mahogany, Firethorn Red, Blue, Silver	
461	Defroster, Rear Window, Electric	
462	Defogger, Rear Window	
434	Door Locks, Electric	
731	Handling Package. Includes GR70-15 Steel-belted Radial Tires, Large Front & Rear Stabilizer Bars	

442	Glass, Soft-Ray, All Windows
612	Guards, Door-Edge
684	Heater, Engine Block
521	Insulation, Added Acoustical
631	Lamp Group—Includes Luggage Lamp, Glove Box Lamp, Instrument Panel Courtesy Lamp
602	Mats, Floor, Front & Rear
601	Mats, Front
652	Mirror, R.H. Visor Vanity
642	Mirrors, L.H. Remote Control Sport, R.H. Fixed
611	Moldings, Body-side
614	Moldings, Wheel Opening
561	Pedal Trim Plates, Custom
411	Radio, AM

412	Radio, AM/FM
415	Radio, AM/FM Stereo
417	Tape Player, 8-Track
441	Tire, Stowaway
524	Seat Belts, Custom
421	Speaker, Rear Seat
541	Steering Wheel, Custom Cushion
544	Steering Wheel, Formula
444	Steering Wheel, Tilt
556	Wheel Covers, Deluxe
558	Wheels, Honeycomb
554	Wheels, Rally II
559	Wheels, Rally II, Body-colored
431	Windows, Power
464	Windshield Wipers, Controlled Cycle

17

Everything seemed to be going right for Pontiac in 1977. The all-new down-sized standard Pontiacs, about which there was considerable trepidation within the division, sold extremely well. The Grand Pix reached new record levels of production. The midyear Phoenix was very well received, too, and the Firebird continued its solid sales growth.

The Firebird had another front end revision for 1977. This time the front bumper/grille was refashioned so as to appear more pointed and GM's new rectangular head lights were included in the ensemble. Other than that, the big appearance news was in the area of special trim editions. The black T-top Trans Am version, known officialy as the "Special Edition," but known informally as the "blackbird" option, returned. An impressive total of 15,567 were produced (all but 1,861 with the T-top). A Skybird option was available on the Esprit. It was essentially a multi-hued blue color option. The Formula Appearance Package was continued over, as well. The tab for these options ranged from the modest to the big-buck category. The Formula option listed at $127, the Skybird at $358 ($385 with velour upholstery) and the mighty Special Edition Trans Am package set customers back $1,143 ($556 without the T-top).

There was quite a bit of engine juggling in 1977. The standard Firebird and Esprit engine was now the Buick 231 cid V-6 rated at 105 hp. The standard engine on the Formula was the new Pontiac 301 cid V-8. It had an 8.2:1 compression ratio, which was high for the times, but a two-barrel carburetor and was rated at only 135 hp—not much for a "high performance" machine. The 350 and 400 cid Pontiac V-8's were still optional, however. The standard engine for the Trans Am was still the 400 cid V-8, but detuned to 180 hp. The 455 cid V-8 was once more deleted, and, in a curious twist, the Oldsmobile 403 cid V-8 was the only powerplant offered on California-bound Trans Ams. Indeed, with various engines being used in various places, the engine line-up was becoming very complex and sometimes very strange.

Prices rose a lot in 1977 and the Trans Am now topped $5,000. The base 'Bird listed at $4,270, the Esprit at $4,551, the Formula at $4,977 and the Trans Am at $5,456. Production reached 155,736 units, of which 30,642 were Firebirds, 34,548 were Esprits, 21,801 were Formulas and 68,745 were Trans Ams.

The only specific Firebird literature for showroom customers in 1977 was the post card (see montage below) and it was really supposed to be mailed to prospects. The Firebird line was included in the handsome full-line Pontiac catalogue (see pages 106-107) and in the color and trim brochure (see page 110). The Firebird spread from the dealer ordering guide appears on pages 108-109.

THE MAGNIFICENT FIREBIRDS.
Four of America's great sport legends.

TRANS AM

The Firebird spirit.

It's grabbing life for all it's worth... doing it with style.

Firebird offers you four dramatic ways to express it.

And the first way may be the most dramatic of all... our ultimate sport, Trans Am.

Aggressive new grille. New squared-off headlamps. New shaker hood. It's a rush just enjoying it from afar.

But as someone with Firebird's kind of spirit, you don't operate from afar. So come closer. Reach for the door. Sit back in those rich all-Morrokide seats.

You're in command.

Everything is right there. The gleaming machine-turned dash with full rally gauges, clock and tach. Thickly padded Formula Steering Wheel. Even Turbo Hydra-matic.

You're cruisin' and you haven't even turned the key. Do it. That surge of excitement is a new 6.6 litre (400/403 CID) 4-bbl. V-8. And if you're looking for something more, there's the new T/A 6.6.* It has the horsepower of last year's 455 V-8 over a broader rpm range.

Now take it to the street. Feel Trans Am's smooth, eager acceleration. And that scatback agility afforded by variable-ratio power steering. Power front disc brakes. And Pontiac's famed Radial Tuned Suspension with GR70-15 radials.

Obviously, this is super stuff.

Formula Firebird has so much spirit it can turn even ordinary drivers into enthusiasts.

Suddenly, you'll insist on the most isolated parking spots. Eager to protect those Formula contours. With new hood and dual air scoop design. Newly standard rear spoiler. Blacked-out grille. Chrome side-splitter tailpipes.

You'll also start driving the long way home. With your finger on the pulse of Formula's all-new 5.0 litre (301 CID) 2-bbl. V-8. (Except California and high-altitude counties.) It's quiet and responsive.

And eventually you'll accept the envious side-glances. Especially if you

*N.A. Calif. & high altitude counties.

Trans Am. It may soon be the most popular road car built in America.

For a dash of excitement.
Trans Am features a machine-turned finish trim plate, rally gauges, clock and tach.

You won't need driving gloves with this richly padded 14" Formula steering wheel. It's standard on Trans Am.

Trans Am's standard 6.6 litre 4-BBL V-8

Just knowing you get Trans Am's rich Morrokide bucket seat interior at no extra cost is a trip in itself.

Spunky 3-speed floor shift is available four-speed shifter from Trans Am's.

Custom all-Morrokide bucket seats standard on Esprit or cloth contoured

DIMENSIONS (inches)	FIREBIRD ESPRIT	FORMULA	TRANS AM
Overall length	196.8	196.8	196.8
Overall width	73.0	73.0	73.0
Wheelbase	108.1	108.1	108.1
Track, front/rear	60.9/600	613/609	612/603
Head room, front/rear	37.5/35.9	37.5/35.9	37.3/35.9
Leg room, front/rear	44.1/29.6	44.1/29.6	44.1/29.6
Shoulder room, front/rear	58.1/54.4	52.1/54.4	58.1/54.4
Hip room, front/rear	52.1/45.8	52.1/45.8	52.1/45.8

Facing page: Firebird (left). Lowest-priced of the magnificent four. † Not available in high altitude countries.
Esprit (right). This one adds luxury to the Firebird legend.

10

order the Formula Appearance Package. With blacked-out lower body and hood scoop. Multi-color stripes and large "Formula" graphics on the side.

If the spirit moves you toward luxury. Esprit is your breed of 'bird.

Every day becomes another oppor-tunity to enjoy its top-of-the-line com-fort. With standard Morrokide or newly available velour bucket seats. And added acoustical insulation.

Every turn of the key signals another spirited performance. This year with a 3.8 litre (231 CID) V-6.

As always, there's the chance to en-joy the little touches that add so much. Sport mirrors. Custom pedal trim plates. Concealed wipers. Deluxe wheel covers.

If you've got a spirit for great value, our base Firebird fills the bill nicely.

It has the features that make Firebird one of the great names in American sporty cars. The sporty good looks. The handling and ride of Pontiac's Radial Tuned Suspension.

It has the fun of a Firebird. Standard 3-speed floor shift †. Spunky 3.8 litre (231 CID) V-6. Morrokide bucket seats.

It's got Firebird's dependability, too. With High Energy Electronic ignition and catalytic converter.

But our base Firebird has something else all its own—the lowest Firebird price.

FIREBIRD

FIREBIRD 2-DOOR HARDTOP
COUPE (S877)

FIREBIRD ESPRIT

FIREBIRD ESPRIT 2-DOOR HARDTOP
COUPE (T877)

FIREBIRD FORMULA

FIREBIRD FORMULA 2-DOOR HARDTOP
COUPE (U877)

FIREBIRD TRANS AM

FIREBIRD TRANS AM 2-DOOR
HARDTOP COUPE (W877)

STANDARD EQUIPMENT

Exterior
- New Grille & New Hood Styling
- Endura Front & Rear Bumpers in Body Color
- Hubcaps with Pontiac Crest
- Dual Horns

In Addition to Firebird Features, Firebird Esprit Includes:
- Body Color Inserts in Outside Door Handles
- Deluxe Wheel Covers
- Outside Sport Mirrors, L.H. Remote Controlled
- Concealed Windshield Wipers
- Esprit Identification

In Addition to Firebird Features, Firebird Formula Includes:
- New Simulated Dual Air Scoops Design
- New Rear Deck Spoiler
- Outside Sport Mirrors, L.H. Remote Controlled
- Black Grille
- Chrome Side Splitter Tailpipe Extensions

In Addition to Firebird Features, Firebird Trans Am Includes:
- Front Center Air Dam
- Black Grille
- Rear Deck-lid Spoiler
- Outside Sport Mirrors, L.H. Remote Controlled
- Rear Wheel Opening Air Deflectors
- Front Fender Air Extractors
- Chrome Side Splitter Tailpipe Extensions
- Rally II Wheels with Trim Rings
- Shaker Hood & Air Cleaner
- Concealed Windshield Wipers
- Trans Am Identification

Interior
- New Deluxe Cushion Steering Wheel
- Nylon-blend, Cut-pile Carpeting
- Simulated Rosewood Applique on Instrument Panel Trim Plate
- Front Bucket Seats in All-Morrokide
- Speedometer Graduated in Kilometres per Hour as well as Miles per Hour (odometer registers miles)
- Single-buckle Seat & Shoulder Belt System
- High-low Level Body Ventilation

In Addition to Firebird Features, Firebird Esprit Includes:
- New Luxury Cushion Steering Wheel
- Custom Interior Trim
  Includes:
  - All-Morrokide or Cloth Bucket Seats
  - Assist Straps on Doors
  - Rear Quarter Ash Trays
  - Luggage Compartment Mat
  - Instrument Panel Assist Strap
  - Lateral Support Bucket Seat Design
  - Custom Pedal Trim Plates
  - Extra Body & Underhood Insulation

In Addition to Firebird Features, Firebird Formula Includes:
- New Luxury Cushion Steering Wheel

In Addition to Firebird Features, Firebird Trans Am Includes:
- Formula Steering Wheel
- Rally Gauges with Clock & Instrument Panel Tachometer
- Engine-turned Instrument Panel Trim Plate

STANDARD & AVAILABLE POWER TRAIN & CHASSIS
(Includes High Energy Ignition & Catalytic Converter)

Standard Engines
- Firebird, Firebird Esprit—3.8 Litre (231 CID) V-6, 2-bbl.—Federal & California
- Firebird Formula—5.0 Litre (302 CID) V-8, 2-bbl.—Federal
- Firebird Formula—5.7 Litre (350 CID) V-8, 4-bbl.—California
- Firebird Trans Am—6.6 Litre (400/403 CID) V-8, 4-bbl.—Federal & California

Available Engines
- Firebird, Firebird Esprit—5.0 Litre (302 CID) V-8, 2-bbl.—Federal
- Firebird, Firebird Esprit—5.7 Litre (350 CID) V-8, 4-bbl.
- Firebird Formula—6.6 Litre (400/403 CID) V-8, 4-bbl.

Standard Transmissions
- Firebird, Firebird Esprit—3-speed Manual Floor Shift (Federal)—Turbo Hydra-matic (California)
- Firebird Formula—4-speed Manual Floor Shift (Federal)—Turbo Hydra-matic (California)
- Firebird Trans Am—4-speed Manual Floor Shift (Federal)—Turbo Hydra-matic (California)

Available Transmissions
- Firebird, Esprit, Formula—4-speed Manual Floor Shift—Federal

Standard Axle Ratios
- Firebird, Esprit—2.73:1—Federal
- Firebird, Esprit—3.23:1—California
- Firebird Formula—2.41:1—Federal & California
- Firebird Trans Am—3.42:1—Federal, 2.41:1—California (Safe-T-Track)

Standard Tires
- Firebird, Esprit, Formula—FR78-15 Black*
- Firebird Trans Am—GR70-15 Black*

Available Tires
- Firebird, Esprit, Formula—FR78-15 Black Fiberglass-belted Radial —FR78-15 White Fiberglass-belted Radial —FR78-15 White*, FR78-15 White Lettered*
- Firebird Formula—GR70-15 Black*
- Firebird Formula, Trans Am—GR70-15 White Lettered*
- All Firebirds—F78-14 Stowaway Spare

*Steel-belted Radials with Radial Tuned Suspension

Standard Steering
- Variable-ratio, Power

Standard Brakes
- Manual, Front Disc, Rear Drum
- Firebird Trans Am—Power, Front Disc, Rear Drum

Capacities

	Firebird, Firebird Esprit
Fuel Tank (gals.)	20.2
Oil, Less Filter Refill (qts.)	4.0

	Firebird Formula, Firebird Trans Am
Fuel Tank (gals.)	20.2
Oil, Less Filter Refill (qts.)	5.0

Trunk Capacity
All models
- Cubic Feet 6.6

STANDARD & AVAILABLE MOLDINGS

Standard Moldings
- Narrow Rocker Panel Moldings (Firebird & Formula)
- Windshield & Rear Window Moldings

In Addition to Firebird Moldings, Firebird Esprit Includes:
- Wide Rocker Panel Moldings
- Windowsill & Hood Rear Edge Moldings
- Roof Drip Moldings
- Wheel Opening Moldings

Available Moldings
- Windowsill & Hood Rear Edge Moldings (std. Firebird Esprit)
- Body Side Moldings
- Door Edge Guards
- Roof Drip Moldings (std. Firebird Esprit)
- Wheel Opening Moldings (std. Firebird Esprit, N.A. on Firebird Trans Am)

MAJOR OPTIONS FOR 1977

- **Formula Appearance Package (UPC W50) Includes:**
  - Black Lower Body w/Stripes
  - Black Painted Grille
- Air Conditioning (UPC C60)
- Cruise Control (UPC K30)
- Fuel Economy Indicator (UPC UR1)
- Canopy Top

- **Custom Interior Trim Package (Firebird Formula & Trans Am only) Includes:**
  - All-Morrokide Bucket Seats
  - Assist Straps on Doors
  - Rear Quarter Ash Trays
  - Luggage Compartment Mat
  - Instrument Panel Assist Strap
  - Lateral Support Bucket Seat Design
  - Custom Pedal Trim Plates
  - Extra Body & Underhood Insulation

STEERING WHEELS

NEW DELUXE CUSHION 3-SPOKE
w/Soft Covered Center & Rim
Standard: Firebird

NEW LUXURY CUSHION
in Interior Matching Colors
(UPC N30)
Standard: Firebird Esprit, Formula

FORMULA
(UPC NK3)
Standard: Firebird Trans Am
Available: Firebird, Esprit & Formula

■ NEW

WHEEL COVERS AND WHEELS

HUBCAPS
w/Pontiac Crest
Standard: Firebird & Firebird Formula

NEW WIRE WHEEL COVERS
(UPC N95)
Available: Firebird, Esprit, Formula

EXTERIOR DIMENSIONS

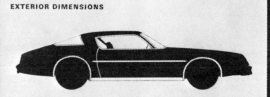

	Firebird & Firebird Esprit	Firebird Formula	Firebird Trans Am
Overall Length	196.8	196.8	196.0
Wheelbase	108.1	108.1	108.1
Overall Width	73.0	73.0	73.0
Front Tread	60.9	61.3	61.2
Rear Tread	60.0	60.4	60.3

NEW DELUXE WHEEL COVERS
(UPC P01)
Standard: Firebird Esprit
Available: Firebird & Firebird Formula

RALLY II WHEELS
w/Trim Rings
(UPC N98)
Standard: Firebird Trans Am
Available: Firebird, Esprit & Formula

**BODY COLORED RALLY II
WHEELS w/Trim Rings**
(UPC N67)
Available: Firebird, Esprit, Formula & Trans Am

BODY STRIPING LOCATION

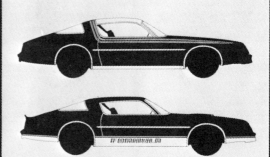

NEW CAST ALUMINUM WHEELS
(UPC YJ8)
Available: Firebird, Esprit, Formula & Trans Am

NEW BODY COLORED CAST ALUMINUM WHEELS
(UPC N60)
Available: Firebird, Esprit, Formula & Trans Am

RECOMMENDED COORDINATION OF EXTERIOR TO STRIPING COLORS

Code	Exterior Colors	Over-the-Roof Canopy Top Colors	Over-the-Roof Stripe Colors*	Formula Appearance Package**	Trans Am Decal Colors	Body Side Moldings
11	Cameo White	White, Silver, Black	Black/White/Charcoal/Argent	Lt. Blue/ Med. Blue	Charcoal/Red	White
		White, Buckskin	Black/Lt. Brown/Dk. Brown/Med. Brown			
		White, Firethorn	Black/Lt. Red/Dk. Red/Med. Red			
		White, Blue	Black/Lt. Blue/Dark Blue/Med. Blue			
13	Sterling Silver	White, Silver, Black	Black/White/Charcoal/Argent	Charcoal/Lt. Red	Charcoal/Red	Black
19	Starlight Black	White, Silver, Black	Black/White/Charcoal/Argent	Gold/Matte Gold	Gold/Matte Gold	Black
		Buckskin	Black/Lt. Brown/Dk. Brown/Med. Brown			
22	Glacier Blue	White	Black/White/Charcoal/Argent	Lt. Blue/ Med. Blue		Blue
		Blue				
29	Nautilus Blue	White, Silver	Black/White/Charcoal/Argent			Blue
		Black, Blue	Black/Lt. Blue/Dk. Blue/Med. Blue			
36	Firethorn Red	White, Black, Firethorn	Black/Lt. Red/Dk. Red/Med. Red			Black
38	Aquamarine	White, Black	Black/White/Charcoal/Argent			Black
44	Bahia Green	White, Black	Black/White/Charcoal/Argent			Black Lt. Green
51	Goldenrod Yellow	White, Black	Black/Lt. Brown/Dk. Brown/Med. Brown	Lt. Red/ Dk. Red	Gold/Orange	Black
61	Mojave Tan	White, Black, Buckskin	Black/Lt. Brown/Dk. Brown/Med. Brown			Buckskin
63	Buckskin Metallic	White, Black, Buckskin	Black/Lt. Brown/Dk. Brown/Med. Brown			Buckskin
69	Brentwood Brown	White, Black, Buckskin	Black/Lt. Brown/Dk. Brown/Med. Brown		Gold/Orange	Buckskin
75	Bucaneer Red	White, Black	Black/Lt. Red/Dk. Red/Med. Red	Lt. Red/ Dk. Red	Gold/Orange	Black
78	Mandarin Orange	Buckskin	Black/Lt. Brown/Dk. Brown/Med. Brown			Black

*Over-the-roof stripe (D98) available on Firebird, Esprit and Formula. Exterior and stripe color availability color keyed to Canopy Top. Without Canopy Top, selection is customer's choice. **Available on Formula only.

FIREBIRD

Standard Bucket Seats

Vinyl Interiors—OXEN
Firebird, Formula & Trans Am 2-door Coupes

Interior Colors	Trim No.	Exterior Colors
White	11R1	11,13,19,22,29,36,38,44,51,61,63,69,75,78
Black	19R1	11,13,19,22,29,36,38,44,51,61,63,69,75,78
Buckskin	64R1	11,19,44,51,61,63,69,78
Firethorn	71R1	11,13,19,36

Seat Mix Interiors
(White Vinyl Seats with Colored Interior)
Firebird, Formula & Trans Am 2-door Coupes

Firethorn/White	97R1	11,13,19,36

Appointment Mix Interiors
(White Vinyl Interior with Colored Appointments*)
Firebird, Formula & Trans Am 2-door Coupes

White/Blue	11R1/26X	11,19,22,29
White/Turquoise	11R1/34X	11,19,38
White/Saddle	11R1/64X	11,19,44,51,61,63,69,78
White/Firethorn	11R1/71X	11,13,19,36

Carpeting, Instrument Panel, Steering Column, Package Shelf.

FIREBIRD CUSTOM INTERIORS

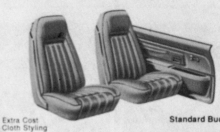

Extra Cost
Cloth Styling

Standard Bucket Seats
(Esprit)

Extra Cost Bucket Seats
(Formula & Trans Am Models)

Vinyl Interiors—DOESKIN
(Standard) Esprit 2-door Coupe, (Extra Cost) Formula
& Trans Am 2-door Coupes

Interior Colors	Trim No.	Exterior Colors
White	11N1	11,13,19,22,29,36,38,44,51,61,63,69,75,78
Black	19N1	11,13,19,22,29,36,38,44,51,61,63,69,75,78
Blue	24N1	11,19,22,29
Buckskin	64N1	11,19,44,51,61,63,69,78
Firethorn	71N1	11,13,19,36

Seat Mix Interiors
(White Vinyl Seats with Colored Interior)
2-door Coupes

Blue/White	92N1	11,19,22,29
Firethorn/White	97N1	11,13,19,36

Appointment Mix Interiors
(White Vinyl Interior with Colored Appointments*)
2-door Coupes

White/Blue	11N1/26X	11,19,22,29
White/Turquoise	11N1/34X	11,19,38
White/Saddle	11N1/64X	11,19,44,51,61,63,69,78
White/Firethorn	11N1/71X	11,13,19,36

(Extra Cost) Cloth Interior—LOMBARDY
Esprit, Formula & Trans Am 2-door Coupes

Black	19B1	11,13,19,22,29,36,38,44,51,61,63,69,75,78
Blue	24B1	11,19,22,29
Firethorn	71B1	11,13,19,36

*Carpeting, Instrument Panel, Steering Column, Package Shelf.
**Included are Pedal Trim Package and Custom Front & Rear Seat Cushioning. Special Door Trim including Pull Strap.

Pontiac's slogan for 1978 was "The Best Year Yet." The division had high hopes of cracking the million mark in model year production. It did not do so, but the 900,380 units actually built hardly constituted an embarrassment. The intermediates, which were all-new, stole most of the thunder, but the Firebirds turned in the best performance at the box office, increasing their sales for the sixth year in a row and setting a new all-time record for the third year in a row.

Nothing much had been done to the Firebirds to spur this buyer interest. They were much the same flock of 'Birds that had been roosting in the tree for the past few seasons but, no matter, the public's fancy with them seemed to have no limits. The black Special Edition and the all blue Skybird options were continued over from 1977, but in midyear were replaced by, respectively, a gold Special Edition and an all red Redbird. Skybird/Redbird production figures were not released, but the Special Editions consisted of approximately 3,680 black (also known as "blackbirds") and 6,000 gold models.

Underneath the skin, the Firebirds were in for their annual engine juggling and, as usual, the news was not very good. The Trans Am engine remained essentially the same as before, with a minor increase in compression ratio, but a higher output 220 hp version was listed. The California powerplant was still the Olds 403 cid V-8, however. The Formula now came standard with the Chevy 305 cid V-8 rated at 145 hp.

Prices were up, once again (surprise, surprise) to $4,593 for the base 'Bird, to $4,897 for the Esprit, to $5,533 for the Formula and all the way up to $5,889 for the Trans Am. Plus options.

Production kept pace with prices, soaring to 187,285 units for the model run and included the millionth Firebird. Of these, 32,672 were base Firebirds, 36,926 were Esprits, 24,346 were Formulas and 93,341 were Trans Ams.

The Firebird customer literature situation was much the same as it had been in 1977. The only regular item specifically on the Firebird was the post card (see the montage below). The full Firebird line was covered in the Pontiac catalogue (see pages 113-119). Also reproduced here are the spread from the ordering guide (see pages 120-122), a typical magazine ad (see page 112) and the available color and trim selections (see page 123).

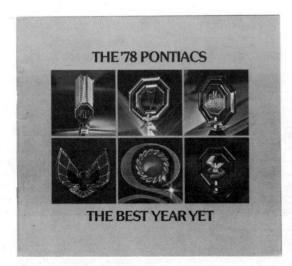

THE '78 PONTIACS

THE BEST YEAR YET

1978 PONTIAC FORMULA FIREBIRD

1978 PONTIAC COLORS

There's a Firebird for every purpose.
Except standing still.

molestias excepteur sint occaecat
sunt in culpa qui officia deserunt mol
Et harumd dereud facilis est er expe
soluta nobis eligent optio est con
Lorem ipsum dolor sit amet, consecte
eiusmod tempor incidunt ut labore
Ut enim ad minim veniam, quis nost
laboris nisi ut aliquip ex ea comm
irure dolor in reprehenderit in volupta
illum dolore eu fugiat nulla pariatur
dignissum qui blandit praesent lupt
molestias excepteur sint occae

sunt in culpa qui officia deserunt
Et harumd dereud facilis est er
conscient to factor tum poen legum c
neque pecun modut est neque no
soluta nobis eligent optio congue nih
reliquard cupiditat, quas nulla pr
potius inflammad ut coercend magi
invitat igitur vera ratio bene sancs a
Lorem ipsum dolor sit amet, con
eiusmod tempor incidunt ut labor
Ut einim ad minim veniam, quis nosti
laboris nisi ut aliquip ex ea comm

irure dolor in reprehenderit in volup
illum dolore eu fugiat nulla pariat
dignissum qui blandit est praesent li
molestias excepteur sint occaecat
sunt in culpa qui officia deserunt mo
Et harumd dereud facilis est er ex
soluta nobis eligent optio est
Lorem ipsum dolor sit amet, consecte
eiusmod tempor incidunt ut labore
Ut enim ad minim veniam, quis nost
laboris nisi ut aliquip ex ea comm
irure dolor in reprehenderit

1978 ⬙ Pontiac's best year yet!

(This ad is a mock-up prepared by the ad agency prior to approval of the actual ad by the division. The ad copy had yet to be written (or approved) at this stage, thus the gibberish in the text section. The brochures are often initially prepared in a similar fashion.)

The ultimate. The 1978 Pontiac Trans Am.

Firebird

A few more gages of Trans Am's success set in a gleaming instrument panel.

Spend your nights spinning gold. Order the available gold cast aluminum wheels.

Trans Am's response is enthusiastic. And so is everyone's reaction to the available custom interior.

How do you track a Trans Am? With this available AM/FM/8-track stereo.

12

Pontiac's sports machines.

Some get it by shooting Colorado's white water in a 12-foot raft. Others by soaring free at 900 feet. Still others by surfing the Bonzai Pipeline and coming through more-or-less intact.

It's an exhilarating feeling. The same feeling you can get behind the wheel of a 1978 Firebird.

Trans Am

The most exhilarating Firebird has to be Trans Am. Trans Am is a red-hot seller. And for good reason. Hearts flutter at its mere mention. And start beating madly with the very first sight....

Look at the styling. That broad, forceful sweep of sheet metal. Punctuated by air extractors, air deflectors and a singular air dam.

A pair of piercing dual rectangular headlamps glare out of the new coal-black grille. Sweeping up from the trunk is Trans Am's distinctive spoiler.

Adding even more flash are the available cast aluminum wheels. Along with a shrieking bird decal for its shaker hood. For when you really want your Trans Am to send pulses pulsing.

If you can pull yourself away from its awesome exterior, slip inside.

Nestle into the rich, all-vinyl bucket seats. Catch the glimmer off the burnished metal dash. With its clock, tach and full set of rally gages. They can help you gage every revolution of Trans Am's powerful 6.6 litre (400 CID) 4-bbl. V-8.†

Grasp the padded Formula steering wheel. And put yourself in command of Trans Am's power steering. It comes standard. So do power front disc brakes. An automatic transmission. And a special Radial Tuned Suspension with GR70-15 steel-belted radials. Together, they can help you tame the most unruly road.

Trans Am. The ultimate Firebird. The ultimate feeling. Once you've driven it, you'll never settle for shooting the rapids again.

†See Facts and Figures page for availability.

11

Formula Firebird

The Formula Firebird is for driving fanatics. Who'd rather spend their nights taking a spin down the road than spinning a dream. Who enjoy exploring back roads. And who wish Sunday drives would last until Tuesday.

The Formula's looks aren't quite as flashy as Trans Am. But it's hardly a wallflower. You could probably spot one 2 miles off in a

fog. Those simulated air scoops out front. Rally II wheels. Body-colored sport mirrors. All standard.

For a little more dazzle, you can order the Appearance Package. It includes some sporty striping. Plus side-lettering that fairly shouts the Formula's name.

When you and your Formula decide to get chummy with back roads, you'll recognize its

supple comforts. Like the luxury cushion steering wheel.

When you get earnest about your late night spins, you'll start to appreciate its responsive 5.0 litre (305 CID) V-8.†

The Formula Firebird. Get one. Then every Sunday, you can take it for a spin over some back roads.

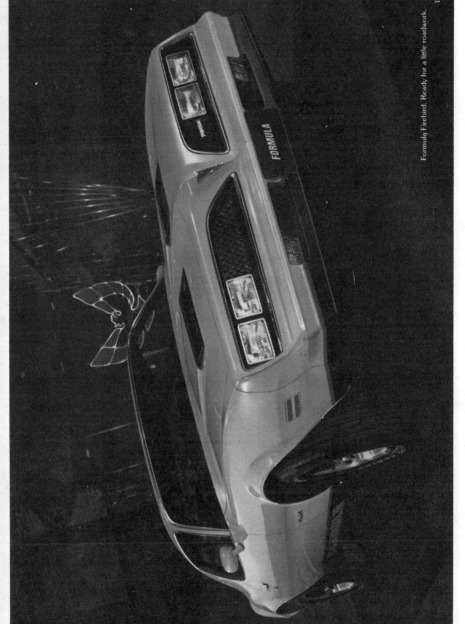

Formula Firebird. Ready for a little roadwork.

13

115

This available defogger helps clear your rear window for a better view of the world you left behind.

Elegant wire wheels are available on Firebird and Firebird Esprit.

Now available on Firebird is this digital quartz clock radio with AM/FM stereo and electronic readouts for station frequency, time, elapsed time and date. It's just one of nine different sound systems available on the Firebird.

Happy ending to another flight for "Sky Bird"

In the vinyl analysis, you'll really appreciate these deeply padded buckets that come standard on Esprit.

Firebird shows its true colors with the available Rally II wheels.

"Sky Bird" proudly displays its available fancy dress blues.

Outings become pleasure cruises—with Firebird's available Cruise Control.

Flip the lid on this nifty available hatch roof, and take on all the airs of a convertible.

14

Firebird Esprit

Esprit is the luxury Firebird.
Not the fragile, frilly "musn't touch" kind of luxury. But Pontiac's kind. A luxury that doesn't interfere with the Firebird driver's love of driving. Esprit's liquid lines are enriched by deep acrylic colors. Enhanced by matching sport mirrors. And gleaming deluxe wheel covers. Its markings are unmistakably Esprit.

And this year you can fly with the special "Sky Bird" Appearance Package that's available. It offers two-tone blue paint. Special trim inside and out. Even sky-blue cast aluminum wheels. All adding up to a 'Bird of a totally different color.

But Esprit's luxury is more than paint deep. Inside, you'll find our luxury cushion steering wheel. Individually cushioned bucket seats of plush vinyl.

Or even plusher available velour you can order. There's deep cut-pile carpeting underfoot. And added acoustical insulation. To help muffle the "oohs" and "ahhs" of appreciative passersby.

Esprit is a perfect melding of luxury and excitement. The kind of luxury that never intrudes. And the kind of excitement that's indelibly Firebird.

A true blue Esprit, the custom "Sky Bird."

15

117

Firebird

When you're looking for a car with all of Firebird's fire....but you need a handsome value, there's just one solution. Our basic 'Bird.

It has the seductive good looks of every Firebird. The boldly sculpted front-end. The sweeping contours.

It has all the appointments you expect in a Firebird. Deep foam bucket seats.

Clear, concise instrumentation. Including a speedometer that speaks in kilometres as well as miles. And a vinyl applique on the dash that looks remarkably like rosewood.

The deluxe steering wheel cushions your hands. While plush nylon-blend carpet flatters your feet.

The car wings down the road with the authority of a Firebird. Thanks to its 3.8 litre (231 CID) V-6.† Redesigned for what engineers say is "even torque interval." And you'll say it's smooth.

Our base model has the wow of every Firebird. Plus one wow all its own. Firebird's lowest price. Now there's no reason you can't move to a Firebird. And kiss the dulls goodbye.

†See Facts and Figures page for availability.

The fundamental Firebird. Great value on any street.

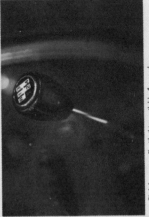

Shift for yourself with this available 4-speed.

Firebird makes another good move with Pontiac's famed Radial Tuned Suspension.

Even our base Firebird belongs to the bucket brigade.

16

FIREBIRD
FACTS AND FIGURES

MODELS

Hardtop coupe offered in four versions: Firebird, Firebird Esprit, Formula Firebird and Firebird Trans Am

POWER TEAMS

Standard engines:
3.8 litre (231 CID) 2-bbl. V-6 on Firebird and Esprit
5.0 litre (305 CID) 2-bbl. V-8 on Formula
6.6 litre (400 CID) 4-bbl. V-8 on Trans Am*

Available engines:
5.0 litre (305 CID) 2-bbl. V-8 on Firebird and Esprit
5.7 litre (350 CID) 4-bbl. V-8 on Formula, Esprit and Firebird
6.6 litre (400 CID) 4-bbl. V-8 on Formula*
T/A 6.6 litre (400 CID) 4-bbl. V-8 on Formula and Trans Am**

Standard transmissions:
Manual 3-speed on Firebird and Esprit
Automatic on Formula, manual 4-speed available at no extra charge†
Automatic on Trans Am

Available transmissions:
Manual 4-speed†
Automatic

*Available 6.6 litre (403 CID) 4-bbl. V-8 mandatory engine in California.
**Not available in California.
†Automatic trans mandatory in California.

Ask your Pontiac dealer for full details on engine/transmission combinations.

STANDARD INTERIOR FEATURES
Standard Firebird Features

Front bucket seats and bucket-type rear seats with all-vinyl trim. Front seat cushions of solid foam trim with integral springs. Deluxe cushion steering wheel in matching interior colors. Nylon-blend, cut-pile carpeting. Simulated rosewood applique on instrument panel trim plate. Speedometer graduated in both kilometres and miles. Single-buckle seat and shoulder belt system. Fluid-on-demand windshield washer. Ash tray lamp. High-low level body ventilation. Thick trunk floor mat.

Special Firebird Esprit Features

Custom all-vinyl bucket seats. Luxury cushion steering wheel in matching colors. Custom pedal trim plates. Distinctive door trim panels. Rear ash trays. Added acoustical insulation.

Special Formula Firebird Features

Luxury cushion steering wheel in matching interior colors. Full-length front console.

Special Trans Am Features

Formula steering wheel. Aluminum machine-turned style instrument panel trim plate. Rally gages, electric clock and instrument panel tach.

STANDARD EXTERIOR FEATURES
Standard Firebird Features

New grille styling with integral body-colored bumpers. Hubcaps with the Pontiac crest. Rectangular headlamps. Bright windshield, rear window and grille moldings. Firebird emblems on sail panel and rear deck lid. Dual horns. Concealed windshield wipers.

Special Firebird Esprit Features

Esprit identification. Deluxe wheel covers. Body-colored sport mirrors, left-hand remote control. Body-colored door handle inserts. Bright moldings—roof drip, windowsills, hood, rocker panels and wheel openings.

Special Formula Firebird Features

Formula identification. Rear deck spoiler. Hood with twin simulated air scoops. Body-colored sport mirrors, left-hand remote control. Blacked-out grille. Rally II wheels.

Special Trans Am Features

Trans Am identification on front fenders, grille panel and on wraparound rear deck spoiler. Front center air dam. Rear wheel opening air deflectors. Front fender air extractors. Body-colored sport mirrors, left-hand remote control. Blacked-out grille. Rally II wheels with trim rings. Shaker hood and air cleaner. Dual chrome splitter tailpipe extensions.

DIMENSIONS

DIMENSIONS millimetres (inches)	Firebird & Esprit	Formula	Trans Am
Overall length	4999 (196.8)	4999 (196.8)	4999 (196.8)
Overall width	1867 (73.4)	1867 (73.4)	1867 (73.4)
Wheelbase	2746 (108.1)	2746 (108.1)	2746 (108.1)
Track, front/rear	1547/1524 (60.9/60.0)	1547/1524 (61.3/60.4)	1547/1524 (61.2/60.3)
Head room, front/rear	945/914 (37.2/36.0)	945/914 (37.2/36.0)	945/914 (37.2/36.0)
Leg room, front/rear	1115/721 (43.9/28.4)	1115/721 (43.9/28.4)	1115/721 (43.9/28.4)
Shoulder room, front/rear	1440/1382 (56.7/54.4)	1440/1382 (56.7/54.4)	1440/1382 (56.7/54.4)

Published dimensions are for a base automobile without optional equipment or accessories. Additional accessories or equipment ordered at the customer's option can result in a minor change in these dimensions.

STANDARD CHASSIS FEATURES
Standard Firebird and Esprit Features

Front disc brakes. Power steering. Coil-spring front and leaf-spring rear suspension. High Energy Electronic Ignition and catalytic converter which requires unleaded fuel. And Radial Tuned Suspension, which includes: FR78-15 specification steel-belted radial tires, computer-selected springs, front stabilizer bar.

Special Formula Firebird Features

Trans Am front and rear stabilizer bars and GR70-15 steel-belted radial tires. Power brakes.

Special Trans Am Features

Safe-T-Track limited-slip differential. Power-flex fan. GR70-15 steel-belted radial tires. Heavy front and rear stabilizer bars.

CAPACITIES

Fuel tank—19.9 litres (21 gals)
Oil refill, less filter—
Firebird/Esprit 3.8 litres (4.0 qts)
Formula/Trans Am 4.7 litres (5.0 qts)

POPULAR EQUIPMENT AVAILABLE

Hatch roof with removable panels. Over-the-roof accent stripes. Canopy vinyl top. Wire wheel covers. Cast aluminum wheels. Body-colored Rally II wheels with trim rings. Deluxe wheel covers. Velour bucket seats (not avail. on base Firebird). Custom vinyl interior trim package (not available on base 'Bird). Air conditioning. Rally gage instrument cluster. Cruise control. Electric rear window defroster. Front console. Nine different sound systems including AM, FM, CB, cassette and 8-track. Formula steering wheel. Added acoustical insulation (std. on Esprit). Remote control deck-lid release. Dome and reading lamp. Formula Appearance Package, including blacked-out lower body and grille, special striping and super-graphics. Special Esprit Sky-Bird Appearance Package, including blue interior trim, two-tone blue exterior, dark blue accent on lower body with gradient blue tape stripe. Medium blue cast aluminum wheels, blue Formula steering wheel, decals, blue grille panels, blue custom seat belts and special sail panel identification. Black Special Edition Trans Am including gold striping and exterior accents, gold cast aluminum wheels.

TRANS AM

FORMULA FIREBIRD

SKYBIRD

FIREBIRD
COUPE (S878)

FIREBIRD ESPRIT
COUPE (T878)

FIREBIRD FORMULA
COUPE (U878)

FIREBIRD TRANS AM
COUPE (W878)

STANDARD EQUIPMENT

Exterior
- New Grille Styling
- One-piece Resilient Endura Front End Panel and Front Bumper
- Endura Rear Bumper in Body Color
- Hubcaps with Pontiac Crest
- Dual Horns
- Concealed Windshield Wipers
- Dual Rectangular Headlamps

In Addition to Firebird Features, Esprit Includes:
- Body-Color Inserts in Outside Door Handles
- Deluxe Wheel Covers
- Outside Sport Mirrors, LH Remote Controlled
- Esprit Identification
- Bright Windowsill & Hood Rear Edge Molding
- Wheel Opening Moldings
- Roof Drip Moldings

In Addition to Firebird Features, Formula Includes:
- New Black-accented Grilles
- Simulated Dual Air Scoops Design
- Rear Deck Spoiler
- Outside Sport Mirrors, LH Remote Controlled
- Formula Identification
- Rally II wheels with Trim Rings

In Addition to Firebird Features, Trans Am Includes:
- Front Center Air Dam
- Black Grille
- Rear Deck Spoiler
- Outside Sport Mirrors, LH Remote Controlled
- Front & Rear Wheel Opening Air Deflectors
- Front Fender Air Extractors
- Chrome Side-splitter Tailpipe Extensions
- Rally II Wheels with Trim Rings
- Shaker Hood & Air Cleaner
- Trans Am Identification

Interior
- New Door Trim Panels
- Deluxe Cushion Steering Wheel
- Nylon-blend, Cut-pile Carpeting
- Simulated Rosewood Applique on Instrument Panel Trim Plate
- Front Bucket Seats in All-vinyl
- Speedometer Graduated in Kilometres per Hour as well as Miles per Hour (Odometer Registers Miles)
- Single-buckle Seat & Shoulder Belt System
- High-low Level Body Ventilation
- Luggage Compartment Mat

In Addition to Firebird Features, Esprit Includes:
- Luxury Cushion Steering Wheel
- New Custom Interior Trim
  Includes:
  —New All-vinyl or Extra Cost Lombardy (Velour) Cloth Bucket Seats
  —New Integral Assist Grips on Doors
  —Rear Quarter Ash Trays
  —Instrument Panel Assist Strap
  —Custom Pedal Trim Plates
  —Added Acoustic Insulation

In Addition to Firebird Features, Formula Includes:
- Luxury Cushion Steering Wheel
- Console

In Addition to Firebird Features, Trans Am Includes:
- Formula Steering Wheel
- Rally Gages with Clock & Instrument Panel Tachometer
- Engine-turned Instrument Panel Trim Plate
- Console

POWERTRAIN AND CHASSIS

Standard Engines
- Firebird, Esprit—3.8 Litre (231 CID) 2-bbl. GM V-6
- Formula—5.0 Litre (305 CID) 2-bbl GM V-8
- Trans Am—6.6 Litre (400 CID) 4-bbl. GM V-8—Federal
- Trans Am—6.6 Litre (403 CID) 4-bbl. GM V-8—California‡

Available Engines
- Firebird, Esprit—5.0 Litre (305 CID) 2-bbl. GM V-8
- Firebird, Esprit—5.7 Litre (350 CID) 4-bbl. GM V-8‡
- Formula—5.7 Litre (350 CID) 4-bbl. GM V-8—Federal & California
- Formula—6.6 Litre (400 CID) 4-bbl. GM V-8—Federal
- Formula—6.6 Litre (403 CID) 4-bbl. GM V-8—California‡
- Formula—T/A 6.6 Litre (400 CID) 4-bbl GM V-8—Federal
- Trans Am—T/A 6.6 Litre (400 CID) 4-bbl GM V-8—Federal

‡A Special Option is Available for High Altitude Operation

Standard Transmissions
- Firebird, Esprit—Manual 3-Speed Floor Shift—Federal; Automatic—California
- Formula, Trans Am—Automatic

Available Transmissions
- Manual 4-Speed Floor Shift
- Automatic

Standard Tires
- Firebird, Esprit—FR78-15 Black*
- Formula, Trans Am—GR70-15 Black*

Available Tires
- Firebird, Esprit—FR78-15 White* or White Lettered*
- Formula, Trans Am—GR70-15 White Lettered*
- Trans Am—225/70R-15 Black*/White Lettered with WS6 Performance Package only

*Steel-belted Radials with Radial Tuned Suspension

Standard Steering
- Power

Standard Brakes
- Manual, Front Disc, Rear Drum
- Trans Am & Formula—Power, Front Disc, Rear Drum

Capacities

Firebird, Esprit
- Fuel Tank..................79.5 Litres (21 gals.)
- Oil Refill, Less Filter..........3.79 Litres (4 qts.)

Formula
- Fuel Tank..................79.5 Litres (21 gals.)
- Oil Refill, Less Filter..........4.73 Litres (4 qts.)

Trans Am
- Fuel Tank..................79.5 Litres (21 gals.)
- Oil Refill, Less Filter..........4.75 Litres (5 qts.)

Trunk Capacity
All Models
- 186 Litres (6.6 cu. ft.)

MAJOR OPTIONS

UPC ITEM
- C60 Air Conditioning, Custom
- U35 Clock, Electric
- D55 Console
- K30 Cruise Control
- A90 Deck Lid Release, Remote Control
- C49 Defroster, Electric Rear Window
- W63 Gages, Rally & Clock
- WW8 Gages, Rally, Clock & I/P Tach
- A01 Glass, All Windows Soft Ray
- CC1 Hatch Roof, Removable
- WW7 Hood Decal (Trans Am Only)
- BS1 Insulation, Additional Acoustical
- Y92 Lamp Group
- C95 Lamp, Dome Reading
- D35 Mirrors, LH Remote Control Sport, RH Man. Adj.
- JL2 Power Disc Brakes, Front
- AU3 Power Door Locks
- A31 Power Windows
- U58 Radio, AM/FM Stereo
- ■ UM1 Radio, AM & Stereo 8-track Tape Player
- ■ UM2 Radio, AM/FM Stereo & Stereo 8-track Tape Player
- ■ UY8 Radio, AM/FM Stereo w/Digital Clock
- ■ UP5 Radio, AM/FM w/40-Channel CB
- ■ UP6 Radio, AM/FM Stereo w/40-Channel CB
- ■ UN3 Radio, AM/FM Stereo & Cassette Tape Player
- N65 Spare Tire, Stowaway
- D80 Spoiler, Rear Deck
- N33 Steering Wheel, Tilt
- CD4 Windshield Wipers, Controlled Cycle

- **W60 Appearance Package, Esprit (Skybird) Includes:**
  —Special Blue exterior
  —Special Striping and Decals
  —Blue Formula Steering wheel
  —Blue-accented Engine-turned Instrument Panel Trim Plate

- **W50 Formula Appearance Package Includes:**
  —Lower Body Paint and Striping
  —"Formula" Lettering on Door and Rear Deck Spoiler
  —Special Striping
  —Wheel Opening Moldings

- **Y84 Special Edition Trans Am Includes:**
  —Black Exterior with Gold Striping and Decals
  —Removable Hatch Roof
  —Hood Decal
  —Gold-accented Cast-aluminum Wheels

- **WS6 Trans Am Performance Package Includes:**
  —T/A 6.6 Litre (400 CID) 4-bbl. GM V-8 engine—Federal (6.6 Litre (403 CID) 4-bbl. GM V-8—California
  —Cast Aluminum Wheels (8" wide)
  —Special Handling Package
  —225/70R15 Steel-belted White Lettered Radial Tires

■ New Item

DIMENSIONS

	Firebird & Esprit Mm. (in.)	Formula Mm. (in.)	Trans Am Mm. (in.)
Overall length	4999 (196.8)	4999 (196.8)	4999 (196.8)
Overall width	1864 (73.4)	1864 (73.4)	1864 (73.4)
Wheelbase	2746 (108.1)	2746 (108.1)	2746 (108.1)
Tread, front/rear	1547/1524 (60.9/60.0)	1557/1534 (61.3/60.4)	1554/1532 (61.2/60.3)
Head room, front/rear	945/914 (37.2/36.0)	945/914 (37.2/36.0)	945/914 (37.2/36.0)
Leg room, front/rear	1115/721 (43.9/28.4)	1115/721 (43.9/28.4)	1115/721 (43.9/28.4)
Shoulder room, front/rear	1440/1382 (56.7/54.4)	1440/1382 (56.7/54.4)	1440/1382 (56.7/54.4)

Published dimensions are for a base automobile without optional equipment or accessories. Additional accessories or equipment ordered at the customer's option can result in a minor change in these dimensions.

FIREBIRD
(Firebird, Formula & Trans Am Models)

Standard Bucket Seats

Vinyl Interiors—OXEN
Firebird, Formula & Trans Am

11R1 White
Recommended Exteriors:
11,15,19,22,24,48,50,
51,63,67,69,75,77

19R1 Black
Recommended Exteriors:
11,15,19,22,24,48,50,
51,63,67,69,75,77

62R1 Camel Tan
Recommended Exteriors:
11,19,50,51,63,69

74R1 Carmine
Recommended Exteriors:
11,15,19,77

Appointment Mix Interiors
(White Vinyl Interior with Colored Appointments*)
Firebird, Formula & Trans Am

11R1/24X
White/Blue
Recommended Exteriors:
11,15,19,22,24

11R1/62X
White/Camel Tan
Recommended Exteriors:
11,19,50,51,61,63,69

11R1/67X
White/Ember
Recommended Exteriors:
11,19,67

11R1/74X
White/Carmine
Recommended Exteriors:
11,15,19,77

FIREBIRD CUSTOM INTERIORS

Standard Custom Bucket Seats
(Esprit)

Extra Cost Custom Bucket Seats
(Formula & Trans Am)

Vinyl Interiors—DOESKIN

11N1 White
Recommended Exteriors:
11,15,19,22,24,48,50,
51,63,67,69,75,77

19N1 Black
Recommended Exteriors:
11,15,19,22,24,48,50,
51,63,67,69,75,77

24N1 Blue
Recommended Exteriors:
11,15,19,22,24,30

62N1 Camel Tan
Recommended Exteriors:
11,19,50,51,63,69

74N1 Carmine
Recommended Exteriors:
11,15,19,77

*Carpeting, Instrument Panel, Steering Column, Package Shelf.

Appointment Mix Interiors
(White Vinyl Interior with Colored Appointments*)
Esprit, Formula & Trans Am

11N1/24X
White/Blue
Recommended Exteriors:
11,15,19,22,24

11N1/62X
White/Camel Tan
Recommended Exteriors:
11,19,50,51,63,69

11N1/67X
White/Ember
Recommended Exteriors:
11,19,67

11N1/74X
White/Carmine
Recommended Exteriors:
11,15,19,77

Extra Cost Custom Bucket Seats
(Esprit, Formula & Trans Am)

Cloth Interiors—LOMBARDY

19B1 Black
Recommended Exteriors:
11,15,19,22,24,48,50,
51,63,67,69,75,77

24B1 Blue
Recommended Exteriors:
11,15,19,22,24,30

62B1 Camel Tan
Recommended Exteriors:
11,19,50,51,63,69

74B1 Carmine
Recommended Exteriors:
11,15,19,77

Firebird Trans Am Decal Colors:

Red/Charcoal—With exterior colors:
11—Cameo White or 15—Platinum

Gold-Yellow/Orange—
With exterior colors: 19—Starlight
Black, 24—Martinique Blue, 69—
Chesterfield Brown or 75—Mayan Red

Gold/Matte Gold—With exterior
color: 19—Starlight Black S.E.

Gold/Bronze—With exterior color:
50—Solar Gold

FIREBIRD

Note: Cameo White—Code 11, will coordinate with all interiors. If a Cordova Top is desired, it should be White—Code 11T or match the interior color. A White vinyl interior is recommended only with an Appointment Mix matching the exterior color.

FIREBIRD, ESPRIT, FORMULA & TRANS AM

Model	Interior Trim	Exterior Paint	Over-the-Roof Stripe (D98)	Decals/Graphics	Body Side Molding (B84)
Firebird and Esprit	Black	19—Starlight Black	Silver		Black
		15—Platinum	Silver		Platinum
		51—Sundance Yellow			
		75—Mayan Red			
	*Blue	22—Glacier Blue	Blue		Blue
	Camel	63—Laredo Brown	Brown		
		69—Chesterfield Brown	Brown		
	Carmine	77—Carmine			
		15—Platinum	Silver		Platinum
Skybird	Blue	30—Lombard Blue			Blue
Formula	Black	19—Starlight Black		Gold/Matte Gold	Black
		15—Platinum		Charcoal/Red	Platinum
		24—Martinique Blue		Light Blue/Medium Blue	
		51—Sundance Yellow		Light Red/Dark Red	
		75—Mayan Red		Light Red/Dark Red	
	Carmine	15—Platinum		Charcoal/Red	Platinum
Trans Am	Black	19—Starlight Black		Gold/Matte Gold	Black
		15—Platinum		Charcoal/Red	Platinum
		24—Martinique Blue		Charcoal/Red	
		51—Sundance Yellow		Gold/Orange	
		75—Mayan Red		Gold/Orange	
	Carmine	11—Cameo White		Charcoal/Red	White
		15—Platinum		Charcoal/Red	Platinum

*Esprit Only.

Pontiac continued its prosperous times well into 1979 before the gasoline crisis, caused by the Iranian revolution, reduced auto sales to depression status. The big news was the introduction of the 1980 Phoenix in April 1979. Although it was officially labelled a "1980", the Phoenix was revised slightly when the regular 1980 Pontiacs were announced in the fall of the year. The Firebirds scored their biggest sales record of all time and were second only to the standard Pontiacs in total production for the 1979 model run. A total of approximately 995,000 Pontiacs were produced during the model year (including approximately 88,000 1980 Phoenix models).

The Firebirds were, except for the Phoenix line, the only models to undergo anything like a normal annual model change. Front and rear ends were dramatically new, while still being in keeping with past Firebird themes. The front end featured a remarkable grille-less look. A new urethane casting included "ported" head lights on top and horizontal louvres in the "bumper" area below. At the rear, Formula and Trans Am models featured a startling "blacked-out" tail light design in which the lamps disappeared when not in use. Other Firebird models had horizontal louvres of a more conventional, but no less attractive, nature. The revised 'Birds were all real head-turners for 1979—which was no more than their fans expected, of course.

Mechanical news was less exciting. The standard powerplant in the Trans Am was now the 301 cid V-8 rated at 150 hp, although the 400 cid V-8 was still optional. A 135 hp version of the 301 V-8 was standard on the Formula, while the other Firebirds used the Buick 231 cid V-6, now rated at 115 hp. In the stopping department, four-wheel disc brakes were listed as Formula and Trans Am options for the first time.

Blackbird and Redbird options were continued over for the Trans Am and Esprit models, respectively, and there was an exciting tenth anniversary Trans Am, as well. Produced in a limited edition, the anniversary Trans Am featured silver exterior paint and matching silver leather upholstery (see facing page).

Firebird prices set two dubious records in 1979. All Firebirds were now over $5,000 and one model cracked the $10,000 barrier (the anniversary Trans Am at $10,620). The base Firebird listed at $5,076, the Esprit at $5,454, the Formula at $6,380 and the regular Trans Am at $6,699.

Production for the year was 211,454. This number included 38,642 Firebirds, 30,853 Esprits, 24,851 Formulas and 117,108 Trans Ams. Of the Trans Ams, 7,500 were tenth anniversary editions.

The 1979 Firebird literature consisted of the normal post card (see the montage below) and the standard spread in the full-line Pontiac catalogue (see pages 126-128). The catalogue came with a companion "Buyer's Guide" supplement which included all the specifications. The Firebird spread from the product manual is included on pages 129-130.

THE 1979 PONTIACS ▽ OUR BEST GET BETTER

1979 COLORS

▽ 1979 PONTIAC BUYER'S GUIDE

FIREBIRD

Announcing the birth of a bold new breed of wow! The 1979 Firebirds. Trans Am, our ultimate, comes on stronger than ever in its eleventh year.

extractors and deflectors. The wide 70-series radials. And front and rear stabilizer bars. All standard issue.

There's never been a 'bird more deserving of our best-of-breed distinction.

Formula with its fiery new two-tone flanks is for those who like a more sophisticated look when they shift down main street.

Yet Formula shares many of the new styling innovations of Trans Am, so it's not hard to guess what lurks beneath

With a broad new forefront cast in durable urethane. Ported headlamps. And a new Pontiac exclusive black tail treatment that runs the width of the rear deck. Trans Am's new visage doesn't just hint at its top-of-the-line position. It shouts it!

And there's still the showy outlay of

Shown below: 1979 Trans Am. Our best of breed. Screaming eagle decal, hatch roof and cast aluminum wheels among available features shown.

those clean contours.

To bring that brawn to the surface, order the Formula Appearance Package. Our new Formula is formidable any

Shown opposite: Trans Am's control board. Air conditioning, 4-speed manual and AM/FM cassette among availables shown.

Shown below: Trans Am, Formula and Esprit's available new hobnail cloth buckets. Some other availables shown: Formula wheel and power windows.

way you dress it.

Esprit, with its well-bred looks, still stands firm as our plushest Firebird. Flashing features like new deluxe wheel covers. Dual sport mirrors. And custom interior package. Check the '79 Pontiac Buyer's Guide for details.

Don't be put off by Esprit's polished appearance, though. It's still dressed to thrill.

Even our base Firebird has fire. We wouldn't dare turn down the excitement

just because it bears our lowest Firebird price tag.

The 1979 Firebirds. A new breed of excitement.

Shown opposite: The '79 Formula. Our newest Formula for intrigue. Formula Appearance Package among available features shown.

Shown below: The dashing new Esprit. Redbird Package (including two-tone red body and red-accented cast aluminum wheels) among availables shown.

FIREBIRD
COUPE (S879)

FIREBIRD ESPRIT
COUPE (T879)

FIREBIRD FORMULA
COUPE (U879)

FIREBIRD TRANS AM
COUPE (W879)

STANDARD EQUIPMENT

Exterior
- New Grille Styling
- New One-piece Resilient Endura Front End Panel and Front Bumper
- New Endura Rear Bumper
- Dual Horns
- Concealed Windshield Wipers
- Dual Rectangular Headlamps
- Hubcaps with Pontiac Crest

In Addition to Firebird Exterior Features, Esprit Includes:
- Body-Color Inserts in Outside Door Handles
- New Deluxe Wheel Covers
- Outside Sport Mirrors, LH Remote Controlled
- Esprit Identification
- Bright Windowsill & Hood Rear Edge Molding
- Wheel Opening Moldings
- Roof Drip Moldings

In Addition to Firebird Exterior Features, Formula Includes:
- Black-accented Grilles
- Simulated Dual Air Scoop Hood Design
- Outside Sport Mirrors, LH Remote Controlled
- Formula Identification
- Rally II wheels with Trim Rings

In Addition to Firebird Exterior Features, Trans Am Includes:
- Front Center Air Dam
- Black-accented Grille
- Rear Deck Spoiler
- Outside Sport Mirrors, LH Remote Controlled
- Front & Rear Wheel Opening Air Deflectors
- Front Fender Air Extractors
- Chroma Side-splitter Tailpipe Extensions
- Rally II Wheels with Trim Rings
- Shaker Hood & Air Cleaner
- Trans Am Identification

Interior
- Fully Upholstered Door Trim Panels
- Deluxe Cushion Steering Wheel
- Nylon-blend, Cut-pile Carpeting
- Simulated Rosewood Applique on Instrument Panel Trim Plate
- Front Bucket Seats in All-vinyl
- Speedometer Graduated in Kilometres per Hour as well as Miles per Hour (Odometer Registers Miles)
- Single-buckle Seat & Shoulder Belt System
- High-low Level Body Ventilation
- Luggage Compartment Mat

In Addition to Firebird Interior Features, Esprit Includes:
- Luxury Cushion Steering Wheel
- Added Acoustic Insulation
- Custom Interior Trim
  Includes:
  — All-vinyl or Extra Cost Hobnail Cloth Bucket Seats
  — Integral Assist Grips on Doors
  — Rear Quarter Ashtrays
  — Instrument Panel Assist Strap
  — Custom Pedal Trim Plates

In Addition to Firebird Interior Features, Formula and Trans Am Include:
- Formula Steering Wheel
- Rally Gages with Clock (Instrument Panel Tachometer-Trans Am)
- Engine-turned Instrument Panel Trim Plate
- Console

Standard Tires
- Firebird, Esprit—FR78-15 Black Fiberglass Radial
- Formula, Trans Am—225/70R-15 Black*

Available Tires
- Firebird & Esprit—FR78-15 White Fiberglass Radial FR78-15 White or White Lettered*
- Formula & Trans Am—P225/70R White Lettered (included w/WS6 performance option)

*Steel-belted Radials with Radial Tuned Suspension

Standard Steering
- Power

Standard Brakes
- Manual, Front Disc, Rear Drum
- Trans Am & Formula—Power, Front Disc, Rear Drum

Capacities

	Firebird, Esprit
Fuel Tank	79.5 Litres (21 gals.)
Oil Refill, Less Filter	3.8 Litres (4 qts.)

	Formula
Fuel Tank	79.5 Litres (21 gals.)
Oil Refill, Less Filter	4.7 Litres (5 qts.)

	Trans Am
Fuel Tank	79.5 Litres (21 gals.)
Oil Refill, Less Filter	3.8 Litres (4 qts.)

MAJOR OPTIONS

UPC ITEM
- C60 Air Conditioning, Custom
- U35 Clock, Electric
- D55 Console
- K30 Cruise Control
- A90 Deck Lid Release, Remote Control
- C49 Defroster, Electric Rear Window
- W63 Gages, Rally & Clock
- U17 Gages, Rally, Clock & I/P Tach
- A01 Glass, All Windows Soft Ray
- CC1 Hatch Roof, Removable
- D53 Hood Decal (Trans Am Only)
- BS1 Insulation, Additional Acoustical
- TR9 Lamp Group
- C95 Lamp, Dome Reading
- D35 Mirrors, LH Remote Control Sport, RH Man. Adj.
- JL2 Power Disc Brake, Front
- J65 Power Brakes, Front and Rear Disc (Formula, Trans Am)
- AU3 Power Door Locks
- A31 Power Windows
- U58 Radio, AM/FM Stereo
- UM1 Radio, AM & Stereo 8-track Tape Player
- UM2 Radio, AM/FM Stereo & Stereo 8-track Tape Player
- UY8 Radio, AM/FM Stereo w/Digital Clock
- UP5 Radio, AM/FM w/40-Channel CB
- UP6 Radio, AM/FM Stereo w/40-Channel CB
- UN3 Radio, AM/FM Stereo & Cassette Tape Player
- N65 Spare Tire, Stowaway
- D80 Spoiler, Rear Deck
- N33 Steering Wheel, Tilt
- CD4 Windshield Wipers, Controlled Cycle

POWERTRAINS

Engine*	Certification	Transmission	Gearshift Location	Axle Ratios Std.	Axle Ratios Avail.
Firebird, Esprit					
**3.8 Litre (231 CID) 2-bbl V-6 (LD5)	Federal, Altitude	Man. 3-Speed	Floor	3.08	NA
		Automatic	Floor	2.56	3.23
4.9 Litre (301 CID) 2-bbl V-8 (L27)	Federal, Altitude	Automatic	Floor	2.41	NA
4.9 Litre (301 CID) 4-bbl V-8 (L37)	Federal, Altitude	Man. 4-Speed	Floor	3.08	NA
		Automatic	Floor	2.73	NA
†5.7 Litre (350 CID) 4-bbl V-8 (LM1)	Altitude	Automatic	Floor	3.08	NA
**3.8 Litre (231 CID) 2-bbl V-6 (LD5)	California	Automatic	Floor	2.56	NA
5.0 Litre (305 CID) 2-bbl V-8 (LG3)	California	Automatic	Floor	2.41	NA
Formula					
**4.9 Litre (301 CID) 2-bbl V-8 (L27)	Federal, Altitude	Man. 4-Speed	Floor	2.41	NA
4.9 Litre (301 CID) 4-bbl V-8 (L37)	Federal, Altitude	Automatic	Floor	2.73	NA
		Man. 4-Speed	Floor	3.08	NA
6.6 Litre (400 CID) T/A 4-bbl V-8 (L78)	Federal, Altitude	Man. 4-Speed	Floor	3.08	NA
6.6 Litre (403 CID) 4-bbl V-8 (L80)	Federal, Altitude	Automatic	Floor	2.56	3.23
†5.7 Litre (350 CID) 4-bbl V-8	Altitude	Automatic	Floor	3.08	NA
**5.0 Litre (305 CID) 2-bbl V-8 (LG3)	California	Automatic	Floor	2.41	NA
6.6 Litre (403 CID) 4-bbl V-8 (L80)	California	Automatic	Floor	2.56	3.23
Trans Am					
4.9 Litre (301 CID) 4-bbl V-8 (L37)	Federal, Altitude	Automatic	Floor	2.73	NA
6.6 Litre 400 CID T/A 4-bbl V-8 (L78)	Federal, Altitude	Man. 4-Speed	Floor	3.08	NA
**6.6 Litre (403 CID) 4-bbl V-8 (L80)	Federal, Altitude	Automatic	Floor	2.56	3.23
†6.6 Litre (403 CID) 4-bbl V-8 (L80)	Altitude	Automatic	Floor	2.56	3.08
**6.6 Litre (403 CID) 4-bbl V-8 (L80)	California	Automatic	Floor	2.56	3.23

*Pontiacs are equipped with GM-built engines produced by various divisions.
**Base Powertrain.
†With Altitude Emissions (UPC NA6) — designed and recommended for high-altitude operation.

DIMENSIONS

	Mm. (in.)
Overall length	4999 (196.8)
Overall width	1854 (73.0)
Wheelbase	2748 (108.2)
Tread, front/rear	1557/1524 (61.3/60.0)
Head room, front/rear	945/914 (37.2/36.0)
Leg room, front/rear	1115/721 (43.9/28.4)
Shoulder room, front/rear	1440/1382 (56.7/54.4)
Trunk Capacity	186 Litres (6.6 cu. ft.)

Published dimensions are for a base automobile without optional equipment or accessories. Additional accessories or equipment ordered at the customer's option can result in a minor change in these dimensions.

FIREBIRD (Firebird, Formula & Trans Am)

Vinyl Interiors—OXEN
Firebird, Formula & Trans Am

12R1 Oyster	**19R1** Black	**62R1** Camel Tan	**74R1** Carmine
Recommended Exteriors:	Recommended Exteriors:	Recommended Exteriors:	Recommended Exteriors:
11,15,19,22,29,50,	11,15,19,22,29,50,	11,19,29,50,51,63,	11,15,19,75,77
51,63,69,75,77	51,63,69,75,77	69,77	

Appointment Mix Interiors
(Oyster White Vinyl Interior with Colored Appointments *)
Firebird, Formula & Trans Am

12R1/74X
Oyster/Carmine
Recommended Exteriors:
11,15,75,77

12R1/16X	**12R1/19X**	**12R1/24X**	**12R1/62X**
Oyster/Gray	Oyster/Black	Oyster/Blue	Oyster/Camel Tan
Recommended Exteriors:	Recommended Exteriors:	Recommended Exteriors:	Recommended Exteriors:
11,15,19,22,29,50,	11,15,19,22,29,50,	11,15,22,29	11,50,63,69
51,63,69,75,77	51,63,69,75,77		

FIREBIRD CUSTOM INTERIORS

Standard
Custom Bucket Seats
(Esprit)

Extra Cost
Custom Bucket Seats
(Formula & Trans Am)

Vinyl Interiors—DOESKIN

12N1 Oyster	**19N1** Black	**24N1** Blue	**62N1** Camel Tan
Recommended Exteriors:	Recommended Exteriors:	Recommended Exteriors:	Recommended Exteriors:
11,15,19,22,29,50,	11,15,19,22,29,50,	11,15,22,29	11,19,29,50,51,63
51,63,69,75,77	51,63,69,75,77		69,77
	74N1 Carmine		
	Recommended Exteriors:		
	11,15,19,75,77		

Appointment Mix Interiors
(Oyster White Vinyl Interior with Colored Appointments *)
Esprit, Formula & Trans Am

12N1/16X	**12N1/19X**	**12N1/24X**	**12N1/62X**
Oyster/Gray	Oyster/Black	Oyster/Blue	Oyster/Camel Tan
Recommended Exteriors:	Recommended Exteriors:	Recommended Exteriors:	Recommended Exteriors:
11,15,19,22,29,50,	11,15,19,22,29,50,	11,15,22,29	11,50,63,69
51,63,69,75,77	51,63,69,75,77		
	12N1/74X		
	Oyster/Carmine		
	Recommended Exteriors:		
	11,15,75,77		

Extra Cost
Bucket Seats

Cloth Interiors—HOBNAIL
(With Lombardy Bolsters)
Esprit, Formula & Trans Am

19B1 Black	**24B1** Blue	**62B1** Camel Tan	**74B1** Carmine
Recommended Exteriors:	Recommended Exteriors:	Recommended Exteriors:	Recommended Exteriors:
11,15,19,22,29,50,51,	11,15,22,29	11,19,29,50,51,63,	11,15,19,75,77
63,69,75,77		69,77	

Exterior Color	Bumper Accent Color		
11—Cameo White	16—Dk. Charcoal	50—Solar Gold	69—Heritage Brown
		51—Sundance Yellow	16—Dk. Charcoal
15—Platinum	16—Dk. Charcoal	63—Sierra Copper	69—Heritage Brown
19—Starlight Black	16—Dk. Charcoal	69—Heritage Brown	16—Dk. Charcoal
		75—Mayan Red	16—Dk. Charcoal
22—Glacier Blue	29—Nocturne Blue		
29—Nocturne Blue	16—Dk. Charcoal	77—Carmine	16—Dk. Charcoal

Pontiac production dropped dramatically in 1980 as the nation entered a recession and as the auto industry seemed to suffer the brunt of the economic damage. With interest rates soaring above 20%, many peole who might have bought new cars held back, and the result was disaster for the industry as a whole. Pontiac production was down sharply to 698,247 for the model run and the Firebirds, which had weathered the 1974-75 recession in fine shape, felt this one and felt it hard. Part of the problem was that, pretty as they were, they just were no longer fresh. This was the eleventh model year with essentially the same models, after all. Nor were they exactly state-of-the-art. Time, to say nothing of technology, had passed them by and it was beginning to show.

That being the case, the big news for the Firebird was, nevertheless, technical. Since the 400 cid V-8 was being discarded, Pontiac was forced to search out another answer to the performance needs of the big 'Birds. What resulted was a turbocharged edition of the 301 cid V-8. This engine cranked out a respectable 210 hp at 4000 rpm despite a relatively low 7.6:1 compression ratio. It was available as an option on the Trans Am and Formula.

The standard Trans Am and Formula powerplant remained the standard 301 V-8. The Buick 231 cid V-8 was still standard on the other Firebirds.

In appearance, the 1980 Firebirds were almost indistinguishable from their 1979 predecessors, with the exception of the turbocharged models. They had a special new hood and, in the case of the Trans Am, a revised screaming chicken hood decal. The Trans Am black Special Edition was continued, but the Redbird Esprit option was supplanted by a similar Yellow Bird option.

Pontiac received a special honor in 1980 when it was chosen to supply a Firebird Pace Car for the Indianapolis 500 race. A special white edition was prepared featuring a multi-toned gray hood decal and an oyster and black interior. Approximately 5,700 of these special editions were built for public consumption.

The base Firebird now listed at $5,948, the Esprit at $6,311, the Formula at $7,256 and the Trans Am at $7,480. Production declined drastically to 107,342 units for the model run. This consisted of 29,811 base models, 17,277 Esprits, 9,356 Formulas and 50,898 Trans Ams.

Firebird literature remained more or less the same as in 1979 with a post card (see montage below) and a spread in the full-line Pontiac catalogue (see page 133). The cover of an Indianapolis 500 map featuring the Pace Car is reproduced on page 136 and a flyer on a special Pace Car jacket is reproduced on page 137. The Firebird spread from the product manual is included here (see pages 132 and 134-135), as is the relevant section from the color and trim brochure (see page 138).

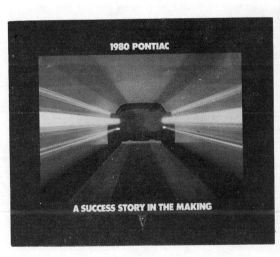

FIREBIRD TRANS AM SPECIAL EDITION (with Turbo V8)

FIREBIRD FORMULA (with Turbo V8 and Formula Appearance Package—W50)

FIREBIRD ESPRIT (Yellow Bird—W73)

SUCCESS STORY NO. 1:

A NEW AGE OF PERFORMANCE FOR THOSE FABULOUS FIREBIRDS.

Just when you thought the days of exciting, sporty performance were over...POW!

Firebird goes turbo! That's right, Trans Am and Formula are now available as the first turbocharged V-8 production cars of the '80s. Which allows Pontiac to give you the advantages of a smaller block V-8 with the performance boost of turbo. But that's just the beginning of the good news!

TRANS AM

You expect something extra from Pontiac's ultimate sport. And you've got it.

Just order your new Trans Am turbofied, and get a specially modified hood. Plus special available decals.

Turbo or no, you still get the full standard contingent of spoilers, air dams, deflectors and sidesplitter tailpipes that say this is Pontiac's sports superstar.

Trans Am's interior is no slouch either. Deep contour bucket seats. Machine turned instrument panel with rally gages, tachometer and clock. Console.

Of course, the real beauty of Trans Am is still on the road. Smooth. Agile. With quick ratio power steering. Heavy duty stabilizers. Power

brakes. A special handling package with four-wheel disc brakes, eight-inch wheels, wide 70-series tires and firmer suspension is available (also available on Formula).

FORMULA

As with Trans Am, new Formula Firebird is available with the new turbo V-8 and sexy new turbo hood.

But Formula has something all its own...a sleek, almost European sophistication.

The lines are trim, bullet-like, with dramatic blacked-out grille and tail

lamp treatment. Simulated dual hood scoops. And now, tungsten quartz halogen headlamps are available to light your path (also available on Trans Am).

And what an exciting path you'll carve with Formula's quick ratio power steering, power brakes and Rally radial tuned suspension.

ESPRIT

A success story in its own right, this new Firebird Esprit shows you can have luxury and sporty performance, too.

Beneath those sensuous contours is the plushest of Firebird interiors. Custom buckets. Luxury cushion steering wheel. And added sound insulation a monk could love.

If you really like it rich, choose from available features like the new seek and scan Delco Electronically Tuned Radio with extended range rear speakers. Power windows and door locks. And electric rear window defroster.

And for a tinge more, there's a new Yellow Bird package available on Esprit for extra flair. It features a two-tone yellow exterior, special striping and decals, yellow cast aluminum wheels, coordinating camel interior and more.

FIREBIRD

If you drive a hard bargain, you've picked the perfect year to drive our base-priced Firebird.

Because it offers so much. That sporty Firebird styling. Resilient body-color bumpers. Handsome buckets. Rich-looking rosewood vinyl accented instrument panel.

All this plus that sensational Firebird ride. With power steering and radial tuned suspension.

The new age of great Firebird performance is here. Come get your share.

Special Edition Trans Am interior with available deep-contoured hobnail cloth bucket seats.

FIREBIRD

FIREBIRD
COUPE (S87A)

FIREBIRD ESPRIT
COUPE (T87A)

FIREBIRD FORMULA
COUPE (V87A)

FIREBIRD TRANS AM
COUPE (W87A)

STANDARD EQUIPMENT

Exterior
- Body-color One-piece Resilient Endura Front End Panel and Front Bumper with Recessed Grilles and Dual Rectangular Headlamps
- Endura Rear Bumper
- Dual Horns
- Concealed Windshield Wipers
- Hubcaps with Pontiac Crest

In Addition to or Replacing Firebird Exterior Features, Esprit Includes:
- Body-color Inserts in Outside Door Handles
- Deluxe Wheel Covers
- Outside Sport Mirrors, LH Remote Controlled
- Esprit Identification
- Bright Windowsill & Hood Rear Edge Molding
- Wheel Opening Moldings
- Roof Drip Moldings
- Wide Rocker Panel Moldings

In Addition to or Replacing Firebird Exterior Features, Formula Includes:
- Black-accented Grilles
- Simulated Dual Air Scoop Hood Design
- Outside Sport Mirrors, LH Remote Controlled
- Formula Identification
- Rally II Wheels with Trim Rings

In Addition to or Replacing Firebird Exterior Features, Trans Am Includes:
- Front Center Air Dam
- Black-accented Grille
- Rear Deck Spoiler
- Outside Sport Mirrors, LH Remote Controlled
- Front & Rear Wheel Opening Air Deflectors
- Front Fender Air Extractors
- Chrome Side-splitter Tailpipe Extensions
- Rally II Wheels with Trim Rings
- Shaker Hood & Air Cleaner
- Trans Am Identification

Interior
- Fully Upholstered Door Trim Panels
- Deluxe Cushion Steering Wheel
- Column-mounted Dimmer Switch
- Nylon-blend, Cut-pile Carpeting
- Simulated Rosewood Applique on Instrument Panel Trim Plate
- Front Bucket Seats in All-vinyl
- Single-buckle Seat & Shoulder Belt System
- High-low Level Body Ventilation
- Luggage Compartment Mat

In Addition to or Replacing Firebird Interior Features, Esprit Includes:
- Luxury Cushion Steering Wheel
- Added Acoustic Insulation
- Custom Interior Trim
  Includes:
  — All-vinyl or Extra Cost Hobnail Cloth Bucket Seats
  — Integral Assist Grips on Doors
  — Rear Quarter Ashtrays
  — Instrument Panel Assist Strap
  — Custom Pedal Trim Plates

In Addition to Firebird Interior Features, Formula and Trans Am Include:
- Formula Steering Wheel
- Rally Gages with Clock (Instrument Panel Tachometer-Trans Am)
- Engine-turned Instrument Panel Trim Plate
- Console

Standard Tires (Steel-Belted Radials with Radial Tuned Suspension)
- 205/75R-15 Blackwall—Firebird, Esprit
- 225/70R-15 Blackwall—Formula, Trans Am

Available Tires

Firebird, Esprit
- 205/75R-15 Whitewall
- 205/75R-15 White Letter

Formula, Trans Am
- 225/70-15 White Letter†

† Included with (WS6) performance option

Standard Steering
- Power

Standard Brakes
- Manual, Front Disc, Rear Drum
- Trans Am & Formula—Power, Front Disc, Rear Drum

**See Car Order Form for additional listings and restrictions.

Capacities (Std. engine)

Firebird, Esprit
- Fuel Tank..................79.5 Liters (21 gals.)
- Oil Refill, Less Filter..........3.8 Liters (4 qts.)

Formula, Trans Am
- Fuel Tank..................79.5 Liters (21 gals.)
- Oil Refill, Less Filter..........4.7 Liters (5 qts.)

MAJOR OPTIONS**

UPC	ITEM
C60	Air Conditioning, Custom (Req. w/305 CID V-8's)
AK1	Belts, Custom Color Keyed (Std. w/Yellow Bird & Custom Trims)
U35	Clock, Electric (N.A. w/ETR Stereo Radio)
D55	Console (Std. Formula & Trans Am — Req. w/Auto. Trans.)
K30	Cruise Control (w/Auto. Trans. only — Req. Power Brakes)
A90	Deck Lid Release, Remote Control
C49	Defroster, Electric Rear Window (Inc. 63 Amp. Alternator)
UR4	Gages, Turbo Boost w/Elapsed Time Clock—Hood Mounted (w/Turbo Engine only—NA Calif.; NA ETR Stereo Radio)
W63	Gages, Rally & Clock (Std. Formula—NA Trans Am, V-6 or 265 2-bbl V-8 Engine)
U17	Gages, Rally, Clock & I/P Tach (Std. Trans Am—NA w/V-6 Engine)
A01	Glass, All Windows Soft Ray
CC1	Hatch Roof, Removable (Inc. w/Black Special Edition)
TT5	Headlamps, Tungsten Quartz Halogen
BS1	Insulation, Additional Acoustical (Std. Esprit)
TR9	Lamp Group (Inc. Luggage & Glove Box Lp., I.P. Ctsy Lp.)
C95	Lamp, Dome—Reading
D35	Mirrors, Sport—LH Remote, RH Man. Convex (Std. Esprit, Formula & Trans Am)
U75	Power Antenna, Automatic
U83	Power Antenna, AM/FM/CB Tri-Band (Inc. w/CB Radio)
JL2	Power Brakes, Front Disc (Req. w/Air Cond. or V-8)
J65	Power Brakes, Front & Rear Disc (Formula & Trans Am w/Limited Slip Axle only; Inc. w/Special Performance Pkg.)
AU3	Power Door Locks
A31	Power Windows (w/Console only)
U69	Radio, AM/FM
U58	Radio, AM/FM Stereo
UN3	Radio, AM/FM Stereo & Cassette Tape Player
UM7	Radio, AM/FM ETR Stereo w/Seek & Scan
UM1	Radio, AM & Stereo 8 Tape Player
UM2	Radio, AM/FM Stereo & Stereo 8 Tape Player
UP6	Radio, AM/FM Stereo w/40 Channel CB (Inc. Power Antenna)
U80	Radio Speaker, Rear (w/Monaural Radios only)
UP8	Radio Speakers, Dual Front & Rear
UX6	Radio Speakers, Dual Front
UQ1	Radio Speakers, Dual Rear Extended Range (Inc. w/ETR Stereo Radio)
N65	Spare Tire, Stowaway (Std. Formula & Trans Am)
D80	Spoiler, Rear Deck (Std. Trans Am & Formula Appearance Pkg.)
N33	Steering Wheel, Tilt
CD4	Windshield Wipers, Controlled Cycle

POWERTRAINS

Engine*	(Order Code)	Certi-fication (1)	Transmission (Floor Shift)	Axle Ratios Std.	Axle Ratios Avail.
Firebird/Esprit					
**3.8 Liter (231 CID) 2-bbl V-6 [LD5] *B		F	**Man. 3-Spd.	3.08	NA
			Automatic	2.56	3.23
4.3 Liter (265 CID) 2-bbl V-8 [LS5] *A		F	Automatic	2.41	NA
4.9 Liter (301 CID) 4-bbl V-8 [L37] *A		F	Automatic	2.41	NA
3.8 Liter (231 CID) 2-bbl V-6 (C-41) [LD5] *B		C	Automatic	2.73	NA
5.0 Liter (305 CID) 2-bbl V-8 [LG4] *C		C‡	Automatic	2.56	3.08
Formula/Trans Am					
**4.9 Liter (301 CID) 2-bbl V-8 [L37] *A		F	**Automatic	2.41	NA
T/A 4.9 Liter (301 CID) 4-bbl V-8 [L37 & W72] *A		F	Man. 4-Spd	3.08	NA
			Automatic	3.08	NA
Turbo 4.9 Liter (301 CID) 4-bbl V-8 [L37 & LU8] *A		F	Automatic	3.08	NA
Formula					
5.0 Liter (305 CID) 2-bbl V-8 [LG4] *C		C‡	Automatic	2.56	3.08
Trans Am					
5.0 Liter (305 CID) 2-bbl V-8 [LG4] *C		C‡	Automatic	3.08	2.56

*Pontiacs are equipped with GM-built engines produced by the following Divisions: A — Pontiac B — Buick C — Chevrolet.
**Base powertrain.
† Also available with Altitude Emissions (UPC NA6) — designed and recommended for high-altitude operation.
‡ Computer-controlled catalytic converter.
(1) F—Federal; A—Altitude; C—California.

DIMENSIONS

	Mm. (in.)
Overall length	4999 (196.8)
Overall width	1854 (73.0)
Wheelbase	2748 (108.2)
Tread, front/rear	1557/1524 (61.3/60.0)
Head room, front/rear	945/914 (37.2/36.0)
Leg room, front/rear	1115/721 (43.9/28.4)
Shoulder room, front/rear	1440/1382 (56.7/54.4)
Trunk Capacity	201 Liters (7.1 cu. ft.)

Published dimensions are for a base automobile without optional equipment or accessories. Additional accessories or equipment ordered at the customer's option can result in a minor change in these dimensions.

FIREBIRD

STEERING WHEELS

Deluxe Cushion
Standard: Firebird

Luxury Cushion
(UPC N30)
Standard: Esprit
Available: Firebird

Formula
(UPC NK3)
Standard: Trans Am, Formula
Available: Firebird & Esprit
(Included with Yellow Bird
Appearance Package [W73])

WHEEL COVERS AND WHEELS

Hubcaps w/Pontiac Crest
Standard: Firebird

Deluxe Wheel Covers
(UPC P01)
Standard: Esprit
Available: Firebird

Wire Wheel Covers
(UPC N95)
Available: Firebird, Esprit

Rally II Wheels w/Trim Rings
(UPC N98)
Standard: Trans Am & Formula
Available: Firebird, Esprit

**Body-Colored Rally II Wheels
w/Trim Rings**
(UPC N67)
Available: Firebird, Esprit, Formula &
Trans Am

Cast-Aluminum Wheels
(UPC N90)
Available: Firebird, Esprit, Formula &
Trans Am (Included with Special
Edition Trans Am & Yellow Bird)

Turbo Cast Aluminum Wheels
(UPC N89)
Available: Trans Am or Formula with
(WS6) Performance Option and (LU8)
Turbocharged V-8 only

- **W50 Formula Appearance Package
  Includes:**
  — Rear Deck Spoiler
  — "Formula" Lettering on Lower Door and Rear
  Deck Spoiler

- **WS6 Trans Am Performance Package
  Includes:**
  — Cast-aluminum Wheels (8" wide)
  — Special Handling Package
  — 225/70R15 Steel-belted White Lettered Radial
  Tires
  — Power Brakes, Front and Rear Disc

FIREBIRD MOLDINGS

Roof Drip Moldings (UPC B80).
Std. Esprit. Available All Others.
(Exc. w/Hatch Roof)

Body Side Moldings (UPC B84).
Available in Body Color on
All Models.

Windowsill Moldings (Includes
Hood Rear Edge Molding)
(UPC B85). Std. Esprit.
Available All Others.

Door Edge Guards (UPC B93).
Available All Models.

Rocker Panel Moldings
(UPC B83). Standard Esprit.
Available Firebird.

Wheel Opening Moldings
(UPC B96). Std. Esprit.
Available Firebird.

C3

PONTIAC
Turbo-Trans Am
Official Pace Car
Indianapolis 500
May 25, 1980

FIREBIRD

Standard Bucket Seats

Vinyl Interiors—OXEN
Firebird, Formula & Trans Am

Interior Colors	Trim No.	Exterior Colors
Oyster	12R1	11,15,19,24,29,51,57,67,72,76,79,80,84
Black	19R1	11,15,19,24,29,51,57,67,72,76,79,80,84
Blue	26R1	11,15,19,24,29
Camel Tan	62R1	11,19,29,51,57,67,72,76,79,80
Carmine	74R1	11,15,19,72,76,79,84

Appointment Mix Interiors
(Oyster Vinyl Interior with Colored Appointments*)
Firebird, Formula & Trans Am

Oyster/Gray	12R1/16X	11,15,19,24,29,51,57,67,72,76,79,80,84
Oyster/Black	12R1/19X	11,15,19,24,29,51,57,67,72,76,79,84
Oyster/Blue	12R1/26X	11,15,19,24,29
Oyster/Camel Tan	12R1/62X	11,19,57,80
Oyster/Carmine	12R1/74X	11,15,19,72,76,79,84

*Carpeting, Instrument Panel, Steering Column, Package Shelf.

FIREBIRD CUSTOM INTERIORS

Standard Custom Bucket Seats (Esprit)
Extra Cost Custom Bucket Seats (Formula & Trans Am)

Vinyl Interiors—DOESKIN
Esprit, Formula & Trans Am

Interior Colors	Trim No.	Exterior Colors
Oyster	12N1	11,15,19,24,29,51,57,67,72,76,79,80,84
Black	19N1	11,15,19,24,29,51,57,67,72,76,79,80,84
Blue	26N1	11,15,19,24,29
Camel Tan	62N1	11,19,29,51,56,57,67,72,76,79,80
Carmine	74N1	11,15,19,72,76,79,84

Appointment Mix Interiors
(Oyster Vinyl Interior with Colored Appointments*)
Esprit, Formula & Trans Am

Oyster/Gray	12N1/16X	11,15,19,24,29,51,57,67,72,76,79,80,84
Oyster/Black	12N1/19X	11,15,19,24,29,51,57,67,72,76,79,84
Oyster/Blue	12N1/26X	11,15,19,24,29
Oyster/Camel Tan	12N1/62X	11,19,57,67,80
Oyster/Carmine	12N1/74X	11,15,19,72,76,79,84

*Carpeting, Instrument Panel, Steering Column, Package Shelf.

Extra Cost Custom Bucket Seats

Cloth Interiors—HOBNAIL
(With Lombardy Bolsters)
Esprit, Formula & Trans Am

Interior Colors	Trim No.	Exterior Colors
Black	19B1	11,15,19,24,29,51,57,67,72,76,79,80,84
Blue	26B1	11,15,19,24,29
Camel Tan	62B1	11,19,29,51,56,57,67,72,76,79,80
Carmine	74B1	11,15,19,72,76,79,84

Exterior Colors and Color Codes

11	Cameo White
15	Platinum
19	Starlight Black
21	Baniff Blue
29	Nightwatch Blue
44	Piedmont Green
50	Mariposa Yellow
59	Stetson Beige
63	Fremont Gold
69	Castilian Bronze
72	Francisco Red
75	Bordeaux Red
76	Montreux Maroon
77	Agate Red
85	Richmond Gray

The automobile industry continued to suffer in 1981 despite repeated predictions of recovery from just about everyone. With fuel prices at last appearing to have stabilized, the big restraining factor was continued high interest rates. Many buyers simply were not prepared to pay 17% interest. And, too, the phenomenon known as "sticker shock" also took its toll. With the price of a base Firebird now almost 2½ times what it had been when the current body was first announced in 1970, increasing numbers of would-be buyers decided to sit it out as long as possible before entering the market. The fact that an all-new-from-the-ground-up Firebird was waiting in the wings for the 1982 model year to roll around didn't help, either, especially not with enthusiasts who knew via the buff magazines what was in the offing (and, by this time, most Firebird buyers were enthusiasts).

Nor did Pontiac Motor Division produce any exciting changes in the 'Birds sufficient to spark buyer interest. Indeed, just about the only interesting development for 1981 was getting Burt Reynolds to pose for the Firebird spread in the Pontiac catalogue. This was done as an upshot of Reynolds' use of jazzed up Trans Ams in his highly successful "Smokey and the Bandit" motion pictures. The other significant news was that the Chevy 305 cid V-8 was listed as an option for the Trans Am, presumably for buyers who wanted some oomph without going the turbocharging route to get it. Also, the Esprit Yellow Bird option was no longer available. Everything else on the Firebirds remained pretty much as before.

Prices were up. The base Firebird cost $6,948, the Esprit cost $7,788, the Formula cost $7,908 and the Trans Am weighed in at $8,419.

Production was way down. A grand total of 70,899 units were built. Of these, 20,542 were base Firebirds, 10,939 were Esprits, 5,925 were Formulas and 33,493 were Trans Ams. Total Firebird production since the first 1967 model rolled off the line had been 1,456,790. A truly impressive record in any league.

Firebird literature for 1981 consisted of more of the same as in previous years. There was a Firebird post card (see the montage below) as well as a spread in the main Pontiac catalogue (see pages 140-141) and in the product manual (see pages 142-143) as well as in the color and trim brochure (see page 144).

FIREBIRD

A new Efficiency System complements Firebird's aerodynamics.
Pontiac engineers know how much you love Firebird. So for 1981 they've kept the thrill while carefully honing Firebird's design for driving efficiency.*

Pontiac know-how puts together low-drag front disc brakes with an early fuel evaporation system and GM's Computer Command Control.

TRANS AM: A new generation of turbo excitement. Beneath the available new hood decal you'll find your favorite sports machine, with standard V-8, still commands the road with fully

What better way to appreciate the thrill of a Trans Am or Formula with available turbo V-8†than by watching turbo boost lights blaze out of the hood scoop?

Flank them with available options like a Delco-GM electronically tuned radio and cruise control with new resume-speed feature.

†Requires air conditioning

functional spoilers and air dams.

It's begging to be ordered with available hatch roof panels and a spectacular turbo V-8 (requires air conditioning), now with a light display blazing out of the hood scoop to indicate turbo boost.

Add the available special handling package. It mates hefty stabilizer bars with four-wheel disc brakes and eight-inch wheels behind 70 series tires. There's even a limited slip differential. (See the Facts and Figures section for more details.)
White-lettered tires supplied by various manufacturers.

FORMULA FIREBIRD: The sophisticated sportster. Fortify yours with a choice of available engines: the formidable turbo V-8 (requires air conditioning) or a 5.0 liter V-8 with manual four-speed.
*See pages 30 & 31 for fuel economy ratings.

1981 Trans Am (left) and Formula Firebird epitomize Pontiac soul and sophistication. Trans Am has been immortalized in the recent "Smokey and the Bandit" movies. Be sure to see "Smokey and the Bandit II," starring Burt Reynolds, Jackie Gleason, Jerry Reed, Dom DeLuise and Sally Field.

ESPRIT: The plushest Firebird. Rich interiors complement the acoustically insulated body. Custom buckets, luxury cushion steering wheel and body-color sport mirrors are standard.

FIREBIRD: Lots of sporty style for the money. Firebird shares many of the Esprit features: V-6 economy, automatic transmission, radial tuned suspension, power steering, power brakes with

new low-drag front discs and a 21 gallon fuel tank, all standard. Firebird meets the future head-on with engineering and classic styling all wrapped in a display of bold new colors.

FIREBIRD DIMENSIONS

FIREBIRD

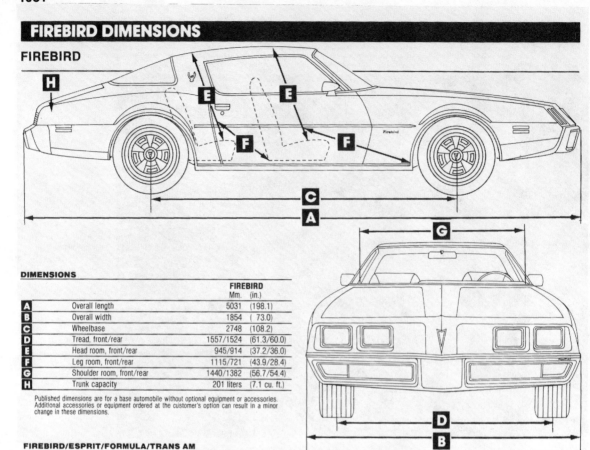

DIMENSIONS

		FIREBIRD Mm. (in.)	
A	Overall length	5031	(198.1)
B	Overall width	1854	(73.0)
C	Wheelbase	2748	(108.2)
D	Tread, front/rear	1557/1524	(61.3/60.0)
E	Head room, front/rear	945/914	(37.2/36.0)
F	Leg room, front/rear	1115/721	(43.9/28.4)
G	Shoulder room, front/rear	1440/1382	(56.7/54.4)
H	Trunk capacity	201 liters	(7.1 cu. ft.)

Published dimensions are for a base automobile without optional equipment or accessories.
Additional accessories or equipment ordered at the customer's option can result in a minor change in these dimensions.

FIREBIRD/ESPRIT/FORMULA/TRANS AM

POWERTRAINS

Engines*†	Certification	Transmissions	Axle Ratios
Firebird/Esprit			
3.8 Liter (231 CID) V-6 2-bbl. (LD5) B*¹	Federal & California	3-Speed Manual¹ 3-Speed Automatic²	3.08 2.56, 3.23‡
4.3 Liter (265 CID) V-8 2-bbl. (LS5) P*	Federal & California	3-Speed Automatic	2.41
4.9 Liter (301 CID) V-8 4-bbl. (L37 & W72) P*	Federal & California	3-Speed Automatic	2.56, 3.08‡
Formula/Trans Am			
4.3 Liter (265 CID) V-8 2-bbl. (LS5) P*¹ (Std. Formula)	Federal & California	3-Speed Automatic¹	2.41
4.9 Liter (301 CID) V-8 4-bbl. (L37 & W72) P*¹ (Std. Trans Am)	Federal & California	3-Speed Automatic¹	2.56, 3.08‡
Turbo 4.9 Liter (301 CID) V-8 4-bbl. (LU8) P*	Federal & California	3-Speed Automatic	3.08
5.0 Liter (305 CID) V-8 4-bbl. (LG4) C*	Federal & California	4-Speed Manual	3.08

*Firebirds are equipped with GM-built engines produced by various divisions: B—Buick, P—Pontiac, C—Chevrolet
†Equipped with Computer-Controlled Catalytic Converter (C-4 System)

‡Available 49 states only
**Available Formula 49 states only

¹Base powertrain
²Required in California, available 49 states

MAJOR OPTIONS**

UPC	ITEM
• C60	Air conditioning, custom (req. w/Turbo V-8s)
• U35	Clock, electric (NA w/rally gages)
■ K35	Cruise control. w/resume feature (w/auto. trans. only)
• A90	Deck lid release, remote control
• C49	Defroster, electric rear window (inc. H.D. 70 amp. alternator)
• W63	Gages, rally & clock (std. Formula—NA Trans Am, or V-6)
• U17	Gages, rally & clock & I/P tach (std. Trans Am—NA V-6 engine)
• A01	Glass, all windows soft ray
• CC1	Hatch roof, removable (inc. w/Black Special Edition)
• TT5	Headlamps, tungsten quartz halogen
• C95	Lamp, dome reading

• D35	Mirrors, sport, LH remote, RH man. convex (std. Esprit, Formula & Trans Am)
• U75	Power antenna, automatic
• U83	Power antenna, AM/FM/CB triband (inc. w/CB radio)
• J65	Power brakes, front & rear disc (Formula & Trans Am w/limited slip differential only; inc. w/Special Performance Package)
• AU3	Power door locks
• A31	Power windows
• U69	Radio, AM/FM
• U58	Radio, AM/FM stereo
• UN3	Radio, AM/FM stereo & cassette tape player
■ UM6	Radio, AM/FM stereo ETR & cassette tape player
■ UM7	Radio, AM/FM ETR stereo w/seek & scan
• UM1	Radio, AM & stereo 8-track tape player
• UM2	Radio, AM/FM stereo & stereo 8-track tape player

■ UX6	Radio speakers, dual front (monaural radios only)
■ UQ1	Radio speakers, dual rear extended range (inc. w/ETR stereo radio)
• UQ3	Radio audio booster
• UR4	Turbo boost gage
• D80	Spoiler, rear deck (std. Trans Am & Formula)
• N33	Steering wheel, tilt
• CD4	Windshield wipers, controlled cycle

TIRES:

• QJW	P205/75R15 white steel-belted (Firebird only)
• QMC	P205/75R15 white letter steel-belted (Firebird, Esprit only)
• QGR	P225/70R15 white letter steel-belted (Formula, Trans Am only); inc. w/Special Performance Package)

FIREBIRD

• W50	Formula Appearance Package Includes: — "Formula" lettering on lower door and rear deck spoiler — Lower body accent color w/striping
• WS6	Special Performance Package (avail. Trans Am & Formula only) Includes: — Cast-aluminum wheels (8" wide) — Special handling package — 225/70R15 steel-belted white lettered radials — Power brakes, front and rear disc — Limited slip differential

**See Car Order Form for additional listings and restrictions.

CI

■ New Item

FIREBIRD STANDARD EQUIPMENT

FIREBIRD

Exterior
- Body-color, one-piece resilient endura front end panel & front bumper w/recessed grilles & dual rectangular headlamp w/bright bezels
- Black-finished grille w/argent grille accents
- Bright windshield molding
- Bright rear window molding
- Endura rear bumper
- Concealed windshield wipers
- Hubcaps w/Pontiac crest

Interior
- All-vinyl front bucket seats
- Floor console
- Deluxe cushion steering wheel
- Column-mounted dimmer switch
- Day/night mirror
- Dual horns
- Fully upholstered door trim panels
- Nylon-blend, cut-pile carpeting
- Door lamp switch
- Simulated rosewood applique on instrument panel trim plate
- Front ash tray
- Cigar lighter
- Center dome lamp
- Luggage compartment mat
- Acoustical insulation

■ New Item

FIREBIRD ESPRIT

Exterior
- Body-colored sport mirrors (LH remote control, RH manual convex)
- Deluxe wheel covers
- Body-color inserts in outside door handles
- Bright windowsill & hood rear edge moldings
- Wheel opening moldings
- Roof drip moldings
- Wide rocker panel moldings
- Body-color, one-piece resilient endura front end panel & front bumper w/recessed grilles & dual rectangular headlamps w/bright bezels
- Black-finished grille w/argent grille accents
- Bright rear window molding
- Endura rear bumper
- Concealed windshield wipers

Interior
- Luxury cushion steering wheel
- Custom interior trim on bucket seats includes:
  — All-vinyl or extra cost pimlico cloth bucket seats
  — Deluxe door trim w/integral assist grips & carpeting on lower portion of doors
  — Rear quarter ash trays
  — Instrument panel assist strap
  — Custom pedal trim plates
- Floor console
- Column-mounted dimmer switch
- Simulated rosewood applique on instrument panel trim plate
- Front ash tray
- Cigar lighter
- Center dome lamp
- Door lamp switch
- Luggage compartment mat
- Added acoustical insulation
- Custom color-keyed seat/shoulder belts

FIREBIRD FORMULA

Exterior
- Body-color, one-piece resilient endura front end panel & front bumper w/recessed grilles & dual rectangular headlamps w/bright bezels
- Black-accented grilles & headlamp bezels
- Simulated dual air scoop hood design
- Body-color sport mirrors (LH remote control, RH manual convex)
- Formula identification
- Endura rear bumper
- Rear deck spoiler
- Rally II wheels w/trim rings
- Special hood w/Turbo V-8
- Black-finished windshield & rear window moldings

Interior
- Formula steering wheel
- Rally gages w/clock (instrument panel)
- Engine-turned instrument panel trim plate
- Column-mounted dimmer switch
- Dual horns
- All-vinyl bucket seats (custom interior trim extra cost)
- Extra cost pimlico cloth trim
- Fully upholstered door trim panels
- Door lamp switch
- Floor console
- Nylon-blend, cut-pile carpeting
- Front ash tray
- Center dome lamp
- Luggage compartment mat
- Acoustical insulation
- Cigar lighter
- Day/night mirror
- Acoustic insulation
- Dual horns

FIREBIRD TRANS AM

Exterior
- Front center air dam
- Black-accented grilles & headlamp bezels
- Endura rear bumper
- Rear deck spoiler
- Body-color sport mirrors (LH remote control, RH manual convex)
- Front & rear wheel opening air deflectors
- Front fender air extractors
- Chrome side-splitter tailpipe extensions
- Rally II wheels w/trim rings
- Shaker hood & air cleaner
- Trans Am identification
- Special hood w/Turbo V-8
- Black-finished windshield & rear window moldings
- Body-color, one-piece resilient endura front end panel & front bumper w/recessed grilles & dual rectangular headlamps

Interior
- Rally gages w/clock, tachometer (instrument panel)
- Formula steering wheel
- Engine-turned instrument panel trim plate
- Column-mounted dimmer switch
- Dual horns
- All-vinyl bucket seats (custom interior trim extra cost)
- Extra cost pimlico cloth trim
- Fully upholstered door trim panels
- Door lamp switch
- Center dome lamp
- Floor console
- Nylon-blend, cut-pile carpeting
- Front ash tray
- Day/night mirror
- Cigar lighter
- Acoustical insulation
- Luggage compartment mat

MECHANICAL/POWERTRAIN/CHASSIS

- 3.8 Liter (231 CID 2-barrel) V-6 engine std. on Firebird & Firebird Esprit
- 4.3 Liter (265 CID 2-barrel) V-8 engine std. on Formula
- 4.9 Liter (301 CID 4-barrel) V-8 engine w/Electronic Spark Control std. on Trans Am
- 3-speed manual transmission (floor shift w/console) std. on Firebird and Firebird Esprit (automatic transmission required in California)
- 3-speed automatic transmission std. on Formula and Trans Am
- Power steering
- Power front disc/rear drum brakes
- ■ Front disc brakes incorporate "Low Drag" feature
- ■ "Quick take-up" brake master cylinder for low brake drag
- 205/75R15 blackwall steel-belted radial tires with 30 psi on Firebird and Esprit
- 225/70R15 blackwall steel-belted radial tires with 30 psi on Formula & Trans Am

■ New Item

- Compact spare tire
- Vented front disc brake rotors & finned rear brake drums
- Coolant recovery system helps prevent costly coolant loss
- ■ New lightweight Delco Freedom® battery never needs refilling w/sealed side terminals to help prevent corrosion buildup
- Early fuel evaporation system on all engines for quick warm-up
- Delcotron generator w/built-in solid-state regulator
- Separator stub frame unit cushion-mounted to body

- Visible ball joint wear indicators on front suspension lower control arms for quick & easy inspection
- Separate stub frame unit cushion-mounted to body
- Independent coil-spring spherical joint front suspension (short & long arm type) w/low-friction non-metallic spherical joint liners & built-in anti-dive control
- Four-link-type multi-leaf rear suspension w/dual bias-mounted upper control arms & parallel-mounted lower control arms
- Cushioned body mounting system helps effectively isolate passenger area from road noise & vibration
- Concealed two-speed non-articulated electric windshield wipers

- Double-panel door, hood & deck lid construction
- Flow-through ventilation system
- Inner fenders front & rear for corrosion protection
- 21 gallon fuel tank capacity
- Counterbalanced hood & deck lid
- Extensive anti-corrosion measures

C2

FIREBIRD

(Silver shown)

Standard Bucket Seats

Vinyl Interiors—OXEN
Firebird, Formula & Trans Am

Interior Colors	Trim No.	Exterior Colors
Silver	15R1	11,16,19,84
Black	19R1	11,16,19,20,21,29,51,54,56,57,77,84
Blue	26R1	11,16,20,21,29
Camel Tan	64R1	11,19,29,51,54,57,67,77
Red	75R1	11,16,75

(Extra Cost) Cloth Interiors—MILLPORT
Firebird, Formula & Trans Am

Interior Colors	Trim No.	Exterior Colors
Blue	26D1	11,16,20,21,29
Camel Tan	64D1	11,19,29,51,54,57,67,77

(Red shown)

Standard Custom Bucket Seats (Esprit)
Extra Cost Custom Bucket Seats (Formula & Trans Am)

Vinyl Interiors—DOESKIN
Esprit, Formula & Trans Am

Interior Colors	Trim No.	Exterior Colors
Silver	15N1	11,16,19,84
Black	19N1	11,16,19,20,21,29,51,54,56,57,77,84
Blue	26N1	11,16,20,21,29
Camel Tan	64N1	11,19,29,51,54,57,67,77
Red	75N1	11,16,75

(Dark Blue shown)

Extra Cost Custom Bucket Seats

Cloth Interiors—PIMLICO
(with Durand Bolsters)
Esprit, Formula & Trans Am

Interior Colors	Trim No.	Exterior Colors
Black	19B1	11,16,19,20,21,29,51,54,56,57,77,84
Blue	26B1	11,16,20,21,29
Beige	63B1	11,19,29,54,67
Camel Tan	64B1	11,19,29,51,54,57,67,77
Red	75B1	11,16,19,75

EXTERIOR COLORS
&
COLOR CODES

11 — White
16 — Silver Met.
19 — Black
21 — Lt. Blue Met.
29 — Dk. Blue Met.
35 — Pastel Champagne
36 — Champagne Met.
45 — Lt. Jadestone Met.
47 — Jadestone Met.
48 — Dk. Green Met.
51 — Bright Yellow
58 — Burnt Orange Met.
63 — Med. Beige
68 — Lt. Brown
69 — Med. Brown
72 — Med. Maroon Met.
75 — Bright Red
77 — Dk. Maroon Met.